MANNERISM

Oryson

30.

MANNERISM

The European style of the sixteenth century

by Franzsepp Würtenberger

Translated from the German by Michael Heron

Holt, Rinehart and Winston · New York · Chicago · San Francisco

Acknowledgments

The frontispiece is a copperplate engraving from *Perspective, das ist die weitberuembte khunst . . . ans licht bracht durch Johan Vredman Frijsen.* The Latin edition was published in two parts in 1604 and 1605. The illustration on the facing page shows a group of caryatids, an engraving by Hans Vredeman de Vries.

The colour photographs were taken by the following: Alinari, Florence, p. 101, 105, 109, 137, 141, 149, 189; A. v. Borsig, New York, p. 69; Crea, Rome, p. 17, 117; Giraudon, Paris, p. 213; Hans Hinz, Basel, p. 45, 240; Kempter, Munich, p. 113, 181, 193, 217; Gerhard Klammet, Ohlstadt, p. 153; Photo Meyer, Vienna, p. 37, 41, 49, 53, 169, 177, 185, 221; Scala, Florence, p. 13, 209, 225; Thames & Hudson, London, p. 85, 145, 173.

The black-and-white photographs were supplied by the following: A. C. L., Brussels, p. 202 (below), 204 (above right); Akademie der bildenden Künste, Vienna, p. 81, 138, 238; Albertina, Vienna, p. 158 (above), 232, 234 (above left), 236; Alinari, Florence, p. 27 (below), 29, 32, 57, 58, 61 (left and below right), 62 (above left), 64 (above left and right), 73, 74 (above), 76 (right), 77, 78, 90 (below), 91 (above and below right), 92, 93 (above left and right, below left), 94, 95 (above), 121 (centre and below left), 122, 123, 125, 126, 127, 130 (above), 131 (below left and right), 132, 157 (left), 161, 164, 197, 198 (above right and below left), 201 (left), 204 (below right), 231 (right); Anderson, Rome, p. 26 (above), 30, 31 (below), 60 (left), 76 (left), 89, 96 (below left), 234 (above right); Archives Photographiques, Paris, p. 31 (above), 160 (below); B. Verwaltung der Staatlichen Schlösser, Garten und Seen, Munich, p. 129; Bayerische Staatsgemäldesammlung, Munich, p. 59 (below right), 230 (above), 233 (below), 234 (below); Bildarchiv Foto Marburg, p. 93 (below right); Blinkhorn, Banbury, p. 130 (below); Ed. Brogi, Florence, p. 25, 63 (above), 95 (below); Foto Cramers, Kunstanstalt, Dortmund, p. 80; Deutsche Fotothek, Dresden, p. 201 (right); Foto A. Dingjan, The Hague, p. 159 (below), 202 (above); Ente Provinciale per il Turismo, Mantua, p. 128; Gabinetto Fotografico della Soprintendenza alle Gallerie, p. 59 (below left), 157 (right), 158 (below right), 162, 163 (below right); Giraudon, Paris, 63 (below), 235; Walter Höflinger, Basel, p. 75; Gerhard Klammet, Ohlstadt, p. 64 (below); Kunsthistorisches Museum, Vienna, p. 159 (above), 199 (above); Landesamt für Denkmalpflege, Munich, p. 121 (centre right); Landesbildstelle Württemberg, Stuttgart, p. 96 (above); Lossen-Foto, Heidelberg, p. 26 (below), 90 (above); Foto Mas, Barcelona, p. 27 (above); Photo Maywald, Paris, p. 200 (below right); Museo del Prado, Madrid, p. 198 (above left and below right), 231 (left); Museum Boymans-Van Beuningen, Rotterdam, p. 229 (below); National Gallery of Art, Washington, p. 62 (below); Österreichisches Museum für angewandte Kunst, Bibliothek, Vienna, frontispiece, p. 96 (below right); from the print collection, p. 55, 115; Österreichische Nationalbibliothek, Bildarchiv, Vienna, p. 28, 124 (above); Pontificia Fotografia Felice, Rome, p. 121 (above); Hans Retzlaff, Tann, Rhöngebirge, p. 79 (right); Foto-Commissie Rijksmuseum, Amsterdam, p. 61 (above right), 66, 203, 204 (left); Jean Roubier, Paris, p. 121 (below right); Schroll-Archiv, Vienna, p. 54, 91, 131 (above right), 163 (above, left and right); Photo E. Schwenk, Vienna, p. 60 (right), 230 (below); Staatliche Gemäldegalerie, Stuttgart, p. 233 (above); Staatliche Kunsthalle, Karlsruhe, p. 229 (above); Städelsches Kunstinstitut, Frankfurt-am-Main, p. 158 (below left); Her Majesty's Stationery Office, London, p. 199 (below); Stichting Lichtbeelden Instituut, Amsterdam, p. 131 (above left); Foto A. Villani & Figli, Bologna, p. 59 (above), 62 (above right); Archiv Prof. Würtenberger, Karlsruhe, p. 74 (below), 79 (above left), 124 (below), 156, 160 (above), 200 (above left and right, below left); the drawing on p. 143 was made by Hans Bonheim, Karlsruhe.

The colour blocks were made by Klischeeanstalten Beissner & Co, Patzelt & Co and Seyss, all of Vienna; the black-and-white blocks by Rasteiger, Graz. The book was printed by Christoph Reisser's Sons, Vienna.

I

Contents

MANNERISM AS AN INTER-EUROPEAN STYLE   6–24   The meaning of the Mannerist style – the style of the humanist ideal of culture – European domestic architecture as an outlet for the new style

MANNERIST ART AS A MEDIUM FOR THE PERSONAL AFFIRMATION OF AUTOCRATIC POWER   33–43   The new evaluation of art – the new relationship between sovereign and artist

THE HUMAN FIGURE IN MANNERIST PAINTING AND SCULPTURE   44–81   The figure *per se* – combining figures into a group – the arrangement of columns in an architectonic context

ARCHITECTURE IN THE MANNERIST SPIRIT   82–101   The new type of architect – lack of restraint in architectural design – the theory of the order of columns

GREAT MANNERIST PAINTING AND DECORATIVE ART   102–156   The intellectual background and origin of the fresco schemes – suitability of the fresco schemes

MANNERIST ART AS A MEDIUM FOR THE GLORIFICATION OF ARTISTIC CREATION   165–190   The artist's creative work and environment as a subject for artistic representation – artists as eccentrics – the artist's palace – provision for posthumous fame

THE ESTIMATION OF MAN IN MANNERIST PORTRAITURE   191–217   The theory of the portrait – the social status of the portrait

HUMAN DESTINY AND THE POWER OF NATURE IN MANNERIST ART   218–240   Human life and the power of fate – nature and the cosmic world feeling

BIBLIOGRAPHY   241–246

Mannerism as an inter-European style

The style known as Mannerism was predominant in the various countries of Europe between 1530 and 1600. Starting in Italy, it spread to France, the Netherlands, Germany, England and Spain. There are masterpieces testifying to its fame in every field of the fine arts — sculpture, painting and architecture. But before appraising any of its individual features, this style has one peculiarity which the art-historian is bound to mention. Mannerism was not a comprehensive, widespread and universally applicable style embracing every kind of contemporary artistic endeavour, as were the Gothic, Renaissance and Baroque. It certainly represented a most important, highly influential artistic outlook which was the most progressive of its day, but the older Renaissance tradition remained continually alive and fertile side by side with it. Throughout the whole of the sixteenth century many works of art were produced which do not belong to the Mannerist style, as works by Titian, Veronese, Palladio, Anthonis Mor and Hans Holbein the Younger prove.

The meaning of the Mannerist style

A decisive feature of Mannerism's appearance on the scene is that it was produced and practised by a completely new, individually gifted type of artistic personality. This fact essentially determined its limited, exclusive sphere of influence. To think and feel in the Mannerist way it was impossible to retain an everyday commonplace outlook on things and the surrounding world; on the contrary, the Mannerist had to be prepared to free himself from the realities of this earth like a visionary and soar into higher spiritual spheres. Faced with the alternatives of being close to reality or remote from it, it was obviously not granted to every artist to commit himself to the second more dangerous course. To be a Mannerist the artist had to have a bent for the eccentric, withstand the exaltation of ingenious mental experiments, subordinate himself to the dominion of the overcultivated intellect instead of natural intuition, enjoy playing with incongruous ideas, place the artificial before normality and cramping convention, be receptive to the theoretical speculative side of artistic creation, be full of enthusiasm for the ideal and delight in the reckless distortion of his materials. All this demanded a mental attitude which naturally enough was only within the reach of an élite. The others, the innately calmer, more traditionally-minded artists of the age, had no access to this ambivalent frame of mind with all its tensions, and consequently quite rightly stayed on the traditional paths of the Renaissance artistic ideal.

The father and creator of the Mannerist movement was Michelangelo. The special groups of artists who copied the *maniera di Michelangelo* in the sixteenth century and as it were accepted a tow from that towering giant were summarily called Mannerists. This designation, at first deliberately used in a pejorative sense, originated with the opponents of these groups, the classicists of the seventeenth century, especially the Caracci brothers and the art critic Giovanni Pietro Bellori. In the first instance the Italian word *maniera* means nothing more than personal style. It is one of the commonest terms in the vocabulary of the most important Mannerist writer on art, Giorgio Vasari. Over and above its usual meaning it can be used to characterize a whole stylistic epoch. Thus Vasari writes of a *maniera greca*, or *bizantina*, or *gotica*, or even the *maniera* of an individual artist. In this usage it is synonymous with our word "style".

Michelangelo's universal influence

Even in his own lifetime Michelangelo made such an impression on his surprisingly numerous disciples that they never broke loose from his hypnotic influence and were overwhelmed by his power. It is a special phenomenon of art-history since the Renaissance that an artist who championed an unmistakably personal, subjective artistic style was nevertheless able to attract such a faithful band of disciples. Here we have the first example of the outspokenly individual style of a great artist having a massive influence on weaker individualists. Rembrandt and Picasso provide similar examples.

The fascinating thing about Michelangelo was his titanic, superhuman quality. The normal spread of artistic ideas alone did not account for its sweeping influence; other favourable outside circumstances had to supervene: the Michelangelesque-Mannerist style was connected at the time with a very definite sociological situation, a factor of some importance for the potential dissemination of a style. Owing to its aristocratic hyper-cultured way of thinking, Mannerism was associated with the intellectual class which was attaining greater power at that time. The middle class, the townsmen, played hardly any part in its exaggerated and audacious mental acrobatics. Mannerism is not a naive style; it is consciously guided by higher vision and disposes of a highly developed theoretical literature which is not merely a by-product; if anything, it gives a philosophical exposition of the driving force behind practical artistic activity. This bent for speculation occurs as early as Michelangelo. Jacob Burckhardt was right when he wrote: "It seems as if Michelangelo thought almost as systematically about art postulating and creating the world, as individual philosophies thought about the world-creating I."

Mannerism in the general development of style

Mannerism was in a very critical situation, historically speaking. To it fell the exceptionally difficult task of linking mediaeval conceptual systematical thought and the Renaissance belief in beauty with the rational scientific thought of the new age. It appears that the leading brains of Mannerism calculated the specific points in shaping life and the world picture where the separate branches and techniques of the fine arts could be used. The Mannerists worried about the classification of the arts in the general edifice of culture, the relation of the arts to each other, the status of their subject matter, where the various ranges of themes should stand in order of importance, how to evaluate historical, portrait, genre and landscape painting and where nudes or draped figures were suitable. The moral and purely aesthetic points of view were partially in opposition. Mannerism had a discriminatory scale of values according to which the branches and techniques of the fine arts could be classified. It established standards.

The quite remarkable result of all this is that the art of Mannerism taken as a whole is one of the most systematic and consequently most fascinating conceptions of the world-picture which the history of art has ever produced. Then the objections advanced from a fragmentary purely aesthetic and formalistic cramped viewpoint pale, for they take no account of the real, greater and more comprehensive aims of this art or in what higher sense and for what loftier purposes the various branches and techniques of the fine arts were employed, even though they often seem to have been employed like formulae.

The style of the humanist ideal of culture

The ancient cultural soil of Italy had long been prepared for the comprehensive mission to which Mannerism laid claim. The Italian Renaissance of the fourteenth and fifteenth centuries saw the development of advances such as the discovery of man as an individual and the world as a scientific object which have become the basic values of all European thought in modern times. The powerful classical creations of the Italian High Renaissance, such as Leonardo's *Last Supper*, Raphael's *School of Athens* and Michelangelo's ceiling in the Sistine Chapel, were not only and no longer purely national Italian monuments. In their clear-cut human greatness they became part and parcel of the new international indispensable cultural heritage. They became great European works. Contemporaries felt that these works of art must be measured by new standards; the transcendent human value of these unparalleled masterpieces allowed of no other attitude.

But neither could the other countries noted for their art, Germany, France and the Netherlands, hold fast to their old tradition-bound cultural heritage; the independent, what we might call territorial repertoire of forms was no longer adequate in the sixteenth century. From then on it was no longer possible to speak of Spanish, Old Netherlands, Old German or even of Nuremberg or Lower Rhineland styles. This classification according to purely territorial points of view was no longer valid, for now the artists belonged to a European cultural community which stretched beyond narrow ancestral frontiers. Even in Italy the local character of the artistically fertile provinces was gradually obliterated. During the Renaissance the different regions had preserved their individuality in the chorus of styles, the Tuscan had contrasted with the Umbrian or Emilian, the Venetian had developed in contrast to the Lombardic style. There were also art schools in the individual towns: Parma, Milan, Cremona, Siena, Perugia and Naples could boast of them. For these places were small centres which preserved their independence and evolved their own styles.

Rome and Florence as cultural centres

All this changed radically with the advent of the sixteenth century, when two world centres, Rome and Florence, virtually dominating all others, crystallized and diffused the culture of their times. Later in the sixteenth century Rome became the spiritual and artistic capital of Italy and the whole of Europe. She received and re-transmitted every new trend; yet in the fourteenth and fifteenth centuries she had been unable to compete with Florence and Siena. The High Renaissance first brought about the decisive transformation. Added to which Florence had lost her pre-eminence after the middle of the sixteenth century.

A single man, the genius of the century, created a universal style. The divine and deified Michelangelo staked out the mental dimensions within which works of art which were to have validity must be envisaged from now on. No one could escape his emotional intensity, his *terribilità*. But the union of genius and intuition with scientific and coldly systematic thought effected by Mannerism was largely responsible for Michelangelo becoming a "world power". Scientific thought is rational and opposed to subjective brilliance in its demands for hyper-exact severely objective criteria. The typically Mannerist combination of these ambivalent approaches was needed before the qualities of genius and supernormality in Michelangelo could be adopted and become a fashion which everyone could adopt. This fashion had such tremendous penetrative powers that it became a universal style. To use a brief formula which naturally does not avoid the danger of generalization, we can say that in Mannerism originality and an international culture which could be learnt replaced the gifts inherent in different national characters.

The struggle between Florence and Rome for Michelangelo was not one of the usual competitions between those two cities or between the Farnese Pope and the Medici for a good artist; the question at stake was whether Florence or Rome was and would remain the artistic centre. Michelangelo's main works, his European works — if one may say call them, are in Rome: the dome of St Peter's, the Julius Monument, the Sistine Ceiling and the *Last Judgment*. On the other hand Michelangelo's works in Florence are more modest in size: his *David*, the *Burial of Christ* in

Florence Cathedral, the Medici Chapel and the anteroom of the Biblioteca Laurentiana. We have a very clear example of the comparative esteem in which Rome and Florence were held in Goethe's *Italienische Reise*. On his arrival in Rome in 1786 he bursts out: "Yes, at last I have reached this capital of the world. My desire to come to Rome was so great... that there was no question of waiting and I only stopped in Florence for three hours." The definitive works were created in Rome; there was the model: antiquity. At the end of the sixteenth century the artists of all nations had gathered at Rome; the Carracci, Caravaggio and Rubens were there.

The special position of Venice

However we must also concede Venice, as well as Florence, a certain independence beside Rome. Even in aesthetics the city of canals had its own line. With trenchant eloquence the Venetian writers on aesthetics defended colour as the highest aim of their art in opposition to the one-sided emphasis on drawing, *disegno*, and the reproduction of the physical, *rilievo*. Michelangelo was played off against Titian. But even these opposites were decided in favour of Florence and Michelangelo. Tintoretto, the main representative of Mannerism in Venice, united the two hostile stylistic concepts in his painting. As the maxim of his technique he is supposed to have written over the door of his studio: "the *disegno* of Michelangelo and the colouring of Titian". It was the behaviour of a true Mannerist to achieve the union of such tension-filled principles and incompatible contrasts. It needed not only feeling and the usual technical ability, but also a highly developed intellect and a marked liking for the exaggerated qualities which Tintoretto's art possesses to an astonishing degree. Neither Titian nor Veronese at Venice had this heightened originality, and because they did not possess these basic Mannerist characteristics they cannot be counted as Mannerists.

Great rivalries sprang up and only in the course of such conflicts was it decided which Florentine artists dared set foot in Venetian circles and which dared not. Federigo Zuccari and Vasari did not manage it; they were rejected and had to leave Venice quickly without success. On the other hand Venice was more tolerant of sculptors. Jacopo Sansovino, a Tuscan by birth, took up permanent residence in Venice in 1527 and was given the big government commissions. He spread Michelangelo's stylistic ideal there. Next to him the main representative of Mannerist sculpture in Venice was his pupil Alessandro Vittoria. But there are also reverse examples of Venetians achieving fame in Florence and Rome. The Venetian Sebastiano del Piombo freed himself from the spell of Giorgione and Titian, and became a loyal and celebrated disciple of Michelangelo who protected him at Rome.

p. 13 Sebastiano produced his *Pietà* at Viterbo, that pathetic and deeply moving composition, in the closest consultation with him. Yet the instinctive Venetian feeling breaks through in the gloomy landscape which is a perfect setting for the emotional intensity of Mary wrapped in grief as she looks up at the moonlit sky. The two contrasting elements of sensitive feeling for sorrow and Michelangelesque heroic physical pathos are merged in a peculiarly subdued harmony in this picture. Then in the second half of the sixteenth century it became possible for Jacopo Ligozzi, born in Verona and trained in Venice, to set foot in Florence and receive big commissions for frescoes *p. 123* which he carried out brilliantly. In 1591 he painted gigantic historical paintings in the Palazzo Vecchio in the style of Venetian ceremonial pictures which demand comparison with the gigantic frescoes by Vasari in the same palace painted twenty years earlier. In 1575 Ligozzi became Court Painter to the Archduke of Tuscany.

The travelling virtuoso as an artistic type

A few scholars and artists seized the intellectual hegemony. The new sociological type of *pittore vago*, wandering virtuosos, rootless art teachers, appeared everywhere. Their main goal was to visit the most important countries in order to spread their own fame. Travel was even expressly called for in the *Dialogo di Pittura* (1548) by Paolo Pino; virtuosos went from one court to another or from one artistic centre to another regardless of their regional and family origins. The artistic repertoire of forms began to become a general European cultural concern. In the process the language of art yielded to a pressure and ritual just as conventional and international as for example the court ceremonial of the sixteenth century which stemmed from the Spanish-Hapsburg royal households and gradually became binding on all Europe, at first under Charles V and later under his son Philip II.

It was obviously only possible for the practice of art to become a cultural concern because artists dared to shake off the fetters of their mediaeval craft status and number themselves among the humanistic intellectual élite. Artists too began to ascend to the class of scholars and men of letters who felt at home everywhere. The academies which were so characteristic of the practice of art during the next two centuries came into being. During and towards the end of the sixteenth century artistic knowledge and teaching were turned into a theory and finally became mental equipment which could be learnt. Now numerous methodical art theoreticians appeared on the scene with even more influence than in the Renaissance when Leon Battista Alberti and Leonardo da Vinci developed their theories. The most important representatives of this entirely new artistic mental attitude with its literary background were Giorgio Vasari, Giovanni Battista Armenini, Giovanni Paolo Lomazzo and Federigo Zuccari. The end of this development saw the founding of the first real academies by Zuccari in Rome and the Carracci brothers in Bologna. There are echoes of this trend in Karel van Mander's didactic poem and the so-called Haarlem Academy which Hendrik Goltzius, Cornelis Cornelisz. van Haarlem and Karel van Mander founded jointly for the general study of antiquity. In the seventeenth century the idea of the academy was extended. The artistic politics practised by Louis XIV through Colbert made special use of it. It became an exceptional privilege to be an academician.

Journeys to Italy by Dutchmen

Artists lived in the intellectual environment of their patrons, the princes, as participants with equal rights in a cultural ideal. Anyone who wanted to play a part in this European concert almost inevitably had to go to the actual source. This started the numerous journeys to Italy. Re-discovered antiquity and modern Rome became journey's end for a great number of northern artists. The term Romanism is used to describe this stylistic movement in which Dutchmen mainly predominated. Nearly all important Dutch painters of the sixteenth century travelled to Italy. Formerly they had gone south as pilgrims, on religious rather than artistic grounds. For example Rogier van der Weyden came to Rome in 1450 for the great Jubilee Year. But his painting also profited from his knowledge of Italy. Abroad he allowed himself to be influenced by the more monumental manner of composition. In the same way Jan van Scorel visited Venice and Rome on his journey to the Holy Land as a member of the congregation of travellers to Jerusalem. Jan Gossaert, known as Mabuse, undertook his journey to Rome in 1508/09 in the retinue of his patron Philip of Burgundy and from then on his painting is permeated by the stimulus of Italy. The conflict between north and south is seen in his pictures for the first time, with Italy as the seminal contributor. But works by Italian artists also reached the Netherlands and had a stimulating influence. In 1506 Flanders merchants bought the marble group by Michelangelo now known as the *Bruges Madonna* and installed it in the Church of Our Lady at Bruges. In 1517 Raphael's tapestry cartoons reached Brussels. They came as a revelation; for young artists like Barend van Orley they became the advanced school of the great ideal style. The influence of Leonardo's character studies of heads on Quinten Massys and his sons Jan and Cornelis is a chapter on its own. Their physiognomical penetration and their grotesque farcical element apparently suited the Dutch (and northern) inclination for dissecting the human soul. They contain tendencies which had their forerunners in the diabolical human faces and caricatures of Hieronymus Bosch, except that in the new works they emerge more aggressively.

Martin van Heemskerck

The Dutch painter for whom the journey to Rome became the most vital cultural experience in the Mannerist sense was Martin van Heemskerck. Because he was dissatisfied with his training by Jan van Scorel at Haarlem he went to Rome in 1532 and stayed there until 1536. He embarked on an intensive study of antiquity, drew from it zealously and used it strikingly in his compositions. Simultaneously he was influenced by Michelangelo from whom he acquired the titanic attitudes of the figures on the Sistine Ceiling and elsewhere. Heemskerck's urge to portray Herculean ostentatious strength is particularly evident in the muscular limbs of his figures. In this manner he succeeded in mastering the heroic world of Michelangelo in grandiose and successful altar compositions as well. But as a northener he was also impressed by the Roman landscape. He drew the ruins around Rome. In this monumental cultural landscape his fantasy went even further and he conceived a handsome series of engravings
p. 234 of the *Seven Wonders of the World*. In his self-portrait of 1553 he explicitly names himself as a drawer of ruins.

Circles of Dutchmen formed in Rome itself. It was the meeting place not only of the painters who specialized in great historical pictures, but also of the landscape painters who were enraptured by the beauty of the Italian countryside. The brothers Mattheus and Paul Brill became the most celebrated. Their activity was not limited to small cabinet pictures. They enlarged their field by using their skill to produce monumental works, i.e. fresco painting. For there grew up a custom of introducing insets of small landscapes in the subsidiary areas of large fresco schemes, and the brothers Brill produced this type of landscape fresco. Then this juxtaposition was adopted by Agostino Tassi under whose direction even Claude Lorrain, the famous glorifier of the Roman landscape, worked. From this we can see that c. 1600 something of the naturalistic Dutch conception of landscape had already infiltrated into important Italian fresco painting. At the end of the century the Italians were no longer so averse to the northern taste as they were at the beginning.

New possibilities for the dissemination of artistic ideas

In the sixteenth century Europe was criss-crossed by a new cultural communications network, and new discoveries, especially printing, spread surprisingly quickly. The sixteenth century has been called the century of the publisher. The great publishing firms blossomed everywhere: Froben settled in Basle, Plantin in Antwerp, Jobin in Strasbourg, others in Lyons or Venice. Works of art benefited by being reproduced graphically. No sooner was an artistic idea, a pictorial composition or an ornament conceived than it was engraved or a woodcut made of it, to be distributed in the form of prints. Artists could study the "inventions" at home without laboriously seeking out their place of origin; they could be admired everywhere and adopted by everyone. Printed woodcuts and engravings with their potential for wide and speedy circulation became a technical commercial medium which can hardly be overestimated in helping the development of the overall European style. Thus it was possible, for example, for the Italians to adopt and assimilate the whole of Dürer's artistic production as part of the basis of their art. As a result an undreamt of possibility opened up. We have the striking fact of compositions and pictorial ideas existing in duplicate in different spheres, firstly as originals in the actual palaces, castles and churches, in the form of monumental frescoes, large painted altar pieces or panel pictures, and then again as reproductions in the form of handy portable engravings or woodcuts of the kind kept in portfolios in cabinets of engravings today.

Engraved reproductions

Side by side with the original creative work a reproduction of it frequently existed on another level as an engraving. The vast flood of engravings is an essential feature of the general picture of Mannerist art. In them the humanistic didactic character to which such exceptional importance was attached could be stressed even more unmistakably by means of captions. In this contradictory relationship between lofty exclusive uniqueness and reproduction as published distributable art there is a partial reflection of the difference between *Ars* and *Usus*, between high and humbler art, which is very characteristic of the Mannerist mental attitude. The Mannerist artist attached great importance to having his ingenious pictorial ideas published graphically; for during that epoch the accent and also the quality of the work of art had shifted from Italian monumental painting to the Late Mannerist Dutch art of engraving. Hendrik Goltzius and Jacques de Gheyn are better as engravers and draughtsmen than Federigo Zuccari or Giuseppe Cesari d'Arpino are as monumental painters.

The influence of northern artists in Italy

There is no doubt that in the process of evolution the gap between the northern and Italian attitudes to art narrowed during the second half of the sixteenth century. The northern artists were not always simply the receivers and learners; there were also cases of northerners achieving renown in Italian artistic circles and playing an active part in them. In this respect two Dutch artists deserve special mention: Jean de Boulogne, known as Giovanni da Bologna, and Jan van der Straat, known as Giovanni Stradanus. Karel van Mander complained that these artists were lost to their native land because they remained in Florence: "Our Belgian Netherlands and their daughters the towns have no small reason for seriously reproaching the greedy florid beautiful Florence because she not only holds the flower of the art of sculpture, the Dutchman Jean de Boulogne, but also the distinguished Hans van der Straat, painter from Bruges and Flanders, whom she keeps away from their fatherland as a sly Circe, beseeching Calypso or bewitching Alcina, allows them to grow grey and white there and also wishes to preserve their bones in her walls for her own renown."

Giovanni da Bologna

Giovanni introduced a new note into Florentine sculpture. In spite of his Flemish origin he is exclusively a figure of Italian and in particular Florentine art history. He was one of those *stranieri*, those immigrants, who only felt at home when they had set foot on Italian soil, because then they could create in the environment which suited them. It was natural for them to take part in the life of foreign countries and never want to leave them. So Giovanni da Bologna was not one of those northern Romanists who enjoyed breathing the artistic air of Italy and Rome but left once they had collected enough impressions and, transformed though they were, went contentedly back to the north. He was one of that special class of travellers to Italy who had to shape their whole existence and artistic endeavour by settling permanently in its atmosphere. In this he could almost be compared with Nicolas Poussin or Ingres, both of whom felt that life was only worth living on the hallowed cultural soil of Rome. Nevertheless Giovanni da Bologna seems to have been free of such fanaticism and to have fitted in perfectly naturally among his colleagues in the Italian artistic world.

It had only become possible for a foreigner to be so completely accepted in the ranks of Florentine artists in the second half of the sixteenth century, when the indigenous power of Florentine art was already on the wane. A figure such as Giovanni only became possible and tolerable from the point of view of artistic sociology and

politics because a certain levelling down and a trend towards the mediocre and popular had become apparent during Michelangelo's last years and after the death of Pontormo. In his art Giovanni da Bologna was an excellent example of the tendency to be conventional and avoid stressing one's origins. An almost international, more flexible and agile intellectualism was united with a dash of northern rationalism in this sculptor. The violence and great pathos of Michelangelo were no longer required; the cry was for the elegant almost over-subtle virtuoso.

Born in 1524 Giovanni da Bologna was a contemporary of Tintoretto. With his slender graceful figures he prepared the way for what Bartholomeus Spranger, the main inspiration of a major group of Mannerists in the north, continued as a painter a generation later and exaggerated even more. It is typical that Giovanni da Bologna renounced working in marble, a hard cumbersome material, in favour of the more delicate and malleable bronze. In this he continued the line of Benvenuto Cellini, the craftsman and goldsmith, rather than that of a Baccio Bandinelli or even of Michelangelo. But for all his conscious highly cultivated stylistic feeling the northern, decidedly Dutch, leaning towards a frequently over-exact naturalism broke through. It was precisely this vacillation and union of extremes which marked him out as a Mannerist artist. In his creations there is a dichotomy between nature and art. Giovanni da Bologna tackled his problems without encountering great difficulties and obstacles. We could say that he was favoured by fortune and found in his own milieu the recognition which was his due.

Giovanni Stradanus

Giovanni Stradanus, who was one year older, occupies a somewhat similar position in Florentine painting to that of Giambologna in sculpture. Like him he only left Florence on rare occasions and he too died there in 1605, three years before his fellow-countryman. Stradanus succeeded in making a reputation in a more limited field, the production of cartoons for manufacturing tapestries. Cosimo I had started this manufactory but it was given its first real impetus by Stradanus. Other artists whose shapes were bolder, such as Pontormo, Salviati and Bronzino, lacked the delicate touch which the cartoons needed, whereas his northern Dutch mind adopted the Florentine artistic sensibility. At the time Florentines had an appreciation for the detailed portrayal of nature, for genre scenes as well as the accurate observation of animals, plants and landscapes. This rather practical Dutch trait centred on the everyday also emerged in Giovanni da Bologna's activity as a designer of animal statuettes and his special liking for garden sculpture. Stradanus provided his tapestries with the necessary luxuriant frames and borders, and as a pupil of the Antwerp painter Pieter Aertsen he was able to develop all the treasures of nature into an eyecatching decoration of fruits, garlands of leaves and still-lifes. His wall tapestries with hunting scenes for the country seat of Cosimo I at Poggio a Caiano near Florence became famous. Stradanus found a pupil and successor in Antonio Tempesta, a native Florentine. Tempesta finally displayed the lavish fantasy of his designs in numerous series of engravings; they appeared in albums of animal pictures of the most varied kind in the form of friezes. These engravings had a wide circulation in the Netherlands as well as in Italy; Tempesta's hunting scenes even served Rubens and Frans Snyders as models. They were frequently used in the applied arts, for example in a sequence of leather tapestries from the life of Charles V in Vienna, or on ceramics.

The special position of El Greco

Domenico Theotocopuli, known as El Greco, occupied a special position, inasmuch as traditional national qualities could also operate and be included in the international ensemble of Mannerism. Traditions were at work in this artist which break the bounds of the usual picture of history. As a Greek (he came from the island of Crete)

El Greco had a different historical origin and an older heritage in his activities as a civilized man than those artists who only belonged to the revival of Roman antiquity, the Italian Renaissance. For European Mannerism is a direct continuation of the Renaissance in spite of all its special tendencies. As an artist who stemmed from the old Byzantine cultural circle which was so pregnant with tradition El Greco could not shake off his cultural heritage; no matter how far he was assimilated, in the last analysis he was always a true Greek in his thought and feeling. The astonishing thing is that when this artist moved to Italy and came into contact with the rationalist Renaissance way of thinking, leaving behind the faith and mysticism of his homeland, he did not merely become a more interesting but otherwise unremarkable immigrant. El Greco did not become an icon painter in Italy; on the contrary he joined in his new historical and cultural environment as one of the most important creative personalities. In order to explain the phenomenon of a foreigner being able to occupy such a high decisive position within the stylistic movement of Mannerism we should realize that art had become something which could be learnt and experienced intellectually. The cultural experience of having been in Rome, Venice or Florence was vital, as we have already mentioned. Consequently a Greek could work in Italy and Spain, and still feel that he was of equal birth and had equal rights. If the crucial characteristics of the Mannerist artist were his intellect, virtuosity and social versatility, then El Greco possessed them to a high degree. He must have been a very intelligent man with exceptional powers of empathy. He was greatly esteemed by his contemporaries as an artist and, like his celebrated colleagues, was swamped with commissions from the noble and ecclesiastical classes and consequently ran a large thriving workshop. El Greco was one of the great entrepreneurs of painting like Raphael, Titian, Tintoretto and Rubens. From the point of view of the Mannerist aesthetic El Greco was an adherent and defender of Ideal art on equal terms with Michelangelo, Vasari and Zuccari. By his predilection for biblical themes matching the Counter-Reformation spirit he contributed to the strengthening and glorification of the Catholic faith.

Denijs Calvaert — a Flemish teacher

During Mannerism foreign artists were not only able to take their place in the Italian artistic world, but also to determine and influence the development of Italian art at crucial moments. A striking example is the painter Denijs Calvaert, known as Dionisio Fiammingo, who became the teacher of important Italian artists. Born in Antwerp c. 1540, he went to Italy at the age of twenty and remained there until his death in 1619. He settled in Bologna, studied under Lorenzo Sabbattini, a successful assistant of Vasari's, and opened a school of painting there. Among his pupils were Guido Reni, Domenico Zampieri, known as Domenichino, and Francesco Albani. Later these painters introduced Early Baroque. The only reason why Calvaert could exert such influence was that the Central Italian schools had lost their inner strength at the end of the sixteenth century. People were almost driven to fetch new blood from elsewhere. The northerners' ability to capture chiaroscuro, intimate space and genre-like narrative scenes gained an importance in accordance with the general inclination of the age to closeness to nature and reality. The reputations of the Upper Italian art schools, which were closer to the transalpine character, grew, while Florentine art threatened to succumb to a decadent formalism. Michelangelo's shapes and forms were used up; artists looked for new sources of strength and this time only the north could supply them. In a sense Denijs Calvaert can be claimed as the harbinger of the genius of naturalism, Michelangelo da Caravaggio.

The universality of Peter Paul Rubens

The real master in the realm of painting, who brilliantly united north and south, Dutch heritage and the lessons of Italy, was Peter Paul Rubens. He cannot be ascribed to one faction or the other; features of both combine to form an indivisible unity in his mighty figure. Rubens is essentially international and universal. He achieved the miracle of standing above the narrow boundaries of all narrow national artistic schools. Insofar as antiquity, humanism, a sense of reality, a desire for beauty and a scientific cultural ideal are recognized indispensable artistic qualities, he is a truly European figure. A most remarkable thing happened around 1600: the works of Rubens could be displayed on an equal footing all over Europe — in Mantua, Antwerp, Rome, London, Paris, in Germany and Spain. Nowhere were they felt to be strangers or intruders. The *Last Supper* by Rubens in the Brera at Milan is quite at home among purely Italian paintings. Nevertheless Rubens is no Italian, his artistic nature is international and it is perfectly capable of assimilating the basic Italian influences. In spite of that Rubens remained a Fleming. This ability to combine cultures shows true world citizenship.

Great efforts had been needed to achieve this universality and breadth: many generations of artists had to help each other, many Nordic artists had to set aside the native modes of expression which they may have preferred in favour of a more conventional, but also more grandiose vocabulary.

European residences an outlet for the new style

Never since the Middle Ages and the end of antiquity had science, art and princely display known such an intimate mutually complementary relationship as during the age of Mannerism. The forms of Italian cultural life were continually expanding. The hegemony of Italy was obvious in every branch of art: palaces, castles, patrician town halls, churches, tombs, fountains, festive decorations, panel pictures, furniture, statuettes for art-lovers, decoration and tableware. The spread of the Italian style was now by no means confined to its country of origin; Italian artists were at work everywhere; they could be found in Paris, Munich, Vienna, Prague, Toledo and Hampton Court. Every European ruler wanted to build his residence in the style appropriate to the age. Rulers were dominated by an entirely new idea of display and in a new sense display became an instrument of political power. No style was more suited for it than Mannerism, steeped as it was in allegory and emblem, besides being exclusive, noble, intellectual and capricious. Consequently within half a century it became a great feudal European fashion. Palaces and castles, royal funeral vaults and chapels, as well as garden layouts, were constructed on a vast scale, with a show of magnificence hitherto unknown. Now artists were able to give concrete form to the idea of the divine right of kings in a kind of grandiose pyrotechnic display.

New figures concentrating intellectual and political power arose in Italy: at Rome the Popes and the Senate, at Florence Dukes Cosimo I and Ferdinand dei Medici, at Caprarola Cardinal Alessandro Farnese, at Mantua Federigo II Gonzaga, at Genoa Admiral Andrea Doria and at Venice the line of Doges from Antonio Grimani to Niccolò da Ponte. The palace of the Vatican, the papal residence, covered more ground. A new feeling for display was exhibited on a lavish scale; the architectural complexes and hall decorations which dated from the Renaissance in their earlier form were given much greater, more comprehensive dimensions. To some extent the extension of the papal residence goes hand in hand with the identical tendencies observable in the gigantic undertaking of St Peter's which was being built at the time.

The Rome of the Popes and the Roman Senate

Michelangelo's frescoes on the ceiling of the Sistine Chapel already formed the prelude to smashing the usual *p. 30* standards; they transcended all previous rules. The violence of the ceiling paintings no longer harmonizes with the architectural details of the chapel. One has the uneasy feeling that the representation on the ceiling projects something much more powerful and dramatic than can be absorbed by the relatively small space. His *Last Judgment*

PERINO DEL VAGA: *St Michael*. Fresco in the Sala Paolina of Castel Sant'Angelo, Rome in the same chapel strives for a similar goal. The formless, the uncomprehended, indeed the inconceivable, are expressed there and that contradicts all the previous conventions of mural painting which strove for the harmony of dimensions between the solidity of the architecture and the space simulated by the painting. In a slightly different way the Sala di Costantino by Giulio Romano also makes the inconceivable acceptable. In it the painted expanses *p. 122* of wall, which are already gigantic enough on their own, produce a titanic effect. The impression of the colossal is further emphasized by the abrupt contrast with the small rooms immediately adjoining (the Stanze) which are most delicately calculated in their painted amplification of space by Raphael's frescoes. And as yet Raphael's loggie show no sign of the spatial top-heaviness of Mannerist works. The striving for excessive dimensions is evident in the gigantic niches of the Nicchione in the Belvedere Court of the Vatican. Begun by Bramante in a restrained manner, it was continued on a vast scale by Pirro Ligorio. Under Pope Paul III the Sala Regia was built to receive embassies from kings; architectonically the hall was grandiosely planned. The themes of the frescoes are significantly appropriate to the room's function: the triumphs of Popes over political opponents or gifts to the Vatican from great princes were portrayed to give the political visitors something to think about. More obviously than ever before the artistic framework and the associated psychological effect of such a state hall were made to serve the ends of government policy.

Additions were made to the general architectonic plan of the Vatican palace which impress by their dimensions and length alone. Suites of rooms were built: long corridors, galleries and halls. The Gallery of Geographical *pp. 27, 93* Maps was laid out by Pope Gregory XIII as a wing which separates the Belvedere Court from the Papal garden. Architects thought in vistas in perspective, such as Vasari introduced in the Uffizi in Florence, and in dimensions such as were used in the Escorial. The Vatican library was established by Pope Sixtus V. The building of the Audience Hall, the Sala Clementina, was completed in 1595 as the last Mannerist work. In a noble apotheosis Clement IX had his namesake and patron, Pope Clement I, glorified here by the monumental bravura pieces of illusionist painting by the brothers Giovanni and Cherubino Alberti.

But the Popes were no more satisfied with the Vatican's complex of buildings than the Medici were with the Palazzo Vecchio at Florence or the Gonzaga with the old Palazzo Ducale at Mantua. Just as the Medici and the Gonzaga built the Palazzo Pitti and the Palazzo del Tè as subsidiary buildings in which to display the development of their magnificence and power, the Popes used Castel Sant'Angelo for great frescoes. In it Perino del Vaga painted the Sala Paolina. The picture of St Michael overcoming the devil was supposed to celebrate the victory of Christi- *p. 17* anity over paganism and naturally also to record the political might of the Popes. The Roman Senate took a long time before it came round to Mannerist state halls. In 1596 it commissioned Giuseppe Cesari d'Arpino to paint the Salone, the gigantic hall in the Conservatori Palace. On the outside of the same palace Michelangelo *p. 123* erected his colossal order of columns, which served as a model for many later palaces. Scenes from ancient Roman history were chosen for the frescoes as being appropriate to the site: the discovery of Romulus and Remus, the Rape of the Sabine Women, the Battle between the Horatii and the Curiati, Numa Pompilius and the Vestal Virgins, and the expedition by Furius Camillus against the Veii. With this monumental commission the secular government of Rome caught up with the *Zeitgeist* at the end of Mannerism and acquired a comparable counterpart to the gigantic historical state frescoes in the Sala di Costantino in the Vatican.

Artistic commissions by the Farnese

Among the families who succeeded in giving visual form to their power were the Farnese, who commissioned many buildings and similar undertakings: the Palazzo Farnese at Rome, on which Michelangelo collaborated, a palace at Piacenza and the Farnese Gardens on the Palatine Hill. However the most impressive and grandiose *p. 26* work of art as a whole — Cardinal Alessandro Farnese was responsible for beginning it — was Caprarola near Viterbo. An old castle had once stood on the same site; later Antonio da Sangallo and Baldassare Peruzzi planned a fortress in the modern style, in the form of a regular pentagon. Beginning in 1559 Jacopo Barozzi, known as Vignola, continued and completed the castle from the modified plans of Peruzzi. Instead of being pentagonal the inner court was an unbroken circle. A series of suites were at the disposal of the royal household; they were used in turn according to the season, in winter or summer. Two tendencies conflict in this building: it is supposed to give the impression of being a real fortress and also to be a pleasant and artistic design. This combination has the effect of making the actual building look as if it was the practical realisation of some ideal plan. Influenced by Caprarola, the Florentine architect and archaeologist Giovanni Antonio Dosio produced designs for castles which were even more fantastic than Caprarola. Dosio said of his own plans: "The building must be both strong and beautiful at the same time." In all this Mannerist stylistic sensibility expresses itself intelligibly and clearly. The painting of Caprarola was undertaken by Taddeo Zuccari and a host of assistants. The frescoes exalt deeds from the Farnese family history. A complement to them is formed by Francesco Salviati's frescoes in the Palazzo Farnese at Rome and the frescoes by Giorgio Vasari in the Cancellaria there. It is an astonishingly rich programme which can compete with the greatest programmes of its time. Caprarola is linked with its immediate surroundings by the effective serpentine staircase in front of the building. In the sixteenth-century plans the garden design was much more discreet than the one which was actually followed from the beginning of the seventeenth century onwards. The building as a whole is particularly ennobled by its majestic scenic setting. It dominates the surrounding countryside as a big single block, rather like the Escorial, which was begun four years later. From the terrace a magnificent panorama can be seen, across to the Soracte and far over the Campagna. It was almost perverse to erect such an expensive building in such a remote district and even to commission an official fresco scheme of such luxury, but the representation of princely power was displayed at all costs, no matter what the locality.

The Medici at Florence

In order to record their dominion the Medici in Florence established their seat of government in the Palazzo Vecchio, formerly the seat of the city government. The exterior of the Gothic palace was allowed to retain its old appearance, but the interior was radically re-modelled by Vasari. This skilful impresario got the last ounce out of what can be done by a subsequent re-organization. State rooms as an expression of the new awareness of *p. 123* sovereignty were created. The Salone dei Cinquecento, which was originally intended for the Assemblies of the Grand Council, was now re-built for public audiences at the order of Cosimo I. Vasari and his assistants decorated the walls with gigantic frescoes taken from Florentine history. In the coffers of the ceiling there were also pictures based on the history of the town and the Medici.

The Gonzaga at Mantua

The Gonzaga made similar arrangements to the Florentine Medici in their own town of Mantua. Duke Federigo II commissioned Giulio Romano to rebuild the interior of the old Palazzo Ducale and decorate it with frescoes which produce an astonishingly grandiose impression of space. In a most progressive way the ceilings in the Sala di Troja were transformed by the painting into an agitated, cloudy sky; the hurly-burly of the Trojan War rolls from the edges in furious haste. Only fragments of the actual battle can be seen: chariots with galloping or *pp. 73, 94, 101* rearing horses. The heroic is captured by new violent methods. In the Palazzo del Tè Federigo II Gonzaga acquired a state building which was not hampered by being reconstructed from an existing edifice; the palace was the ingenious creation of Giulio Romano alone, a perfect whole. In it the great official feasts were celebrated. The palace was first shown in all its enchanting brilliance at the great reception for Emperor Charles V on 2 April 1530. Luigi Gonzaga da Borgoforte described this magnificent feast as follows:

"In the morning Federigo, sumptuously clad, ate with many princes and gentlemen, and rode with them to the castle to wake the Emperor and accompany him to the Palazzo del Tè. On their arrival they entered the great hall, the Sala dei Cavalli. Here they stayed a long time in contemplation. Then they went into the great room, the Sala *pp. 121, 128* di Psiche. His Majesty was most astonished at the sight of this hall, stayed there more than half an hour and praised everything lavishly. Then he went into the other apartment, which was called the Camera dei Pianeti *pp. 137, 141* and Venti, where the Duke lived, and which His Majesty greatly liked. Next they came to another room, called the Camera delle Aquile, which is very lovely with two superb doors of oriental jasper... And His Majesty wanted to see everything in detail. Then they went into the loggia which was not yet completed; but His Majesty imagined how well it would look when it was finished. And then they went into the garden, which pleased him greatly with the whole series of buildings which were laid out around this garden. The Emperor ate alone by the window of the Sala di Psiche and Federigo held his napkin, so that he could dry his august hands, while the retinue ate in the Sala dei Cavalli. After the refreshments a game of handball was organized, which once again pleased the Emperor greatly.

"He went on playing for four hours, being extremely active, and knew a great deal about this game. They played for twenty gold scudi and His Majesty lost sixty scudi. After this exertion, Charles changed his shirt and remained a while longer.

"In the evening sixty of the first and most handsome noblemen and noblewomen to be found in Mantua were invited to a feast. At eleven o'clock all the rooms were lit by torchlight and the carriages of the noblewomen arrived. The Emperor stood at the end of the Sala dei Cavalli to receive their homage. Then, standing with his hand on a chair upholstered with cloth of gold, he watched them dancing until three o'clock in the morning. The Jumping Dance or Gagliarda was performed by many young Mantuan nobles according to our method and custom, an entertainment which His Majesty watched with great pleasure. Then followed a meal of such variety and abundance that it lasted three hours. The ladies and gentlemen ate it at tables which were arranged around the Sala dei Cavalli. After the meal His Majesty withdrew to the Camera dei Venti and had an hour's public conversation with Cardinal Cibò, and expressed great praise of these rooms, and also of their master and inventor... And His Majesty wanted to understand everything in detail. While the ladies gossiped in the Sala di Psiche, the Sala dei Cavalli was cleaned and swept, after which the ball began again.

"The Emperor again stood by his chair and dancing went on until seven in the morning. Then, in the light of more than a thousand torches, night seemed to change into day, the Emperor rode to the castle on horseback, the ladies and gentlemen returned to their houses. Giulio's new fantasies sank into darkness once more and so ended the magnificent festivity which was organized in the Palazzo del Tè."

The Doria at Genoa

On a more modest scale Andrea Doria had a residential palace built in Genoa, actually some way outside the town, but also as an affirmation of his sovereignty. The Papal admiral commissioned Giovanni Angelo Montorsoli, one of Michelangelo's closest collaborators, to construct this building between 1522 and 1529, and surrounded it with a large garden. A statue of Zeus was placed on top of the palace, so that there would be no doubt who lived there. To crown this, the rear side of the palace was decorated with a large fountain of Neptune by Carlone, 1599–1601, with the sea god assuming the features of Andrea Doria. Perino del Vaga, the pupil of Raphael, painted the halls in the interior. In the atrium there were divinities, triumphal processions and the heroic figures of the Capitani dei Doria. The ceiling paintings in the main hall emphasized the patron's importance in the light of ancient mythological history even more. In one hall the picture of Aeneas' shipwreck, now unfortunately destroyed, was to be seen; but one can still gaze in astonishment at the bombastic style of these paintings in the *Fall of the Giants* in the other hall.

Faced with the importance of Genoa, Venice, in conformity with her glorious historical past, made a hitherto unparalleled use of art to illustrate the power of the state. In no other town in Italy, not even Florence, was this so succesfully done, nor did the official monuments combine to form such a wonderful group of civic buildings as those around St Mark's Square and the Piazetta: St Mark's, the Procuratoria, The Doges' Palace, the Mint and the Library of St Mark's. Although Venice's political influence was on the wane in the sixteenth century, magnificent artistic schemes testifying to the city's power were still carried out. The paintings in the Doges' Palace are the outstanding example, but sculpture also contributed. In 1540 the ante-room of the Procuratoria, the Loggetta at the foot of the campanile, was fitted out like a jewelcase with statues and reliefs by Jacopo Sansovino.

The Doges at Venice

In spite of the reconstruction (carried out by Antonio da Ponte and Andrea Palladio) which was necessary after the fires of 1574 and 1577, the mediaeval edifice of the Doges' Palace had not undergone any significant changes, so that the general Gothic appearance was retained. But the paintings destroyed by fire in the interior, among them the great works of the Venetian historical painters of two centuries, were replaced. Making tremendous efforts, the still living but quite aged great masters, Paolo Veronese, Jacopo Tintoretto and Palma il Giovane shared in the redecoration. Within a few years gigantic murals appeared in the state halls. These total transformations of halls competed with contemporary solutions of similar monumental commissions in Rome and Florence. The Venetian decorative canvases differ entirely from the Florentine and Roman frescoes in that they pay less attention to the illusionist architectonic organization of the interiors. Expenditure on frames and niches is considerably less; Venetian painting is much more modest in the decorative architectonic accessories of its pictures. Such rich frames as existed were not on the walls but on the massive heavy carved wooden ceilings. The schemes for their subject matter are also correspondingly simpler and looser in their allegorical allusions. Whatever may be lacking in the richness of the frames and the subsidiary allegorical figures is, in Tintoretto's case at least, made up for by the *bravura* of the composition, the interesting play of light and dark, and the glowing colouring.

If purely narrative historical painting was cultivated in the Doges' Palace during the fourteenth and fifteenth centuries, as well as the portrayal of contemporary life in its realistic sumptuous development, the latter part of the sixteenth century introduced a more solemn and elevated attitude to history: the triumphal concept of the state was directly incorporated into powerful allegories. Very impressive in this connection is the invention of the figure of "Venezia" and her elevation to the Christian-pagan pantheon. Venezia may be guided by Jupiter in the lagoon, appear to the Doge Niccolò da Ponte from heaven or be surrounded by allegorical figures representing the towns of Verona, Padua and Brescia. Together with Paolo Veronese, more realistic and more restrained in the formal organization of a picture, the Mannerist Jacopo Tintoretto carried out a large part of the decoration of the halls. His paintings are mainly divided between the Sala delle Quattro Porte, the Sala Anticollegio, the Sala dello Scrutinio and the Sala del Maggior Consiglio. They are works from the later period of Tintoretto's creative life when he was the absolute master of his media. Even in the realistically portrayed battle scenes he succeeded in making the actual event become a dreamily etherealized supernatural happening. Only a Mannerist painter of genius could succeed in transforming the Battle of Zara in the Sala dello Scrutinio into a vision. The Sala del

p. 29

Maggior Consiglio shows what he could produce when in charge of the decoration of rooms of excessive dimensions. The homage of the civic government to the Goddess Venezia appears on the ceiling as a gigantic picture *p. 29* surrounded by four battle scenes. The whole of the shorter wall is taken up by the painting *Paradise*. This collection *p. 31* of heavenly hosts is the Venetian counterpart to Michelangelo's *Last Judgment* in its masterly artistic handling of the theme. With this picture Tintoretto says the very last word on his creative work. Just as selfwilled as Michelangelo, he freed himself here in his own way from the traditional compositional schema. The Venetian had the inner freedom to transform the giant ceremonial picture whose iconography was intrinsically fixed into a cosmic scenic event in a personal artistic vision. This was only possible because the painter as a modern man stood in opposition to the hieratic theme. The billows of the cloud bank have become more decisive than the arrangement of the persons. Whereas Michelangelo emphasized the primacy of the human figure, Tintoretto gave the palm to landscape in these heavenly scenes. This is the breakthrough of a new concept of the monumental event in mural painting; but it had no serious successor in its uniquely bold solution.

François I of France

Just as in the political field François I fought tenaciously and intrepidly with the great powers of his day, the Hapsburgs and Charles V, and tried every expedient in order to play a part in the European concert of powers, so he strove indefatigably for brilliant effects in the artistic display of his sovereignty. François I wanted to make Fontainebleau which he had chosen as his residence one of the most splendid royal seats in Europe. State rooms *p. 121* such as the Galleries of François I and Henri II were built. François I was also skilful at making conquests in the field of artistic politics. He attracted a host of Italian artists to his court and harnessed the newly blossoming style of Mannerism to his chariot of fame. Side by side with the Italian painters a crowd of stucco workers, designers and bronze-founders were active and a tapestry manufactory was also established. But Greek and Roman works were lacking. Because there were no classical originals in France, François I had plaster casts of famous statues such as the Laocoon and the Apollo Belvedere made and he sent artists to Italy to buy works of art. As a result the great Italian style became important in France, and France was able to play a part in the general development of art in Europe. These endeavours were continued by his son Henri II and after Henri's death in 1559 by his widow, Catherine de Medici, culminating in the cycle by Rubens glorifying the government of Maria de Medici in the Palais de Luxembourg.

Minor princes in Germany

There were so many minor princes in sixteenth-century Germany that their residences were of necessity on a more modest scale. The castles at Aschaffenburg and Heiligenberg were built. Mostly it was a case of old fortresses which needed modernization. They were frequently given a more modern appearance by the simple introduction of magnificent portals. The Bavarian Duke Wilhelm V erected his residence on Mount Trausnitz and summoned *pp. 121, 129* German and Italian painters to decorate it. An attempt was made to enlarge the old-fashioned narrow apartments by *trompe l'œil* frescoes. The castle contains the original so-called *Clown's Steps* with comic scenes from the *Commedia dell' Arte*. None of this can compare with Italian or French royal households, but there is one edifice still standing in Germany which can compete with the great international works: the Ottheinrich wing of Heidelberg *pp. 26, 90* Castle. This work too is not an independent new design of a whole castle but merely a section introduced into the old existing building. The Ottheinrichbau with its magnificent grandiose façade, unique on German soil, was inserted between older buildings, the Glass Hall to its left and the Ludwig building to its right. With it Count

Palatine Ottheinrich erected, between 1553 and 1562, a façade which takes its place among the great monuments of the new international Italian style. In the organisation of its storeys and the richness of the statuary decoration it stands comparison with the palace façades at Rome, for example that of the Palazzo Spada. Here, as there, the cycle of statues of the antique gods is called on to endow the palace with the highest, most ceremonial and majestically exalted character possible. Ottheinrich had studied the famous architectural works of his time and the contemporary revised editions of Vitruvius, as well as the books on architecture by Serlio, and he collected ornamental engravings after Raphael, Michelangelo and Giulio Romano. From this world of the imagination the Count created a polyphonic synthesis of architecture, statuary decoration and ornamental building. A triumphal door which is reminiscent both in form and content of the Julius Monument by Michelangelo was erected as the entrance. But in spite of all these allusions and reminiscences a harmonious masterpiece arose, of a completely original character. The Dutch sculptor Alexander Colijn was called in, as he had already worked on Maxmilian's tomb at Innsbruck. He produced the best and most advanced examples of all sculpture executed in Germany at the time.

Philip II and the Escorial

Spain acquired its residence in the new Mannerist court style relatively late. Charles V spent much of his life travelling and his constant political troubles did not give him time to build himself a central residence. His son

p. 27 Philip II first decided to record his sovereignty in the total work of art of a princely seat. It became the Escorial. It was erected between 1563 and 1586 at a speed which is astonishing in view of the enormous undertaking. It is typical of the original conception of this residence that, freed of all historical ties in the choice of site, it was produced as a complete and freely inventive creation. The Escorial stands neither in Toledo, the old royal city, nor in Madrid, the new royal town. It owes its site to strictly rational considerations. A commission was sent out from Madrid to find the best place for the residence from the hygienic and geographical points of view, and the choice fell on the mountain village of El Escorial, which lies at a height of 3,341 feet and enjoys cool, clear air. A memorial chapel and a monastery were included in the plan of the residence. In this way irreconcilable points of view unite, and different ends, meanings and levels of life intersect. Only Mannerism could bring off the feat of uniting monastic life, secular display, a royal household and the encouragement of knowledge in one single monumental building.

Rudolf II at Prague

The latest great European cultural residence in the Mannerist sense was Prague. When Rudolf II was crowned Emperor of Germany in 1575, he chose the Hradschin as his permanent royal seat. He was an introvert and as far as possible avoided wearing himself out in external entanglements and distinguishing himself in warlike arguments. During his reign he attached importance to seeking a settlement between the warring creeds and ensuring a peaceful dignified existence for the peoples under his sway. He himself suffered from fits of depression; a believer in astrology, he felt that he was under the sign of Saturn, the planet of men of melancholy disposition. He took the keenest interest in the projects of artists, scholars and alchemists, and spent many hours in their laboratories and studios. When it came to the encouragement of art Rudolf II was particularly fond of the more intimate arts of sculpture and painting; significantly enough he had not sufficient energy to construct a new residence. He remained in the family castle, the Hradschin, to which he made only minor additions. The north wing with the "Spanish Hall" was built on the slope of the Hirschgraben and on the south side the "Lambrecht-stube" was built on to the eastern wing of the palace. But Rudolf devoted himself fervently to his ruling passion, art-collecting. He erected his famous Chamber of Art and Wonders and in 1577 appointed as its keeper a well-known numismatist, Jacopo Strada, a native of Mantua, who dabbled in painting himself. The elegant, refined movement of Mannerism was strongly represented in the international circle: in sculpture by one of Giovanni da Bologna's main pupils, Adriaen de Vries; in painting by the Fleming Bartholomeus Spranger from Antwerp, the German Hans von Aachen and the Swiss Josef Heintz, while the ludicrous eccentric Giuseppe Arcimboldi was brought from Italy. Hans Vredeman de Vries and his son were engaged as architectural painters. They were responsible for the decoration of the north wing of the Hradschin. Their endeavours to create considerable enlargements of space with the help of perspective are parallel to those of the Italian *quadraturiste* working at the same time, such as the brothers Cherubino and Giovanni Alberti. Paul Vredeman de Vries painted "a ceiling-painting on canvas 200 feet long and 80 feet wide in such a way that he raised the vaulting by means of foreshortened pillars, decorated the curved surfaces of the arches with grotesques and introduced a large opening in the middle, all in exact perspective", as Karel van Mander tells us. The optical illusion alone was the main attraction of this undertaking. "In another smaller hall Paul Vredeman de Vries painted another ceiling, in equally exact perspective." The fact that many halls were done in the same manner testifies to a flagging of invention. "Here the twelve months were portrayed and in the middle was a large circular picture of Jupiter armed with thunderbolts, using foreshortening..." "At the Emperor's wish Paul also painted in perspective a picture of a gallery giving a view of a garden with a fountain, through which the Emperor often wanted to pass in error. He frequently came to watch the painter."

Decorative art, once so complicated and ingenious in its subject matter and apparatus, which were cleverly puzzled out, ended in purely visual tricks and surprise effects. The feeling for genuinely monumental display seems to be missing in the Emperor. A sovereign who should have represented his dominion, turned into an individualist wrapped up in himself, who even used architecture and monumental painting for the restricted needs of his living space. Paul Vredeman de Vries had to arrange his rooms so that he could hang in them his paintings in order. So for the Emperor the arrangement of his private gallery was the most important, most architectonic task: the easel picture wins the day over monumental state decorations. In addition, de Vries had to arrange things so that the Emperor could go everywhere in his castle unseen and through covered rooms: architecture became protective armour for an unbalanced crank.

The ruler is the central figure in his court of the Muses: painters, sculptors, architects and poets are waiting for commissions; some of the artists hold models and plans of the projected buildings and fountains

GIORGIO VASARI: *Archduke Cosimo I Medici surrounded by his court artists. c* 1570. Palazzo Vecchio, Florence

25

Caprarola, near Viterbo. Built for the Farnese family 1559–1573

The Ottheinrichbau of Heidelberg Castle. Built for the Count Palatine 1553–1562

The country-setting of their palaces and the massive dimensions of the buildings were an expression of the rulers' desire to assert their sovereignty

The Escorial, built for Philip II of Spain. It was begun in 1563 and finished in 1586

The Vatican. A view of the Belvedere Court and the wing of the Galleria delle Carte Geografiche. The different phases of its construction were executed under Popes Nicholas V, Julius II, Pius IV, Gregory XIII and Sixtus V

MICHELANGELO: *The Last Judgement* on the altar wall of the Sistine Chapel was completed in 1541. This illustration was compiled from several large plates after the engraving by Giorgio Ghisi

28

'In wartime the Muses are silent': the seven liberal arts which have fallen asleep during the war are re-awakened. Significantly the scene unfolds on Roman soil; the ruins on the Palatine Hill and Trajan's Column are identifiable

LUKAS DE HEERE (1534–1584): The Seven Liberal Arts in Wartime. Pinacoteca, Turin

TINTORETTO: The Battle of Zara. Sala dello Scrutinio, the Doge's Palace, Venice c 1584–1587

MICHELANGELO's frescoes in the Sistine Chapel in the Vatican

The impressive architectural organization of an interior, like the magnificent pictorial treatment, is a means of paying tribute to the dignity and power of the ruler; contemporary political events can be recorded in the sublimer form of solemn historical scenes with allegorical embellishments

The Sala Regia in the Vatican, completed in 1573

30

Jacopo Tintoretto: *Paradise*. Sketch for the gigantic canvas in the Sala del Maggior Consiglio in the Doge's Palace at Venice. *c* 1579. Louvre, Paris

Francesco Salviati: Frescoes in the Palazzo Farnese at Rome, post-1550. *The glorification of Pope Paul III*. François I and Charles V can be seen on the left, and Martin Luther and Cardinal Gaetani on the right. The winged figure on the far right is Fama, the allegory of fame

BENVENUTO CELLINI: Base of the
Perseus group, dated between
1545 and 1554. Loggia dei Lanzi,
Florence

*In the niches are statuettes of Diana
and Zeus, and at the corners busts of
Diana of Ephesus; above, tragic
masks and goats' heads comment on
the tragedy ('tragodia' means goat-song)
of the beheading of the Medusa*

32

Mannerist Art as a medium for the personal affirmation of autocratic power

The new evaluation of Art

A survey of the works of art produced after the Renaissance immediately betrays not only the new problems they deal with but also the new accent with which they were expressed. The arts as a whole have entered another stage of evaluation and painting in particular had a clear cut mission to fulfil. Symptomatic of this are the statements in the *Dialogo della Pittura* by Lodovico Dolce, which appeared in Venice in 1557. The important thing about it is the stand taken against the idea that painting is only a kind of handicraft. He also opposes the low evaluation of the fine arts in the Middle Ages, when they were classed among the *artes mechanicae*, in contrast to the more highly-thought of *artes liberales* or liberal arts. Even during the Renaissance educated artists, among them Leon Battista Alberti, Francesco di Giorgio and Piero della Francesca, strove for the elevation of the fine arts, especially painting with its theory of perspective and proportion, to the ranks of the exact sciences. By this means the arts could later play an effective part in the general cultural activities of the time. Leonardo da Vinci, Francisco de Hollanda and other writers on art rated drawing so highly that they recommended placing it as an eighth art beside the seven old *artes liberales*. Painting was attributed a universal value. In his treatise on painting (1538), de Hollanda goes so far as to put the hyperbolical claim in Michelangelo's mouth "that there is only one single art and science on earth, namely that of drawing or painting, from which all others stem and form part of; for if we rightly weigh up everything we do in this life, we will find that everyone in the world paints, without knowing it: both in the creation and production of new forms and shapes, and in clothing and drapery; in filling space with buildings and houses, which are like paintings; by arranging the fields and acres of the earth in lines and designs; by sailing the sea with the help of sails; in the battles and arrangements of army ranks; and lastly when dying and being buried, in short during each and all of our activities." The same writer tells of a conversation between Michelangelo and his learned and pious friend Vittoria Colonna about the "noble art of painting": they could not have found a nobler or more elevated subject for conversation, because painting stems from God himself, who, as "painter above all painters", created us, p. 37 after he had painted the earth for us. A picture in Vienna by Dosso Dossi shows how alive this concept was; it portrays Zeus creating the butterfly as a painter sitting at his easel.

The dignified status of art

The act of painting attained to a hitherto unimagined dignity and became almost a religious activity. Francisco de Hollanda states that, apart from his Christianity, there is truly no greater dignity nor honour for a man than the desire to be a painter. At the end of Mannerism Federigo Zuccari, in his theoretical work, *Idea* (1608), places the art of *disegno* in the immediate vicinity of theology, indeed of Good. The word *disegno* was interpreted as *signo di Dio*. This extravagantly high evaluation of painting is new. Painting was still a long way from it in the more rational thinking of the Renaissance. Leonardo called it grand-daughter of nature and he only considered

33

it as related to God in that capacity. In addition he only called the painter sir, *signore* or *padrone*, and God stood high above; he was the creator of everything.

From its attitude to spiritual things Mannerist art also adopts a very definite unmistakably sociological position. The high esteem in which painting was held is shown by the epithets applied to it: Michelangelo Biondo named his book which came out in 1549, *Nobilissima pittura*, and Karel van Mander speaks of the *Edel vry Schilderkonst*. The social classification of art in the upper and noble classes obviously comes from an important sentence by Ludovico Dolce: "It is certain that an art is all the nobler, the more it is respected by higher personalities and intelligences. Now at all times painting was held in high esteem by Kings, Emperors and scholars..." Equally significant is another of his arguments: "So I can quite easily understand why the Greeks, who fully recognized the high worth of the art of painting, forbade their slaves to paint", or when Condivi relates about the activity at Michelangelo's school "that he always wanted to entrust the painting to noble persons, as the ancients did, and not to the plebeians". Such views are inside confirmation that the art of the sixteenth century, and to an outstanding extent that of Mannerism, was an art of the princely, courtly and cultured circles. Art was something exclusive, something which could and should only be accessible to men who socially and mentally were able to exist in the upper and highest spheres. There was no question of the art of the Mannerists being bought and commissioned by townsmen and farmers, seamen and innkeepers as was later true of Dutch genre painting in the seventeenth century.

Lodovico Dolce also legitimized the superiority of painting with historical arguments, which rely on great names. He goes back to antiquity and produces the patrons of the Greeks and the Roman emperors as witnesses. Thus he tells us "that even Nero, who was otherwise debauched and cruel, painted and modelled admirable clay bas-reliefs, just as Julius Caesar was renowned for his paintings and intaglios". This close connection between the painter and potentates of world history went without saying; "the painters were rightly always held in special esteem, because it appears that they are the men who excel the rest in brains and courage in that they dare to imitate by art what God has created..." Both Michelangelo and Leonardo da Vinci were given the title of *il Divino* by their contemporaries as a mark of the highest respect. The reason why Michelangelo in particular was worthy to be called "the Divine" is given by Vasari in the introduction to his lives of the Italian artists. Michelangelo not only mastered one or the other of the fine arts, all three of which are indebted to *disegno*, drawing, but "in our age *la Bontà divina,* the divine goodness, sent us Michelangelo Buonarroti, in whom all three arts shine forth with equal perfection". Painters could not help being amazed by his paintings and sculptors by his sculpture, on top of which there was his architecture. So he must deservedly be called the unique sculptor, greatest painter and most distinguished architect. "We can certainly confirm that those who call him divine do not err in the least, for in a divine way he has used the three most praiseworthy and ingenious arts to be found among mortals like a god."

The markedly political and didactical value of the pictures was also recognized and fully appreciated. Dolce uses a historical metaphor in this connection: Quintus Fabius and Publius Scipio were supposed to have urged themselves to noble deeds whenever they contemplated the portraits of their ancestors. But the purpose of painting was not always restricted to such lofty aims by the Mannerists.

Art and practical science

An example is the attempt to include the extraordinary achievements of scientific cartography in the overall field of art. With the Mannerists the difference between purely mechanical reproductive techniques and created art forms was not yet quite clear, for charts were also used in the big schemes of decoration. The period saw the building of the long corridor of the *Galleria delle carte geografiche* in the Vatican; in the Palazzo Vecchio at Florence a whole room was distinguished in that its built-in cupboards were painted with bright maps. Nor can we assume that this introduction served a purely practical purpose, for its aim was more ideal and artistic. Only from this attitude to the scientific technique of reproduction, which was highly developed just then, was it possible for scientific and geographical decorative painting to play a very big part even in fresco painting. But on the whole there is no doubt that in the age of Mannerism, in spite of every frequently acrobatic gamble, intellectual extravagance and barely comprehensible fantasy, great decorative painting still met an inner need and was generally regarded as an essential part of the cultural possibilities of enhancing life. Consequently Dolce could claim that in public and private buildings "without the adornment of beautiful paintings, the crown of delightful decoration" was missing. Painting belonged to the civilized life; doing without it was considered in the sixteenth century as a lack of strength in cultural development leading to barbarism.

Art and cultural propaganda

Works of art were introduced as a means of campaigning for the maintenance of ideological and moral values among men. Not until this century of fierce ideological religious controversies could art be given such a large-scale propagandist task. From it resulted the strikingly marked moralistic and didactic nature of the Mannerist work of art. Art could become a part of politics. It was a new phenomenon in the history of culture when an ecclesiastical council, the Council of Trent, worked out a detailed plan stating how works of art could and should be deployed on the ideological, cultural and religious battlefront. Views on artistic matters were now much more frequently brought under the official control of the ruling classes. Pope Pius V declared war on the antique and the achievements of humanism were in danger of being lost. Pope Paul IV wanted the Passion of Christ portrayed with greater reverence as befitting its high seriousness. He had a picture which portrayed Mary with child removed from Sta Maria Maggiore. Even an event such as the founding of the Accademia di San Luca in Rome in 1577 did not take place merely owing to the artists' need to organize themselves. The letter of foundation from Pope Gregory XIII expressly emphasized the aim of leading art back to the old faith and not surrendering it to the heathen way of thinking. In 1588 the Academy was allotted the church of Sta Martina in the Forum as its headquarters by Pope Sixtus V. Religious ties were expressed even in the housing of this Academy.

Decorum and ecclesiastical art

In many of its ordinances the Council of Trent was intent on reforming ecclesiastical art. It was forbidden to exhibit pictures in churches which had any relation to a false dogma. Everything impure and all provocative features were to be avoided in pictures. Ecclesiastical works of art would be inspected for their decorum, i.e. their seemliness, and their religious content. Commentaries explaining this were written by both priests and laymen. In 1564 a book by the priest Giovanni Andrea Gilio appeared: "Two dialogues, the first deals with the obligations concerning propriety and morality of courtly men of letters..., in the second the subject is the errors of the painter with reference to history, with many observations about the *Last Judgment* painted by Michelangelo Buonarroti". In it the author objected to *mostrare la forza del'arte* (demonstrating the violence of art) and the autocratic artistic endeavours of the Mannerists. For example he reproached them for not depicting the dead body of Christ on his descent from the cross covered with wounds as historical truth as the religious content of the theme demanded, but as a beautiful body full of vigour. The *Flagellation* by Sebastiano del Piombo in S Pietro in Montorio at Rome was merely a beautiful nude, yet this was exactly the sort of theme where the ugly was appropriate and even required by decorum. In such remarks a peculiar emotional naturalism emerges, which makes sweeping demands. St Lawrence must actually be shown in his torments on the red-hot gridiron, and in the depiction of St Sebastian, Gilio insists on an instruction which is very typical of the man in the street who wants his horrors depicted clearly: the saint should appear bristling with arrows like a porcupine.

He claimed that artists must be educated and well read, that is, *letterati*. Their main interest was directed to things artistic and the result was that they neglected the religious content of the work of art. The Inquisition held inquiries to ensure the appropriate *decoro* of altar paintings. Paolo Veronese was accused of not having matched the dignity of the scene in his *Feast in the House of Levi*, because he put a Negro's head next to Christ's. The painter justified himself by pointing out that he had needed darkness at this very spot for reasons of artistic contrast. El Greco was reproached because he had placed the heads of the myrmidons of the law higher than the figure of Christ in his painting the *Despoiling of Christ*, which was unfitting. Owing to the need for spiritual purity in artistic conceptions, people now found fresh attraction in late mediaeval devotional pictures. Pope Pius V had the *Last Judgment* by Fra Angelico copied by Bartholomeus Spranger; later this painting was even inserted in his tomb as a decoration. The lack of purity of content in pictures was felt so urgently that it led to the publication in Rome in 1593 of the *Tractatio de Poesi et Pictura ethica* by a Mantuan scholar, Antonio Possevino, who was secretary to Ignatius Loyola.

All questions of the religious admissibility of works of art, which had to serve in the ecclesiastical domain and were possibly compromised by virtuosity, were brought under official control by the establishment of an ecclesiastical censor. On 13 November 1603 Cardinal Camillo Borghese issued an edict that every ecclesiastical work must be submitted to him or his representative for appraisal.

In case of non-compliance with the regulations, the artist was threatened with heavy punishments. The artist was recommended to submit preliminary sketches or cartoons for examination when executing a commission. The measures went so far that they even invaded private spheres. In 1596 the Synod of Salerno decided to have religious pictures in private collections examined by the priests, who had to report to the bishop when offences against the ecclesiastical rules or good morals were detected.

The new relationship between sovereign and artist

As yet there has not been enough research into the history of the new relations between the nobleman and artist in the sixteenth century for us to be quite clear about its general cultural and political significance. A novel phenomenon was that politics alone no longer sufficed the modern sovereigns, whether they were temporal or spiritual rulers. It was also true that politics had to be practised in the spiritual cultural field to satisfy the general will of the age. Side by side with the military battlefield was the metaphorical battlefield of the spiritual penetration and conquest of the world in art and science. Here too the prince had to be a genuine ruler, he had to set the fashion, be a leader, determine trends. At this epoch art and science were still much more intensively yoked in state and dynastic concerns than after the French Revolution by which culture was removed from its direct relation to public life and political activity. In the last sentence of the introduction to his treatise on painting Francisco de Hollanda was able to announce that he had intended to examine "what purpose all the distinguished and necessary science of drawing serves and is useful for in the state, in both peace and war..."

Dosso Dossi: *Jupiter, Mercury and Virtue*. Kunsthistorisches Museum, Vienna

This theme was also treated in large-scale paintings. Lucas de Heere painted *The Seven Liberal Arts in Wartime*. *p. 29*
We see the personifications of the arts sleeping on Mount Parnassus, while a pitched battle is in progress on earth; but the gods on Olympus decide to make peace and send Mercury to awaken the arts. Vasari's fresco in the Cancellaria at Rome, in which Pope Paul III is glorified as the prince of peace, alludes to the flowering of the arts in peacetime; the inscription reads: *In pace optimae artes excoluntur, ingenia ad frugem coalescunt, publicae privataeque opes augentur* (In peacetime the best arts are cultivated, minds unite in fruitful activity, public and private fortunes are increased).

Enhancement of the ruler's reputations by works of art

The sovereigns were in a fever for specific artistic projects to be completed during their reign. In this way their fame was increased and the idea was that their name would go down to eternity. This was the case with the building of St Peter's, when the Popes Sixtus V and Gregory XIII pressed for the completion of the first monument of Christianity while they were still in office. Works of art were frequently placed on an equal footing with great political events; on the completion of an artistic project medals would be struck, as after a victorious battle. It happened on the occasion of the completion of the paintings in the Escorial by Federigo Zuccari. Gandolfo Posino wrote a sonnet on the unveiling of the *Last Judgement* by Michelangelo which culminated in the lines: "O holy Roma, never did Caesar or any of the illustrious emperors grant thee the joy of such a triumph", and Vasari wrote on the same theme: "Paul III, thou art fortunate, because God has granted that under thy protection spreads the fame which the pens of the writers will preserve for thee and him (Michelangelo)! How greatly are thy merits elevated by his art!"

It is to the credit of fourteenth and fifteenth-century humanism that mental victories could appear on an equal footing with purely military victories. This spiritual movement resulted in thought, art and science being conceived of as independent special domains alongside religion and the state which had their own rights and respect to claim. In the new world of the sixteenth century art became an important instrument of power for the reputation of the ruler, and the princes had to recourse to art; they did not want to be backward in the field of spiritual and cultural penetration of the world, or worse still be cut off from it. They had to play cultural politics and support or spiritually confirm their dominion with this weapon too. If one can so express it, the princes had to draw up their troops on the field of art, issue their orders, defend their claims; they had their battles to fight, their victories to celebrate. The numerous court artists now belonged to the princely households of necessity and with more justification than before.

The ruling houses and their court artists

A new phenomenon was the intimate exchange of ideas between rulers and artists which prevailed at court; the Medici in Florence are a good example. The best illustration of this new relationship is the *tondo* by Giorgio Vasari on the ceiling of the Palazzo Vecchio, which shows Cosimo I sitting in the midst of his circle of artists and demon- *p. 25*
strates how they all flourish under his protection. He tried to portray the whole circle. The following artists appear: San Marino, Bartolommeo Ammanati, Tasso, Vasari, Baccio Bandinelli, probably Bacchiaca, Francesco di San Jacopo, Cellini, Tribolo and Nanni Ungliero. All these men actually did apply all their ability and volition to serving the house of Medici and spreading its cultural fame. And this or similar situations existed everywhere. The princes for their part were intent on winning the best, most famous and effective names. Michelangelo, who as an artistic figure staked out entirely new dimensions of universal historical impact for himself, occupied a special

position. His biographer Condivi was astonished at the efforts princes made "to possess him". Apart from the four Popes, Julius, Leo, Clement and Paul, the Grand Turk was interested in him, not to mention King François I of France and the Signoria of Venice. Condivi remarks about this: "These are no ordinary things, such as happen every day, but new and outside normal usage, and tend only to occur in the case of quite unique and outstanding excellence." In order to quote someone comparable the biographer mentions Homer who was claimed as a son by so many Greek cities.

In the sixteenth century it was the fashion for every ruling house in Europe to have its court artists: Popes Julius II and Paul III had Michelangelo; Emperor Charles V Titian and Seisenegger; King Philip II Titian, El Greco, Tibaldi, Coello, Leone Leoni and Pompeo Leoni; Emperor Rudolf II Bartholomeus Spranger, Hans von Aachen, Josef Heintz, Giuseppe Arcimboldi and Adriaen de Vries; King François I Rosso il Fiorentino, Niccolò dell'Abbate, Primaticcio, Cellini and the Clouets; King Henry VIII Holbein the Younger; Duke Cosimo I Medici Vasari, Cellini, Bandinelli and Giovanni da Bologna; the Doges of Venice Titian, Tintoretto and Veronese; the Farnese Vasari and the brothers Zuccari; the Gonzaga Giulio Romano, Tintoretto and Rubens; Elector Johann Friedrich of Saxony Cranach the Elder and Cranach the Younger; Duke Albrecht V of Bavaria Hans Mielich; the Margraves of Baden Tobias Stimmer; Duke Charles III of Lothringen Jacques Bellange; Archduke Albert and Archduchess Isabella, the Spanish Governors in the Netherlands, Otto van Veen and Rubens. Ruler and artist were brought very close together. Only Michelangelo broke through every single barrier which had previously been erected between a ruler and an artist. He behaved exactly as if he was of the same rank as his patrons the Popes. His work was determined solely by the dictates of his own will, and the Popes submitted to his will. His contemporaries knew about this and we know from his own mouth, via Francisco de Hollanda, what Michelangelo himself felt about this question: "I must tell you that precisely my important artistic position has given me such freedom that I keep my felt hat calmly on my head during a conversation with the Pope and speak quite unconstrainedly with him. But he does not kill me on that account; rather did he first make life possible for me. To be sure I impose restrictions on myself in his service, because there it is necessary, but not in personal communication with him". Condivi calls Pope Julius I the Prince of Christianity and Michelangelo Prince of the Fine Arts. In other words each was sovereign in his own domain; the ruler is master in the kingdoms of Jupiter, Mars and Bellona, the artist in the kingdoms of Mercury or Minerva. It was proud self-assurance of this kind which enabled the late Mannerist Gerrit Pietrsz. of Amsterdam to say, as Karel van Mander tells us, that he "would not change the brush for the sceptre of the King of Spain, he would rather be a good painter than a great prince".

Friendly relations between princes and artists

However the princes did not only value the artists in their pursuit of political aims, they also took a frequent and particularly human personal interest in things artistic and respected the creative artist highly. Prince and artist could coalesce and share the same symbiotic destiny. When the Elector Johann Friedrich of Saxony was put in prison after losing the battle of Mühlberg in 1547, Lucas Cranach the Elder shared the same fate out of personal loyalty to his prince. From the fifteenth century onwards the Medici cultivated a particularly good and friendly relationship with the artists at their court, and when the family were banished from Florence from 1527 to 1530, the Florentine sculptor Bandinelli followed his chief patrons and protectors into exile. After their return he naturally received even more numerous commissions from them and was allowed to execute the tombs of the Medici Popes Clement VII and Leo X. Duke Federigo II Gonzaga was so enthusiastic about Giulio Romano and the works he executed for him that he felt he could not live without them.

Artists had to provide more and more for the private amusement of the art-loving princes; enjoyment of art was an increasingly important characteristic. The difference in rank between the sovereigns and artists generally relaxed in favour of less formal freer mutual intercourse. Benvenuto Cellini, for example, relates that Duke Cosimo Medici took him into his palace and liked to watch him at his goldsmith's work. In return Cellini had access to the Duke's private apartments. Cosimo enjoyed cleaning antique findings himself with an engraving tool. Cellini was even drawn so far into the Duke's private artistic interests that he was afraid of being diverted from his own public commissions, notably his work on the statue of Perseus. When the artist privately showed the ducal pair the statuettes for its base, the Duchess deplored that such subtle works should be exhibited in a public place and said that she would have preferred to keep them for herself. In his earlier years Cellini had, as we know from his autobiography, been much more official and humble in his communications with princes, for example his meetings with King François I and Emperor Charles V. Many artists took the liberty of playing witty jokes on their princely protectors. So it is understandable when Hans Mielich depicts his patron, Duke Albrecht V of Bavaria, as a visitor to his studio in a small scene on the last page of his volume of motifs (1559); his noble guest is looking on with interest at a painting on the easel, while the painter himself hides behind the easel and points to the title of the scene, which casts doubts on the connoisseurship of the extremely art-loving sovereign — although only in jest. It reads: "nec sutor ultra crepidam", let the cobbler stick to his last. In reality the prince was a very profound connoisseur of art; occupation with works of art took an increasingly decisive part in his private life. King Philip II of Spain was a passionate collector of the paintings of Hieronymus Bosch and attached the utmost importance to living in the immediate atmosphere of the works of the Dutch painter.

Princes as dilettante artists

It was only one step from princes having a sympathetic understanding of works of art to their dabbling in the arts themselves, as frequently happened. They often produced plans for architectonic projects. Because it was their duty to commission buildings they were especially conversant with such projects. Thus in 1586 Don Giovanni de Medici, a natural son of Cosimo Medici, submitted a model, which has been preserved, in the competition for the façade of Florence Cathedral, in which Bernardo Buontalenti and Giovannantonio Dosio also participated. For a layman the prince handled the rules of the contemporary conventional organization of the façade with considerable skill. We know that Archduke Ferdinand of Austria personally devised the strange ground plan of *p. 43* the Stern Hunting Lodge in the Tiergarten on the Weissen Berg near Prague. It consists of a six-rayed star with complicated geometrical, ingenious complications. The building was constructed by Italian and German master builders after the foundation-stone was laid in 1555. It obviously was not necessary to understand very much about architecture to invent such a layout; if anything it expresses that aspect of a dilettanteish Mannerist experiment which strives for effect. In addition to the architectural designs, we also know plans for fountains from the Archduke's own hand, e.g. for one in the Tiergarten at Innsbruck. The model was made by Alexander Colijn and cast by Hans Christoph Löffler. Presumably the Elector Palatine Ottheinrich was also active as an architect, for he certainly designed the façade of the Ottheinrichbau of his Castle at Heidelberg himself, based on the study of architectural treatises in his possession. He was not only a collector of engravings and books, and the founder of the world famous Bibliotheca Palatina, he also knew how to handle the pencil himself and sketch landscapes. His drawing of the upper castle on the Heidelberg Schlossberg, which was destroyed in 1537, still exists and Sebastian Münster states in his *Kosmographie* of 1550 that he engraved a view of Heidelberg from a sketch by Ottheinrich. Karel van Mander relates of Duke Henri of Nemours (1573—1632) that he too often practised the arts for his

BARTHOLOMEUS SPRANGER: *Hercules and Omphale*. Kunsthistorisches Museum, Vienna

own amusement; that may be why the prince even showed sympathy for the most daring and eccentric jokes of the Dutch painter Cornelis Ketel, for he bought a picture of a weeping philosopher which the painter had painted with his feet.

Emperor Rudolf II as patron of the arts

The relation between prince and artist changed during late Mannerism at the end of the sixteenth century. The Emperor Rudolf II so intensified his love of art and his connoisseurship that these interests were more important than the activities of government and politics. There were agents of the Emperor in all the major artistic towns in Europe. He acquired the main works by Albrecht Dürer. He kept on pestering the town of Nuremberg to sell him the *Allerheiligenbild* until it satisfied his desire; the painting came to Prague in 1585. However Nuremberg did not part with the Paumgärtner Altar and the Four Apostles. The Elector Christian II presented the Emperor with the *Adoration of the Magi* from the Allerheiligenkirche at Wittenberg. The *Martyrdom of the Ten Thousand* from the estate of Cardinal Granvella came from Spain to Prague at a cost of 13,000 thalers. The finest Dürer drawings also came into the Emperor's possession from Granvella's estate. Through Hans von Aachen Rudolf II was also able to acquire the *Madonna of the Rose Garlands* which the German merchants in Venice had commissioned from Dürer in 1506, again in return for a high price. In 1601 strong men carried this great altar-painting, hanging from poles so that it would not be damaged by shaking, over the Alps and up to the Hradschin. Another master, whose works Rudolf II collected avidly was Pieter Bruegel the Elder. During his visit to the Emperor's collection in Prague, Karel van Mander saw the *Tower of Babylon*, the *Bearing of the Cross* and the *Massacre of the Innocents*. When the Emperor could not acquire the originals he had them copied, for he was immensely interested in everything depicted in these paintings, in their lavish subject matter. Pieter Bruegel the Younger copied for the Emperor, and his brother, Jan Brueghel the Elder, also stayed in Prague in 1604. Thanks to his intense personal passion for collecting Rudolf II acquired a whole series of works, which we consider treasures of art history today. It was not so much the individual works of the masters named which were to his taste as the attitude to the world of Dürer or Bruegel. In a similar way Philip II of Spain felt himself drawn into the fantastic world of Hieronymus Bosch. But Rudolf II also acted as a great patron of contemporary masters. He summoned a whole colony of artists to his court and spent much of his time with them. He expressed his true interests and fancies when he sent the Flanders landscape and animal draughtsman Roelandt Savery to the Alps so that he could bring back particularly pleasing rocky motifs from his expedition. The Emperor's love of art became his main occupation which is equivalent to saying in the Mannerist sense that Rudolf II exchanged the kingdom of Mars appropriate to him as a ruler for the kingdom of Mercury, of the fine arts. He preferred to be on as friendly terms as possible with artists. In his pedantic way Karel van Mander praises the relation between ruler and artist in a comparison with antiquity: "Thus Hans von Aachen, as his art deserves, found the greatest and foremost friend of the arts in the world as protector, in whose service he thenceforth worked as court painter, and with which great Alexander, by whom he was greatly respected, he cultivated a friendship like that of Apelles." Finally van Mander gives a detailed account in his biography of Bartholomeus Spranger of how close the relations between the Emperor and the artists were, how intimate they were with each other. When the Emperor had to go to Vienna, Spranger and all his household followed him. Once there the artist no longer wanted to work at home in his private studio as before but in the room in which the Emperor used to spend his time, and so he began to work in the presence of the Emperor, to his great pleasure. When he returned to Prague from Vienna:

"he continued to paint in the Emperor's apartment, with the result that few or none of his works were available to others, for he had no assistants and only worked when he felt like it. And since God had so richly endowed him that he was not forced to work for his livelihood, his sole care was to satisfy his Emperor and give him pleasure, and so he worked for about seventeen years in the rooms allotted to him and in the frequent presence of the Emperor. But as he was not especially cut out for a courtier (they really need to be shameless) he found it very difficult to bring himself to request favours persistently with the result that he received little. Yet he can boast that he was always freely granted by his Emperor every grace and favour which he did request. But his patience finally bore good fruit: for in 1588, at a banquet in Prague, the Emperor in his bounty hung a three-stranded gold necklace round his neck in the presence of his whole court with the command that he should always wear it, certainly the greatest favour and honour that could be conferred on Spranger and one by which the Emperor honoured not only him, but also the art of painting in general. In addition the Emperor had admitted him as a freeholder some years before at a Provincial Diet in Prague in the presence of all the country's great men and conferred on him and all his descendants all the privileges of the nobility."

Ground-plan of the 'Star' hunting-lodge near Prague. Devised by Archduke Ferdinand of Austria, pre-1555

The human figure in Mannerist painting and sculpture

The recherché virtuoso element in Mannerist figures and especially those of Michelangelo struck even his contemporaries. In the *Dialogo di Pittura*, by Paolo Pino, published in Venice in 1548, the artist is enjoined to show the *difficile*, the difficult, in art, to introduce a *figura sforciata, misteriosa o difficile* into his compositions. The connoisseur could recognise the *valente*, the virtuoso, by his success in so doing. In fact artists were experts at the most peculiar foreshortenings, distortions and twistings of the human figure. Karel van Mander tells a very significant story about the Late Mannerist French painter Martin Fréminet: "In the presence of his sovereign he rapidly sketched on the canvas first a foot, then a hand and a head as if at random. In the end, to the King's great astonishment, a whole figure appeared." In other words, artists were quite prepared to dismember the human figure and mix up its limbs so that the normal organic combination was barely recognizable.

The figure per se

Mannerism is by no means a naive style. A fierce conflict raged about figures, which is also dealt with in the book *Aretino, or a Dialogue about Painting* by Lodovico Dolce. In this discussion the moderate Venetian Aretino expressed the opinion that the artist should not purposely pursue foreshortening, but only use it seldom in order not to disturb the charm of the effect. On the other hand Michelangelo, the representative and defender of Mannerism, says very informatively "that foreshortening is among the greatest of all difficulties in the art of painting... I for my part, if I were a painter, would use it not always but frequently, convinced that I would win myself more fame by doing so than by a sparing use of the technique". Consequently the Mannerist artist, on grounds which are no longer relevant, assumes the right to use his sensational personal ability and in the process eagerly applies extraordinary methods of representation. In his personal search for fame he permits himself the most extravagant artificialities and peculiarities. Already in his artistic technique he is wooing the fame, the *gloria*, which he often painted as a figure. *Gloria* was one of the most popular allegories of the time.

Giovanni da Bologna's Mercury

There is no doubt that Giovanni da Bologna reached a high point of the ideal Mannerist figure with his statue *p. 57* of Mercury. To catch a figure conquering the force of gravity, in fleeting flight, just suited the new stylistic sense. The artist solved this extremely difficult problem in a really brilliant way. Where the Gothic artists placed their figures on consoles to raise them from the earth, Giovanni da Bologna used a quite different technique for an outwardly similar purpose. The figure of Mercury is blown into the air by the head of a wind god, which by way of comparison assumes the function of a base. The messenger of the gods only touches the puff of wind with the tips of his toes. From that point onwards the youthful nimble god dominates space. With expansive, upward

EL GRECO: *The Baptism of Christ*. Prado, Madrid

reaching movements, he speeds through the air. He has thrown up his right arm and right foot, and his gaze tries to follow the index finger pointing steeply to the skies. This produces in the figure an inordinate sense of striving for a goal, and we experience the direction of the movement most intensely thanks to an almost inconceivable "dynamization" of the problem of the movement of the human body.

Previously the theme of flight could only be solved and represented by painting. We might compare the flying figures of the gods by Raphael in the Villa Farnesina at Rome, where a similar subject is portrayed. There in the story of Cupid and Psyche, Mercury fulfils the same function: he is flying. The movement of this figure is related to that of the Mannerist sculptor. The extravagant boldness of Giovanni da Bologna consists in the fact that a condition bordering on the unreal and surreal, as the flight of a human figure is, was artistically fashioned by a sculptor, while in the process all the technical limitations of the material seem to have been overcome.

The figure of Mercury is the literal incarnation of Mannerist man's relation to the world. It is obviously placed between the two striking poles of tension between which Mannerist thought basically oscillated: the supernatural and heavenly, and the practical earthly. In this figure the state of tension is given concrete, visible, not unsuccessful, sentimental form; this Mercury does not surrender himself to the zone between the finite and the infinite in romantic dissatisfaction, he combines the two poles in his body, in that the play and counterplay of the limbs are artistically and formally mastered. This masterly piece of bravura surprised even Giovanni's contemporaries. Vasari called it "molto ingegnioso". This brilliant work of High Mannerist figurative sculpture was executed about 1563/64 — about the time of Michelangelo's death.

The stylistic ideal of the "figura serpentinata"

Giovanni da Bologna's statue of Mercury also represented in a particularly pronounced way the universal stylistic ideal of the human figure which Mannerism created, namely the *figura serpentinata*. By this was understood an irrationally proportioned human figure depicted in the shape of the letter S. The art theoretician and painter Lomazzo compared it to a leaping flame, by which he referred to the spiritual element overcoming matter. In this a-natural artificially conceived ideal figure the standard Renaissance theory of proportion, the teaching of Leonardo and Dürer, was annulled. Michelangelo's *Victor* was looked on as the first figure to embody the new p. 58 ideal. A triumphant lofty mood is expressed by the slim, upward spiralling, gracefully stretched figure of the youth who has conquered vice. In a different way it revives something neo-Mediaeval, comparable to the figures on the columns of Gothic cathedrals. Beginning with Michelangelo's group the new concept of the figure continued its triumphal march, both in the fields of sculpture and painting. A proper understanding of this work provides the key to Mannerist figurative art in general.

The discovery of the *figura serpentinata* proved that the artist was able to create the human figure out of his own imagination, over and above the naturalistic external realities. In the century of advancing naturalism the Mannerists turned eagerly to the idealistic *figura serpentinata* in order to preserve their inner vision from dull reality. With it they intentionally recorded a mental attitude surpassing mere imitation of nature. But the *figura serpentinata* is only a symptom, it merely points to the other possibilities of modelling, such as the unrestrained emergence of figures in motion. Sculptures rich in *contrapposto* provide the most varied aspects, depending from which side the spectator looks at them. Painters in particular seized on this possibility of complicating the human body by using daring angles of vision; they were easily lured into depicting the most strange contortions, instead of reproducing the normal attitudes of the body. Vasari said of the so-called *di sotto in su* (literally, "from below upwards")

46

that the figures "pierce the vaults" and was highly delighted with them, saying that the utmost grace and beauty lay in their difficulty. They evinced a "terribilissima arte". So the aim is to arouse a feeling of the overpowering.

Figures seen from exaggerated, artificial angles of vision

p. 59 Stimulated by the slaves painted by Michelangelo on the Sistine ceiling, Pellegrino Tibaldi produced the *non plus ultra* of distorted angles of vision in the Palazzo Poggi at Bologna. The most daring is perhaps that of a wind god, balancing in a half-sitting position on the entablature. There is no longer anything to be seen of his trunk; only the legs, arms and head are juxtaposed as seen in an unusual disjointed view from below. The Mannerist artist took a real pleasure in such studied works of art and concentrated his powers of invention on them. The different times of day by Michelangelo in the Medici Chapel also gave rise to similar unrealistic views of the figures. If *Night*, for example, is photographed from the side, as it was by Charles de Tolnay, we realise what contortions are included in this figure too. The painters sought for and discovered such side views, which were so to speak,

p. 59 only for the special admirer and refined connoisseur. There are drawings by Tintoretto after Michelangelo's *Evening*. The Venetian achieves a *Verfremdungseffekt* and further distorts the side view of the figure which is already extreme, by viewing it from above and even making allowance for the fact that as a result the head unexpectedly appears below and the legs point upwards.

In the middle of the sixteenth century it was no longer a matter of drawing up rules for painting, as Leonardo had done in his treatise of painting. Now the question arose whether such rules were to be kept or whether they could be disregarded in order to snatch effects and attract attention in every possible way. Lodovico Dolce, as a Venetian with a moderate and orthodox attitude, felt impelled to warn people: "Just as excessive economy in draping the body leads to a miserable appearance and robs it of all grace, so too much casting of drapery creates confusion and unpleasantness. Here too the middle course which is so clearly indicated in all things must be taken." But the Mannerists did not take this middle course. Their genius led them along higher, narrower and more dangerous paths.

El Greco's draped figures

The paintings of El Greco show what draped figures could mean to a Mannerist in addition to nudes. We find
p. 45 a reaction in his work. He abandoned the Florentines' preference for painting nudes, that is to say, the naked body in its earthly sensuality was not unquestioningly considered by him as the suitable medium for illustrating holy incidents. On this point El Greco, as a man of the Counter-Reformation, adheres to a more spiritual conceptual art. We know his remarks about the over-painting of Michelangelo's *Last Judgment* under Pope Pius IV. He adopted the attitude of "purifier of art" and claimed that if the whole work were demolished, he would "do it again in an honourable and moral way, which would in no way be inferior to the other in artistic merit". There are no delusions with El Greco, of the type induced by the Inquisition, as, for example, in the case of the Florentine architect and sculptor Bartolommeo Ammanati. As a zealous adherent of the Jesuits the latter in his old age in 1582 addressed a letter to the Florence Academy and included in it a moral confession. Worried about his salvation, he regretted having fallen into temptation during his life-time and produced nudes. He hoped that under the rule of Pope Gregory XIII no more indecent objects would be displayed in holy places, and called for a censorship by decent-living people with impeccable judgment. El Greco on the other hand to some extent portrayed a new ideal figure on inner artistic grounds. From his whole attitude to mankind he moved away from nude painting

and favoured draped figures, indeed he conceived his figures as shapes already clothed, and not as bodies on which drapery was placed. No anatomical figures are concealed beneath the draperies of his figures. He did not sketch his compositions like Leonardo, Raphael or Parmigianino, all of whom first prepared drawings of the nude figures as a framework for the composition and only added the drapes when actually painting the picture. El Greco achieves his expression in the formation of the main large folds of drapery; one might almost say that his drapes are limbs; and in cases where there are nudes by him, their anatomy is completely subordinated to the striving for spiritual expression. This attitude comes close to a re-Gothicising of the ideal figure. But his procedure in no way implies an imitation of old models, rather does his Byzantine heritage break through. In El Greco's draperies we can even trace the new conceptions of space and the contrasting effect of light and shade. The draperies are "freely organic" in their folds, as is the case in the landscape formations of Mannerist pictures. His draperies also have long-drawn-out crests; they have ridges, broad level plains, chasm-like inroads and sharp spurs. All these phenomena are very clearly evident in his late masterpiece, *The Opening of the Fifth Seal*, which was painted about 1610.

For all its individuality El Greco's art is not really so far removed from Michelangelo's. For all their dematerialisation the figures of El Greco and Michelangelo have one thing in common: their incomparable pathos, an expression of lofty demeanour, a new dynamic energy-filled drama. These qualities remove El Greco's art basically and unmistakably from the Middle Ages. As I have mentioned, El Greco did portray nudes, in fact large numbers of them, but they are disembodied and the shinbones, legs and muscles are more like folds of drapery than real plastic fleshy parts of the body. The situation was the exact opposite with Michelangelo who suppressed draperies as far as possible, making them cling closely and tautly to the frame. Naturally Michelangelo did not introduce naked bodies as an end in themselves; he only attached importance to them in the service of a loftier idea. For Michelangelo man is the tragic prisoner of matter; hence the tortured, dissatisfied quality of his figures. In his late period Michelangelo denied the corporal and sensual and to some extent also what he still retained of naturalism, the Rondanini *Pietà* being the most obvious example. With this work he achieved forms and an *p. 60* interpretation which comes very close to what El Greco continued with his dissolution of the anatomical corporal figure: a new spiritualization of the human figure was at stake.

Colouring

We learn something else from the treatise by Dolce which was displeasing to him as a Venetian with an orthodox attitude. He recommends "paying attention to the colouring and the soft shade of the flesh; for full many paint flesh whose colour and hardness look like porphyry... For my part (here speaks the cautious Venetian and partisan of Titian) I would prefer a brown to an exaggeratedly light colour and generally banish from my pictures those scarlet cheeks and coral lips which make the faces look like masks". And then he goes on to reject the over "harsh brilliance of the colouring" and "a studied affectation of the figures", and, full of horror, remarks: "Yet there are still painters who present their figures so quaintly enamelled that they seem to be made up; moreover with such a strained deliberate arrangement of the hair, that not a single hair in it is disturbed. But that is a fault and no merit; for through it people fall into that affectation which robs everything of grace". Hence the understanding Petrarca describes the hair of his Laura as "intentionally, artlessly uncurled and flying". Horace too teaches, as the last classical authority, that all exaggerated adornments should be avoided in poetic descriptions. Here Dolce rejects all the peculiarities on which the Mannerists laid the greatest value and emphasis. Then he goes on with moralistic objections to the ideal figure of Michelangelo. It is unseemly "merely to demonstrate the difficulties

TINTORETTO: *The Flagellation of Christ*. Kunsthistorisches Museum, Vienna

of art, continually and licentiously to expose those parts of the body which shame and propriety keep covered, and this without having any sort of consideration either to the holiness of the persons represented or to the localities in which they are depicted". Finally he says: "Nevertheless, owing to his great art we condone in Michelangelo what we would never condone in anyone else"; but then comes the rider: "It would be far better for the figures of Michelangelo if they, showing more modesty, were even less accomplished in the drawing, instead of being, as is the case, equally accomplished and shameless."

The theory of the figure

The central problem around which Michelangelo's art revolved was the movement and the capacity for expression of the human figure, its dynamic spiritual and psychological potentialities. Michelangelo was so intensely absorbed by this problem that he intended to write an anatomical treatise based on his findings, although he did not find time for it. Condivi emphasizes Michelangelo's unsurpassable knowledge of anatomy and the inimitable perfection of his figures. Michelangelo was no longer satisfied with the books hitherto written on this subject, not even Dürer's theory of proportion which was much used in Italy at the time. He was interested in something more than the self-possessed classical beauty of the Renaissance figures in repose. Consequently he rejected Dürer's theory of proportion. Condivi writes, in the same vein: "Dürer deals with the masses and the diversity of the body, about which it is impossible to formulate definite rules, and makes the figures stiff boards." Undoubtedly classical restraint was not suitable and desirable for the cult of the stormy Mannerist ideal figure. Condivi says — and here he is the spokesman of Mannerism — that Dürer says nothing about human gestures and movements, which are the most important after all. But the movements of the human body would have been the main theme of Michelangelo's treatise; for on this point Michelangelo and his Mannerist disciples demanded the extraordinary, and Michelangelo gives examples in his art of all the extraordinary possibilities of movements of the human body. Thus Condivi could rightly say in this description of the *Last Judgment* that apart from the divine composition of the fresco one could see everything depicted there which nature could make out of human bodies.

Although no theoretical essay on the new ideal figure from Michelangelo's immediate circle has been preserved, an outsider felt it incumbent on him to produce a theoretical substructure for this central theme. He was the sculptor Vincenzo Danti from Perugia. In 1573 he made plaster casts after Michelangelo's times-of-day for the Accademia del Disegno in his home town. The plaster statues were transported there at the academicians' expense and set up in the study rooms *nella stanza de' loro esercizi*. Danti began to publish his book on the "perfect proportions", but his project remained a fragment. Of fifteen planned volumes only the first, as prodromus and trial, was printed in Florence in 1567. The grandiosely conceived work, if completed, would have been "one of the most important intellectual documents about Mannerism", as Julius von Schlosser has said. But the contents page at least has been preserved. It is reproduced here for its characteristic systematic importance. Book I was to deal with the basis of the theory of proportion in general; books II—VII to give a complete summary of the entire anatomy of man, illustrated by drawings; Book VIII to deal with the functions of all the individual limbs; Book IX to give the reasons which condition the shape of the outer parts; Book X to show attitudes and gestures; Book XI the physical symptoms of emotional states; Books XII and XIII to include the composition of historical, landscape and similar pictures; Books XIV and XV to make the transition to architecture, and their main subject for discussion would have been the relationship of one part to another based on the proportions of the human body. To sum up, the early volumes of the projected work would deal with the preliminaries, the knowledge of the human body. Then the reasons which condition the appearance of the human body form a transition to more artistic matters; to them belong attitudes and gestures and the physical characteristics of emotional states, which lead to the inner psychic life of man. Astonishingly enough only then comes what is today considered as the fundamental part of a work of art: the composition; but for the Mannerist artist it was of secondary importance, the figures came first, they formed the main attraction, namely as a figurative composition and not as disposition in a space continuum. All other subjects in the Mannerist representational repertoire, such as landscape, plants and animals play a subordinate role (and also in Danti's case) vis-à-vis the overemphasized figures. And so long as there were artists who clung to the principle of placing the virtuoso artificialities of the figures above normal representation, Mannerism existed as an art movement. Two or three generations after Michelangelo's death, there were still artists who believed in this style; in Italy there were Giuseppe Cesari, known as Cavaliere d'Arpino (died 1640), and Domenico Passignano, actually Domenico Cresto, who died in 1638 aged about 80; in the Netherlands Abraham Bloemart (died 1651) and Joachim Wtewael (died 1638), while in France we can name Martin Fréminet, who died in 1619.

Artificial poses and genre figures

However it should be emphasized that Mannerism did not merely concentrate on figures in exaggerated movements — this style is dominated by too complicated and many-layered a philosophy for that — it also created a whole scale for portraying figures. There are paintings and compositions which exclusively use the exaggerated *figura serpentinata*, but also compositions which juxtapose the various possibilities of rendering figures. In Passignano's

p. 131 fresco in the Capella di S. Antonino of San Marco at Florence exaggerated muscular nudes take up the foreground; in the picture proper on the other hand normal figures in contemporary costume appear and worthy commonplace people take part in the saint's funeral procession. We find similar transitions from excessively mobile artificial figures to normal genre figures in the compositions of Pieter Aertsen. But the direct opposites of the over-refined alert and agile human figures are the motionless awkward peasants of Pieter Bruegel the Elder, who vegetate apathetically in their bulky envelope of clothing; they have little connection with their surroundings.

The artificiality of the procedure is also recognizable in the fact that the Mannerist artists were more or less indifferent about the subject matter or themes they represented. The contents of the picture were neglected in favour of virtuoso formulation. The methods and techniques of the figure draughtsman became largely an end in themselves; the inclination to such formalism became widespread and was even noticeable in the commissions given. It might be that the patron was completely uninterested in the subject of the picture commissioned, that he was only concerned with acquiring a product of the inventive gift of the artistic genius. A passage from a letter from Annibale Caro to Vasari is significant here. The former ordered a painting from Vasari but left the painter a free hand when it came to the subject: "It may be two naked figures which are the principal subjects of your art." However Caro allowed himself to hint in which direction he was thinking: "But you should know my preference: Venus and Adonis seems to me a composition of two very beautiful bodies which you could fashion."

Mannerism had the historical merit of still being a style which put the human figure *per se* in the centre of its world vision. In that it is closely related to antiquity, as well as the Middle Ages. Like those epochs, Mannerism also considered that man was incontestably the highest being of creation, exclusively the highest subject for art. In his own way the Mannerist artist defended himself against man being swallowed up by other powers, for example that rational background which we call landscape and which was beginning to assimilate man in the sixteenth century. Contemporary thinking fought against letting man be pushed into second place vis-à-vis the space surrounding him, as happened in the next age, with the advent of Baroque.

Combining figures into a group. The motif of victors and vanquished

In addition to the problem of the individual figure there was a problem of the group of figures. This too was solved with astounding perfection. Michelangelo's *Victor* shows it, or the groups *Charles V Triumphing over Envy* by Leone Leoni and the *Victory of Honour over Deceit* by Vincenzo Danti. Hans Baldung Grien also gives us an example with his fine drawing of *Hercules and Antaeus*. The interlacing of the figures portrayed is carried so far in the course of the development that in the end they can scarcely be disentangled. Once again Giovanni da Bologna particularly distinguishes himself. At first he followed Michelangelo's *Victor* with the composition *Florence Triumphs over Pisa*. This group was given a place of honour in the great hall of the Palazzo Vecchio as a state monument and displayed opposite Michelangelo's *Victor*. Giovanni da Bologna's work is more complicated *p. 61* and technically facile than Michelangelo's. His group of Samson slaying the Philistine with the club-shaped jawbone of an ass seems to have been produced more out of pure enjoyment in dominating his medium than for any other reason. He has literally delighted in compressing and violently dislocating the body of the enemy; indeed below we have an almost indecipherable tangle of limbs, which are directed diagonally against each other, while high above Samson raises his arm for the fatal blow. His world-famous bravura piece of this kind is the group the *Rape of the Sabines* in the Loggia dei Lanzi at Florence. It was a bold undertaking to confine such a complicated and tumultuous scene as this rape to a block of marble about twelve feet high. Normally sculptors tried to chose the most static situations possible as their themes. In this example procedures which hitherto seemed to be exclusively reserved for painting are mastered through the medium of sculpture and in its way sculpture outdoes its sister art, painting. A violently agitated group towers up: the upward impetus and with it the way to freedom out of the man's firm grasp, is also emphasized here, much as in the statue of Mercury, by the woman's arm stretching far up into the air. Although each of the three individual figures adopts a highly complicated wound up attitude, it is their trebling and interpenetration which really produce surprising effects. On the panel on the base Giovanni handled the theme of the Rape of the Sabines once again, in relief allied to the flat architectural scenery of a street vista. Within the rigid perspective lines of the façades of the houses the piled up wild actions of the rape with their rapid violently elegant movements are strongly emphasized and as a result are almost more charged with expression than in the sculptured group. The artistic virtuoso indulges even more lavishly in the most complicated interpenetration and entwining of the flexible bodies of men, women and horses, and the whole confused mass looks like the acrobatic star turn of a ballet. The Dutch painter Cornelis Cornelisz. van Haarlem *p. 61* conceived his panel painting of the *Massacre of the Innocents* from a closely allied imagination. Even the biblical theme becomes a welcome pretext for showing off with the most audacious criss-crossing of figures and foreshortening. To heighten the artificiality of the idea the myrmidons of the law are portrayed as nudes and the women in part with naked torsos.

The influence of the Laocoon

Since the problem of interlacing figures was already posed in general, it is not surprising that the classical group of Laocoon with his two sons, excavated as early as 1505, should become a favourite model for the Mannerists in their creative work. They did not need to follow it directly; even in free new creations it was clear how profoundly close it was to them. Giulio Romano approached this theme in the Sala di Troja in the Palazzo Ducale at Mantua. The aim was, over and above the purely formal, to show how the human and the animal can interlace. There is no doubt that Ovid's poetic description had nearly as much effect as the classical marble group; for his

PIETER AERTSEN: *The Four Evangelists*. Kunsthistorisches Museum, Vienna

The Ape Laocoon. Woodcut by TITIAN

Metamorphoses enjoyed such popularity at the time that Karel van Mander published them as a separate book and pronounced it the painter's bible. But artists could scarcely make enough direct copies of the Laocoon either. One executed by Baccio Bandinelli in 1525 is today in the Uffizi, and the group was cast in bronze by Primaticcio's *p. 62* school for François I's collection of antiquities at Fontainebleau. Parmigianino and Hendrik Goltzius made drawings after it, and a drawing by Federigo Zuccari depicts a young art student sketching the group in the Belvedere Garden of the Vatican. In Tintoretto's studio the Laocoon group stood next to the reproductions of the Belvedere torso, the Farnese Hercules, the Medici Venus, as well as replicas of busts of Roman emperors and classical bas-reliefs. In the biography of Bartolomeus Spranger by Karel van Mander it is expressly stated that on being nominated papal painter he was allotted a magnificent apartment in the Belvedere right above the Laocoon group, which was naturally regarded as a special stroke of luck.

Nearly every artist made use of the Laocoon in some way or other: Titian published his woodcut of the Ape Laocoon, El Greco paraphrased the theme ingeniously in a painting produced between 1610 and 1614, and *p. 62* Adriaen de Vries, in his group in Drottningholm, turned it into an almost inextricable tangle of men, in which the coilings of the snakes finally complicate the whole. Pellegrino Tibaldi uses a variation of Laocoon's agonized expression in the Palazzo Poggi at Bologna in his fresco of Poylphemus who is blinded by Odysseus. The way in which the head is bent back and the peculiar protrusion of the musculature of the trunk are appropriate to the desperate situation, but with Tibaldi the movement of Polyphemus is in some ways even more tense than that of the Greek priest; with the more modern artist it is strikingly formalistic and exaggerated. Lastly the Laocoon was commended as an especially appropriate model for portraying the torments of the martyrs by the moralizing priest Giovanni Andrea Gilio in his remarks on the *Errors and Abuses of the Painter in History Paintings*. Thus antiquity could also be of use to the painter of religious themes.

Busts and caryatids

But deliberate grandeur, cultivated sublimity and formal elegance are not the only characteristics of the Mannerist depiction of the human figure; just as often Mannerism does exactly the opposite — disfiguring and more or less freely degrading it. The Mannerist artists were fond of using the traditional decoration of busts and caryatids which to some extent force human bodies to become architectural details. They were especially inventive with *p. 5* such combinations. The French theoretical writer on architecture Ducerceau and the Dutchman Hans Vredeman de Vries produced whole series of engraved examples. Frequently realistic details were included, e.g. baskets of flowers on the heads of the figures.

Ornamental engraving by PETER FLÖTNER

The Venetian sculptor Alessandro Vittoria placed two majestic caryatids at the entrance to the Library of St Mark at Venice. These strikingly agitated figures, conceived naturalistically in their powerful shapes, contrast with the arch of the door which is orthodox and serene, and weighs heavily over their heads. This contrast is fully exploited in the composition of the portal. The most exquisite and perfectly shaped caryatids were executed by the French sculptor Jean Goujon for a music gallery in the Salle des Gardes in the new wing of the Louvre at Paris. The con- *p. 63* tract for this work was concluded in 1550 and it was executed in collaboration with the architect Lescot. The noble *contrapposto* and treatment of drapery of the four white marble female figures approaches the standard of the best classical art and they were constantly compared with the kore on the Erectheum. The counterpart in fresco painting is provided by Parmigianino's wonderful rhythmically moving female figures carrying baskets on their heads in his fresco on the vaulting of the Church of Madonna della Steccata at Parma. But for all their beauty neither the figures of Jean Goujon nor those of Alessandro Vittoria soar into the ultimate harmony of the human figure. There are peculiar harshnesses and flaws in the overall figure: Goujon's figures are truncated. Their arms are intentionally cut off suddenly and smoothly at breast height. This emasculated figure, the torso, was unknown to artistic theory before; it was a discovery of Mannerism with its passion for disturbing effects. With it began the history of the incomplete as a fully acceptable art form in the modern evolution of art.

The cult of monstrous creatures

Mannerism did not even shrink from playing with the human figure in free combinations, especially in the grotesque ornaments which likewise belong to its odd discoveries. This gave rise to heated theoretical discussions, which were recorded in the *Four Dialogues on Painting* by Francisco de Hollanda. The Spaniard Zapata and no one less than Michelangelo figure as partners in the dialogue.

Zapata: "Messer Michelangelo I still wish to be rid of one doubt. For there is something in painting which I cannot understand: why is it the custom, as one can see in many places in this city, to make a thousand and one monsters and strange figures, such as women's bodies with fishes' fins and tails, tigers' claws and wings, or even animals with human faces? In short why does the artist frequently only make what pleases him, although it is not found in reality?" *Michelangelo*: "To that I gladly reply. In fact people tend to paint a great deal which is never to be seen in the world, and this artistic freedom has perfectly good reasons and grounds. Yet there are persons who do not realize it and claim that Horace aimed the following lines at the painter as a sharp reproof:

> Painters like poets
>
> Have the power, always to dare one and all.
>
> I know it...

He claims this freedom for himself and gives it to others. But these verses are not meant as an attack on the painter. Perchance Horace is praising and encouraging them when he says poets and painters have the power to dare, I emphasize to dare, what pleases them. This freedom of vision and this power they have always possessed. But if, as seldom occurs, a great painter creates a work which seems to be false and untrue, yet there is nothing but truth concealed behind this apparent falsehood. For never will he fashion anything which could not exist. He will never give a man's hand ten fingers; never paint the leg of an elephant in the same shape as that of a horse; nor will he lend the arm or face of a child the movement or expression of an old person; still less will he force eyes or ears as much as a finger's breadth from their place, or introduce the hidden veins of an arm just where he pleases; for all that would be radically wrong. But if, in the right connection and the right place, for the sake of the beauty of the composition, he transfers a limb or part of a creature to another species (in the case of gro-

The force of gravity seems to have been overcome by extreme elegance and virtuosity attaining the highest goal of Mannerist art

GIOVANNI DA BOLOGNA: *Mercury.*
c 1564. National Museum, Florence

The earliest realization of the ideal Mannerist figure, the 'figura serpentina'. The inventive spirit of countless successors was stimulated by the example of this slim, artfully twisted youth

MICHELANGELO: *The Victor*. 1506. Palazzo Vecchio, Florence. The group is over eight feet high

58

The human figure seen from unusually daring viewpoints: virtuosity and almost acrobatic feats go far beyond the conventions of normal bodily postures

PELLEGRINO TIBALDI: *Wind God on an Entablature*, post-1552. Palazzo Poggi, Bologna

TINTORETTO: A drawing in the Uffizi after Michelangelo's figure of *Evening*, in the Medici Chapel, Florence.

Far right:
BARTHOLOMEUS SPRANGER (1546–1611): *Mourning of Christ*. The picture, painted on copper, measures only 5 ⅝ by 4 ¾ inches. Alte Pinakothek, Munich

59

CORNELIS CORNELISZ. VAN HAARLEM (1562–1638): *The Massacre of the Innocents*. Rijksmuseum, Amsterdam

Individual figures virtually abandon their usual detachment; whole groups of human bodies knot themselves together

Left: GIOVANNI DA BOLOGNA: *Rape of the Sabines*, post-1580. *Below:* A representation of the incident in a contemporary setting, in bronze bas-relief on the pedestal. Loggia dei Lanzi, Florence

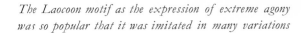
*The Laocoon motif as the expression of extreme agony
was so popular that it was imitated in many variations*

Above left: BACCIO BANDINELLI (1493–1560): *Laocoon and his Sons.* A copy after the classical group. Uffizi, Florence

Above: PELLEGRINO TIBALDI: *Polyphemus.* Ceiling fresco in the Palazzo Poggi, Bologna. Post-1552

EL GRECO: *Laocoon. c* 1610. National Gallery, Washington

A palace façade can be given impetus by the introduction of figures in agitated motion, and an interior can achieve classical serenity by the use of caryatids which do not quite conform to the classical prototypes

LEONE LEONI: Façade with busts. Palazzo degli Omenoni, Milan. Post-1565

JEAN GOUJON: Caryatids supporting the gallery in the Salle des Gardes in the Louvre. Post-1550

63

BERNARDO BUONTALENTI (1536–1608): Façade and interior view of the grotto with Michelangelo's Slaves. Boboli Gardens, Florence

The realistic subjects appropriate to an idyll disappear completely owing to the irresponsible use of a technical trick

GIOVANNI DA BOLOGNA (*c* 1524–1608): Detail of a pastoral scene in the grotto of the Boboli Gardens, Florence

tesques, which would lack charm and inner truth without such freedom), for example changing the lower part of a griffin or deer into a dolphin, or giving the upper half a figure which pleases him, if he paints wings instead of legs and leaves out the arms, because wings look better, yet every limb that he so alters, regardless whether it comes from a lion, horse or bird, corresponds to the most perfect of that species to which it belongs. We can only call such things, even if they appear false, well invented and wonderful. It is intelligible and thoroughly artistic, when a monstrosity is included in a picture in order to delight the senses by variety and making the picture more attractive to mortal eyes; for sometimes people want to see something they have never seen before and which seems more absurd to them than the likewise strange natural figures of animals and men. From this too the insatiable human longing for enjoyment took its freedom and sometimes preferred to a simple building with columns, windows and doors, an edifice which is decorated with invented deceptive grotesques, whose columns are depicted as children climbing out of the calyxes of flowers and whose portals are supported by reeds and other things. This variety seems to be impossible and senseless, and yet it is magnificent if it has an educated spectator who understands it."

Turning the human figure into matter

In fact there were great contemporary masters in the curious practice of dismembering the human figure and *pp. 149, 189* transforming it into inanimate objects. No one excelled at this more than Giuseppe Arcimboldi who must be considered as the zenith and culmination of this tendency, but who was in no way unique with his monsters and *p. 96* bogies. Federigo Zuccari restricted himself to one part of the face for his follies; he made window frames and portals out of human mouths. One illusion of this type was very practically conceived, not merely conjured up as painting. The visitor can actually use the mouth as a portal and walk through its lips, which form the doorframe, into the garden of the artist's palace at Rome. The conception of men in the spell of the material world which was *p. 230* current among the Mannerists is also found in the work of Pieter Bruegel. It is even possible, on the descending scale of reducing man, the highest creation, to a thing, for people, released from the divine will, from the gravity of our earth, to be stretched inertly on the ground and lie there like felled trees, as we can see with the peasant, the knight and the scholar in Bruegel's painting the *Fools' Paradise*. But these three central figures, the representatives of the classes, are not completely released, they are still in the protection of the trees and the round table, which in the sense of Mannerist pictorial organization take over the function of architectural details and lend *p. 66* them stability. It is worse in Bruegel's engraving *The Battle of the Chests and Coffers*, in which human figures are amalgamated with the lifeless world of things, in this case money-boxes. Giulio Romano makes use of similar *p. 141* ideas in the Sala dei Giganti in the Palazzo del Tè at Mantua. There the limbs of the giants are often completely mixed up with the fragments of stone; trunks, heads and semi-human forms become an inextricable heap of ruins together with the debris of the Cyclopean masonry. Every conceivable mixture of this type was portrayed, the showpiece clearly being Polyphemus blinded by fire and covered with stones.

Primaticcio was inspired by this possibility of mixing the human figure with rough undressed stone to make use of it architecturally. In the *Grotte des Pins* (1549) nude caryatids are represented as rough rustic stone fragments — man as raw material! Arcimboldi went one step further down the scale. He made the human figure partially *p. 149* dissolve into the earth and its fruits: the human being became a heap of vegetables, part of the earth itself. That is what happens in the series of pictures of the seasons in the Pinacoteca at Brescia. At the extreme end of this process of dissolution the difference between human head and landscape scenery ceases completely; it is obliterated in those pictures which seen straight on represent a head and through the trick of turning the picture

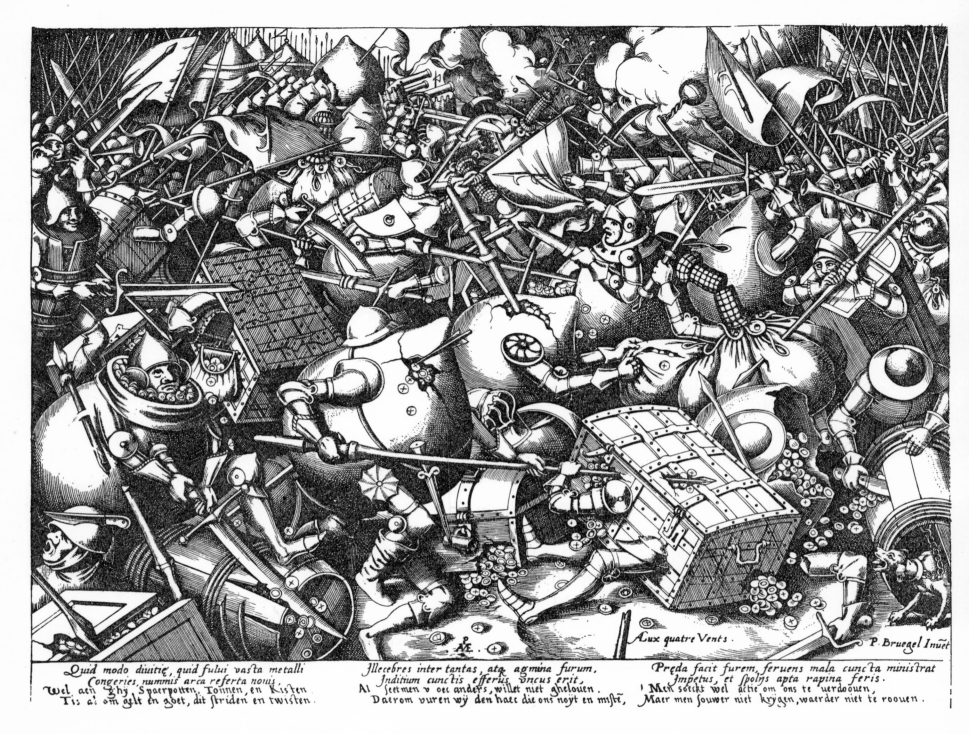

The Battle of the Chests and Coffers. Engraving by PIETER BRUEGEL THE ELDER

through ninety degrees show a landscape. The same shapes in a picture can be a human ear or a castle wall; a beard can change into a tree. That such distortion and debasement of the human figure was not the by-product or perhaps the incidental aberration of a minor artist is shown in Arcimboldi's case by the high quality of these paintings, as does the extraordinary esteem which the monstrosities earned for the artist as the ennobled Court Painter of Rudolf II. He did not even shrink from depicting his royal protector, the Emperor himself, as the god Vertumnus in inhuman "botanical" fashion, dissolving his head and body into pumpkin, cucumber, cabbage, radish, dandelion, beans, apple, pear, figs, grapes, ears of corn, cherries, onions, leek, celery, roses and lilies.

A peculiar attitude of mind goes with the idea of the human figure being composed of vegetables or merging with the inert masses of the earth. The result is even odder when this attitude dominates the sculptor. Giovanni da

66

p. 69 Bologna adopted it when he created his landscape allegory of the Apennines at Pratolino: the human figure has become a mountain mass. We scarcely dare compare sub-humanity made matter, as these figures which have dissolved into natural raw materials literally are, with that other pole of the human image, with the idealistic ambivalent delicately limbed nude, entirely freed from the law of gravity, which the same artist created in his *Mercury*. A monstrous, almost unbearable tension: the highest dignity and ideality contrasting with the deepest baseness and disintegration of form; the same Giovanni da Bologna created the heavenly, airy, weightless, elegant, distinguished statue of Mercury as a *figura serpentinata*, as the highest product of the epoch, and he also dredged up from the primitive depths of his creative spirit the elemental, heavy, sagging, ponderous, cloddish figure which symbolized the mountain range.

Contrasts between physical states and environmental tension

Mannerism was equally fond of depicting the contrasts in men's physical state. It thrives on the tension between asceticism and gluttony, it sees the contrasts between thin and fat men. In the process it is resonant with moralistic reflections and questions of the practical philosophy of life. Pieter Bruegel the Elder published his two engravings of "thin" and "fat" fare. In sculpture there are the delicately limbed statue of Mercury by Giovanni da Bologna *p. 204* already mentioned and at the same time Valerio Cioli's obese Pietro Barbino riding on the broad back of a turtle. In prose Cervantes invented, equally out of a feeling for human polarity, the figures (needed to complement each other) of the knightly Don Quixote and the rustic Sancho Panza; Panza means paunch, and Sancho smacks of the bucolic. Extremes of the kind just described are a real experience for the Mannerist epoch. People could dispense with neither one side nor the other and even actually confronted them, often merely for the sake of effect. This tendency probably explains why Buontalenti placed the uncompleted statues by Michelangelo intended for *p. 64* the Julius Monument in the grottoes of the Boboli Gardens at Florence. Thus the statues which *per se* were conceived in a completely idealistic spirit were placed in a miserably small area which was unworthy of them. Immediately next to their smooth marble and brilliant *contrapposto* an idyllic rural genre-like scene unfolds: one shepherd plays the bagpipes, sheep graze, another rests. This group of figures in the grotto exhibits another fanciful technical peculiarity. It has had dripping chalk poured over it and in their simulated dripping condition men and animals look as if they had actually become, materially speaking, a part of their environment, a grotto with stalactites. The idealistic monumental statues of Michelangelo would properly only suit such a carefully chased background as would have been the case on the tomb of Julius II with its noble handsome stones, and now they have suddenly been moved into the crude rustic setting of a garden grotto. A quite deliberate discrepancy which the novel façade of the grotto already prepares us for — but in the opposite way. Outside dressed stone and organized architectural features preponderate, inside the atmosphere of undressed natural stone takes the upper hand. An ingenious obliteration and confusion of actuality — and a singular joke.

The arrangement of figures in an architectonic context

It is a viable opinion that the human figure and architecture have scarcely any points of contact when considering the way in which they should be constructed. Renaissance and Mannerist artists thought otherwise; for them the theory of the orders of columns, on which the science of architecture at the time was essentially based, and the theory of human beings definitely had a common root: both were subject to proportion. The orders of columns were to be deduced from human proportions. This view was an old heritage; in antiquity Vitruius referred to the close connection between the two (Book IV, Chapter 1, para. 1). This knowledge was not lost in the Middle Ages and continued down to modern times. It belonged to the treasury of human thought in the field of art especially architecture. Nowadays architecture is not conceived in such direct connection with the human figure.

The human figure and architecture

As early as Vincenzo Danti's treatise we can read of the intimate connection between figure and architecture which the Mannerists believed in. A letter which Michelangelo addressed to a cardinal c. 1557—1560 is also significant for the living feeling of organic connection:

"Most reverend Monsignore,
If a design has different parts, then all of them which are of the same value and size, as well as their counterparts, must be decorated in the same way. But if the plan alters its form, then it is not only permissible, but actually necessary, to alter the decoration and the objects as well. The middle can always be freely treated, just as the nose which is in the middle of the face is dependent on neither one nor the other eye. But one hand must be like the other, always having regard to the sides and the fact that they are counterparts. Therefore one thing is certain: the limbs of architecture have their model in the limbs of men. Anyone who was, or is not, a good artist in the shaping of bodies, and particularly not an expert in anatomy, can understand nothing of this.

Michelangelo Buonarroti"

Gothic architectural sculpture with its figures on columns undoubtedly effected the most intimate connection between the human figure and architectural features, especially columns. If Italian Renaissance sculpture strove rather to separate architecture from individual sculptural figures, Mannerism embarked on a renewed powerful symbiosis of figure and architecture. During its dominion the combination of figure and columns became closer and closer by stages which are clearly discernible. A simple encounter between a human nude and a column is found in Michelangelo's *Last Judgment*. In the two upper spandrels the implements of Christ's passion are shown *p. 73* and nudes circle round the cross and the columns. These nudes behave as if they wanted to measure their bodies against the size, volume and proportion of the columns. A deep inner and mysterious harmony exists between columns and human figures; it could almost be called a loving relationship, so similar are their powers, so comparable their dynamism. In the *Fall of the Giants* in the Palazzo del Tè at Mantua, Giulio Romano aims at amal- *p. 137* gamating the falling columns and the falling giants in an inseparable common fate. He wants to show how similar is the fall of both and succeeds in this; giants and columns fall in the same diagonal direction; one giant continues in a striking parallel the direction of the shaft of a column snapping off from another one; the same giant has his forearm in the crack in the column, and next to his head appears a falling capital, the head of a column. Giulio Romano was only able to imagine this scene, because he was aware of the relationship between the human figure and columns and demonstrated its validity in the common catastrophe of the collapse. Parmigianino also alludes to the relationship between figure and column in his painting of the *Madonna del Collo lungo*, *p. 74* the Madonna with the long neck, and he used it to stimulate a train of thought in the spectator. The figure of the Madonna stretches up from her platform as statuesquely as a devotional picture; in her isolation she is placed in relation to the equally solitary "figure" of the column towering into space in the middle of the picture. This relation is stressed even more in the picture's existing unfinished state than in the original design, which provided for coupled columns with an entablature. When looking at the painting today the spectator is challenged to compare

GIOVANNI DA BOLOGNA: Landscape allegory of the Apennines, in the park of the Villa Demidoff at Pratolino

the two impressively isolated images and measure them against each other. This exercise shows that the over-refined elegance of the ideal Madonna shown here is actually established in its form by the column.

Figures and columns

Columns and figures are also interchangeable in their functions. In the picture *Day* by Hans Bock the battle of *p. 75* the giants which rages in the landscape is dominated by the allegorical figure of Day and she occupies the whole height of the canvas. When Hans Vriedeman de Vries produced the orders of the columns in his manual he first *p. 74* placed the columns — see the illustration of the composite order — in a separate field in order to show them in all their majestic dimensions, and secondly in their practical application where we look into a columned courtyard. In the same way that in Hans Bock's *Day* the figure lends the composition support, the column in Vredeman de Vries's engraving gives his didactic picture its special impressive accent. Columns like figures are thrown into relief as dominating exemplary elements; their majestic, poised, lofty quality makes columns and figures appear as precious and noble images. Great importance was attached to portraying this closely felt bond between architectural features and human figures as closely and ingeniously as possible. In this we can also see one of those traits which fundamentally link Mannerist thought with mediaeval, even cathedral-style thinking.

Fountains

Mannerism developed completely new branches of art, in which this inter-play of architectural features and figures could unfold luxuriantly but quite organically. The art form of the fountain was particularly adapted to this endeavour; the fountain afforded the possibility of making unrestricted combinations, of arranging erect and recumbent figures more or less freely on an architectonic framework. After modest beginnings in the Renaissance, the free-standing monuments of the fountains achieved the status of independent artistic organisms. From the middle of the century onwards they exercise a similarly decisive function for free space to that performed by the palace and church façades of the epochs of Mannerism and Baroque. One of the ideal solutions, in the Mannerist sense, of the problem of the harmony of fountain architecture and figurative decoration was found in the *Fontana delle p. 76 Tartarughe*, the turtle fountain, in the Piazza Mattei at Rome. Two artists shared the commission: the architect Giacomo della Porta designed the actual fountain and the Florentine sculptor Taddeo Landini the figures. The turtles from which the fountain takes its name were not added until much later, in 1658. The fountain was erected in 1585 and it is the first fountain in Rome to display itself in isolation as an important work of this branch of art. The slender limbs of the four youths which connect the upper and lower basins are twisted in exaggerated *contrapposti* to fulfil this function. The effective motif of the arms which reach high up to the upper basin is not sufficient; in addition one leg is lifted sharply upwards and looks for support to the dolphins of the outer corner basins, while the other leg steadies itself behind on the inner edge of the base. The unsteady complicated gestures of the figures keep the intrinsically rigid composition in motion, although it is a strange automatonlike motion. The first really large-scale Italian fountains with many figures and wide round basins were originally erected not in Central Italy, the seminal district, but in Lower Italy. Significantly enough their creators stem from the school of Michelangelo. They make use of the design of the Medici Chapel which combines sitting and standing figures with recumbent figures in one spatial ensemble. In 1547 Michelangelo's close collaborator Giovanni Angelo da Montorsoli erected the *Fontana di Orione* in the cathedral square at Messina, and Francesco Camilliani and Michel

Naccherini ornamented the Piazza Pretoria at Palermo with a spacious fountain in 1554/55. Then the great Italian cities, especially Rome, Florence and Bologna, accepted this new possibility of display as a model. In Germany this art form made its impact in the wealthy bourgeois towns, Nuremberg, Augsberg and Treves.

Giovanni da Bologna's Neptune Fountain

p. 77 The *Neptune Fountain* by Giovanni da Bologna in the Piazza del Nettuno at Bologna is one of his most famous masterpieces. A few influential rulers pushed on the execution of this project: Pope Pius IV, Cardinal Carlo Borromeo, Bishop P. D. Cesi and the government of Bologna. The contract with the artist was concluded on 20 August 1563. He was to carve the following figures: one, a fountain figure (nine feet high); two, four *putti* (four feet high) with vases from which water streams; three, four harpies (three feet high) which were to be related to the main figure in their movement; four, four escutcheons of the patrons with festoons and other ornaments. Everything was to be completed within ten months, but the work dragged on until December 1566. When Giovanni da Bologna left Bologna again for good in January 1567, the government of Bologna wrote a letter of thanks to Francesco Medici, who had given Giovanni da Bologna leave of absence from his duties as his Court Sculptor, with the acknowledgement that his sculptor had finished the commission to everyone's satisfaction. The artist had produced a work which is assembled from many individual components, with several tiers and gradations. In spite of the rich apparatus of subtle details nothing of the unified animation of the whole is lost. Of course we cannot overlook the fact that through this richness of detail a certain craftsmanlike element has intruded on the big sculpture — one thinks of contemporary table ornaments, for example by Wendel Jamnitzer, but also of the

p. 32 composite structure of Cellini's *Perseus*. The structure rises steeply and proudly upwards in steps with a refreshing combination of living figures and agitated ornamentation. It was a happy notion to place figures at the corners. As a result all heaviness is removed from the structure and the way in which the figures reach up into the air is emphasized. The *putti* sit on the corners of their platform, full of playful movement, the harpies easily accept the swing of the volutes and above the whole stands Neptune, God of the Sea. It is as if the twisting spiralling movement of his figure had been built up to in the tiers of the pedestal; the whole structure has the effect of an extended *figura serpentinata*. Neptune stands there with his trident like a conductor, with the crowd of figures below him responding to the rhythm of his movement. The jets of water are a welcome additional animating element in the overall composition. They are graphic, pencil thin, delicate, as the stylistic sensibility of Mannerism required. Above, the jets flow from the mouths of the dolphins held up by the *putti* into the small basins on the lower corners. The harpies squeeze their breasts from which thin streams pour into the large basin. The contrast between the smooth undisturbed surface of the water and the thin jets is fully exploited, while another pleasing contrast is the way in which a broad sweeping flight of steps below makes the transition from the lofty aspiring monument to the flatness of the square.

Tombs

Mannerism had a predilection for using tombs to pose and solve the highly exciting ambivalent problem of confining human figures, which are rendered independent in their naturalism and artistic freedom, within the context of an architectural structure. We find this dilemma in the most famous example. In Michelangelo's tomb in the Medici Chapel every effort seems to have been taken to make the figures in general fit in with the wall architecture. The statues of the dead at least fit in the niches of the wall, yet the figures of the times of day seem as if they were only loosely placed on the lid of the sarcophagus. The undressed bands of the base, left rough, show clearly enough how little attention these figures pay to the architecture surrounding them. A pair of river gods appearing to lie on the ground were to have completed the whole, as we know from preserved *bozzetti* and the sketches of the design. In spite of such contradictions the Mannerist artist aimed at leaving the human figure in its architectonic context, indeed he even seeks out this harmony. In Michelangelo's Julius Tomb there *p. 78* are forces at work which the architecture can only restrain with the greatest difficulty — ultimately the powerful face of Moses which is so full of energy escapes from its architectural framework. If there were no interim figures to ensure the connection with the architectural components, its effect as a solitary figure would be unbearable. But there are also the figures of Rachel and Leah which have a calmer aspect and are more compatible with the niches and pilasters. Lastly the busts of the four temperaments form a close alliance with the architecture. On many other sculptured tombs we can see the same struggle to chain to the architectural structure human figures whose energy has set them free; for example on the tomb of Marchese Gian Galeazzo Medici, which was erected in Milan Cathedral between 1560 and 1562 by Leone Leoni, or on the tomb of the Benavide which Ammanati executed in the Eremitani Church at Padua from 1564 onwards. As a painter Titian was equally aware of this contemporary problem; for not the least of the fascination of his late painting, the *Pietà* in the Venice Academy, lies in the fact that the emergent movement of Mary Magdalena is in dramatic conflict with the background of magnificent architectural niches. On the tomb of Michelangelo himself in Santa Croce at Florence the free- *p. 164* standing figures have largely freed themselves from the architectonic context. The three allegorical figures of the arts of *disegno* sit in relaxed positions in front of and beside the sarcophagus, but once again a consolidation in the structure of the tomb matches this relaxation. The tension within the structure passes from the painted ornamental picture to the freed figures sitting at the corners of the sarcophagus. The most astonishing example of this tendency is found in the Mausoleum of Prince Ernst von Schaumburg-Lippe at Stadthagen which was built *p. 80* by von Nosseni and decorated with figures by Adriaen de Vries between 1617 and 1620. What we have here is a monumental tomb resembling a chapel. In the middle of the central space the resurrection of Christ is represented. The free-standing tomb of Christ is completed by the two pairs of columns with pediments on the walls of the chapel. The guardians of the tomb become threatening figures to the spectator standing in the confined space.

However there are some Mannerist tombs where the opposite effect is achieved. In them the figures do not break loose from the architecture and as it were debase it; on the contrary the architecture is the paramount element and the figures on it shrivel up to uneasy negligible particles. The tomb of Pietro Bembo in Sant'Antonio at Padua is an example. The architect San Michele produced a portal motif for it which consists of very tall double columns made to seem even taller by their fine fluting. The sculptor Danese Cattaneo placed the diminutive bust of the poet on a pedestal with an inscribed panel between these columns. The poet portrayed is almost completely lost in the dimensions of the architecture. The choir of the church in the Escorial is where we are most conscious of the tension between the smallness of the human figure, and typically enough of the realistic actual figure, and the vastness of the architectural setting. Leone Leoni deliberately displayed the figures of Charles V, and Philip II and their closest relatives, without the direct support of the gigantic height of the coupled columns with their empty space. Only a Mannerist artist could imagine and exploit with such trenchancy the discrepancy between the cold grandeur of the architecture and the insignificance of man within this setting.

In their own way German sculptors also tackled the same problem of linking figures with the architecture on the tombs they made. The naturalism of the figures in Germany led to even odder productions. In the tomb of Mar- *p. 79* grave Karl of Baden (died 1577), his wife Kunigunde (died 1588) and the Countess Palatine Anna (died 1587) in the Collegiate Church at Pforzheim the architecture obviously makes the most extreme efforts to assimilate itself

*Columns and human figures are
intimately associated*

MICHELANGELO: *The columns of
Christ's Agony*. The angels carry
the instruments of the Passion, in
the fresco of the Last Judgment,
upper right arch, Sistine Chapel,
Vatican. Completed in 1541

*The tragic common destiny of columns
and supermen*

GIULIO ROMANO: *The Fall of the
Giants*. Sala dei Giganti, Palazzo
del Tè, Mantua. Completed in 1534

73

Columns and human figures in direct comparison; the majesty of columns in themselves and in their setting

PARMIGIANINO: *The Madonna with the Long Neck*. *c* 1535. Uffizi, Florence

COMPOSITA.

I de vriese inventor.

HANS VREDEMAN DE VRIES: The composite order of columns. Engraving from *Les cinq rangs de l'Architecture*, Henricus Hondius, Amsterdam, 1620

The human figure, isolated from the composition, attains architectural grandeur

HANS BOCK: *Allegory of Day:* Zeus Fighting the Titans, 1586. Kunstmuseum, Basle

*The human figure was used in combination with
fountain architecture and strikingly displayed*

GIACOMO DELLA PORTA (architect) and TADDEO LANDINI
(sculptor): Fontana delle Tartarughe (the Tortoise
Fountain), Rome. The fountain was erected in 1585

GIOVANNI DA BOLOGNA: Neptune Fountain, Piazza del Nettuno, Bologna.
Right: The harpy squeezes refreshing jets of water from her breasts

76

The harmonization between the human figure and its architectural framework

Far left: TITIAN: *Pietà.* 1573–1576. Now in the Accademia di Belle Arti, Venice

DANESE CATTANEO (*c* 1509–1573): Tomb of the poet Pietro Bembo. Sant'Antonio, Padua

MICHELANGELO: Lower section of the monument to Pope Julius II. The figures are of Moses in the centre, with Rachel and Leah to his left and right – allegories on the contemplative and the active life – and four busts above. 1513–1542. San Pietro in Vincoli, Rome

78

Tomb of Margrave Karl of Baden, his wife Kunigunde and the Countess Palatine Anna. Pre-1590. Stiftskirche, Pforzheim.

Tombs of the Counts of Solm and their wives, c 1550. Marienstiftskirche, Lich (Oberhessen)

Monumental architecture and figure-composition in a harmonious yet restless relationship

ADRIAEN DE VRIES: Tomb of Count Ernst von Schaumburg-Lippe, crowned with the *Ascension of Christ*, 1617–1620. Mausoleum, Stadthagen

to the world of shapes of the costume figures. The figures stand there, startlingly realized in their corpulence and respectability. Consequently the embarassing stylistic problem arose of what architectonic structural setting could possible suit such costume figures. A classical architectural solution to the problem is almost inconceivable. Hence the accompanying architecture which in essence is just as unarchitectonic as the costume figures are mis-shapen and out of proportion, is still quite in keeping with them. The ambivalence is also noticeable in the relation of these figures to their background. It is left undecided whether the figures stand in front of or inside the archi-tecture. Margrave Karl of Baden at all events is not in the setting of coupled columns intended for him; in its way the architectonic structure conforms to the deformity of the actual figures. Many accompanying motifs are introduced and the escutcheons, the ornamented shafts of the columns and the inscribed panels try for their part

p. 79 to bring stability to the structure. An even more startling solution was found in the tomb of Count Solm in the Stadtkirche at Lich, which was built between 1545 and 1562. The figures stand forth in all their corpulence, straddling pose and unconstrained humanity. One feels more that they are in definite contrast to the simple pilaster frames on the tomb than that they were composed together with them. The function of the architectonic framework is further suppressed by the large escutcheons, whose naturalistic shapes are uncontrolled, and the unwieldy helmets on the ground next to the standing figures. The figures and their emblems have achieved an importance and solidity which the architecture is no longer able to support.

Gateway Number 17. Woodcut by Sebastiano Serlio
from *Tutte l'opere d'architettura.*
The first edition appeared in Venice from 1537 onwards

Architecture in the Mannerist Spirit

In the eternal dispute as to which of the fine arts ranks first, architecture is often considered the most important, as the foundation of the other arts. Architecture does not assume such a high position in the stylistic picture of Mannerism. Mannerist art is far too interested in ideas, far too unrestrained and focused on an artistically liberal attitude in its inventions for that. The Mannerist artist was over-fond of giving his caprices full rein, instead of giving serene balanced expression to the classical solidity and unequivocal harmony appropriate to architecture. He sacrificed the objectivity current up to the Renaissance and preferred pursuing more subjective effects and ingenious gambles. Even in his buildings he was often trying produce psychological effects on the spectator, disregarding the basic rules of traditional architecture.

This is largely true even of the great founder and model of the Mannerist style, Michelangelo. However unusual, powerful and brilliant his buildings are, yet we cannot from their very essence regard them as the creations of a genuinely architectonic mind. Even as architect Michelangelo remains the born sculptor and faces the creation of buildings with an unusually unrestrained, completely new and self-willed approach to the design. In this connection it is significant that the architecture and the plastic decoration in the Medici Chapel at Florence seem to fuse into an inseparable unity. They have the effect of a perfect whole, because for Michelangelo the individual architectonic features — pilasters, windows, frames, corbels — are also three-dimensionally charged organisms, stamped with personality.

The new type of architect. Painters and sculptors as architects

It is particularly interesting to note the class of artists by whom Mannerist architecture was mainly produced. The driving forces are not professional architects, but talents whose main interest often or in the first instance lay in quite different fields. A great many of them were originally painters or sculptors. In other words they were practising artists in fields which are more accessible to the fantasy and facility of creation than architecture can be, owing to the unwieldiness of its materials. The most important painter-architects, among them Baldassare Peruzzi, Giulio Romano, Francesco Primaticcio, Giorgio Vasari, Pellegrino Tibaldi and Pirro Ligorio, appear in Central Italy, Michelangelo's immediate sphere of influence. Jacopo Barozzi, known as Vignola, began his career, which led him to become both practising architect and architectural theoretician, as a designer of intarsios, on which representations of buildings in perspective were a speciality at the time. Others too were not originally or exclusively architects: Giulio Mazzoni was a painter and stucco worker, Bernardo Buontalenti painter and theatre designer, Bartolommeo Ammanati a sculptor. In addition many of them had strong scientific interests, for example Pirro Ligorio and Giovannantonio Dosio, who both made extensive antiquarian studies. Significantly enough, those architects who were architects by profession kept apart from the Mannerist mentality and its disruptive effect on architecture. Examples of such artists are Antonio da Sangallo the Younger, Giacomo della Porta and Andrea Palladio, of whom the two last named are to be counted among the most important architects of all time.

The confusion and watering down of the professional branches was aggravated by Mannerist architecture's marked addiction to the decorative and the improvised. The systems of decorative ornamentation of architecture and decorative painting approximate to each other. Thus there is a well defined type of individual decorative shapes which we can easily see could only have been invented by the two-dimensional art of painting, for example in Vasari's buildings where the vaults are finished off with a flat framework instead of being divided with projecting coffers or genuine ribs. Often there was a striving for picture-like effects which were not conceived as part and parcel of the construction but chosen for the attraction of their delightful and ingenious appearance. Owing to this tendency, palace façades were presented as separate entities and special structures, and treated as frequently brilliant experiments with form having no organic connection with the construction of the buildings themselves. But the architectural composition of the façade can also include highly painterly elements. For example big relief panels and festoons of flowers looking like paintings were introduced as the main motif on the rear of the Villa

p. 91 Medici at Rome.

This invasion of architecture by painters and decorators also took place in the north. There they were not so much important creators of buildings, as in Central and Upper Italy, as the designers of pattern books which were widely distributed by the publishers. Cornelis Floris and Hans Vredeman de Vries took part in this activity as writers on perspective, painters of architectural pictures and designers of model engravings, and at the end of the

p. 96 sixteenth century they were joined by Wendel Dietterlin, who moved from painting into the field of architectural design. The extravagant and brilliant effects achieved by the Italians in this decorative art which was still firmly based on the old crafts turned into frills and ludicrous eccentricities, and a quite special frivolous kind of decoration in the hands of the Germans and Dutch. This preference for completely undisciplined superabundant decoration with scroll-work and strap-work is manifest on the town halls and the façades of the houses of guilds and burghers in Strasbourg, Nuremberg, Antwerp, Brussels, Ghent and Danzig.

Lack of restraint in architectural design

It is characteristic of the Mannerist style of architecture that its practical impact rarely extended to official buildings; its almost frivolous and basically unarchitectonic nature could be realized with much less resistence in easily improvised minor edifices. So there is no monumental Mannerist architecture in the real sense of the word.
Church architecture which previously was always the leading branch of the art takes a comparatively modest place. The really representative sacred buildings in the sixteenth century such as St Peter's and Il Gesù at Rome and Palladio's Church of Il Redentore at Venice do contain isolated Mannerist elements but already tend more to Baroque in their overall style.

Original villa lay-outs

The vital achievements are the secular castles and palaces, and in particular an imposing number of original villa lay-outs: a pronounced pagan bias was characteristic of Mannerist architecture. The most famous villas are the Villa Medici, the Villa Giulia of Pope Julius III and the Casino of Pius IV, all three at Rome, the Villa Lante and the Villa at Bagnaia, both near Viterbo. All these villas represent curiously isolated creations, which are sited in conscious contrast to their natural surroundings and stand out against them as separate entities. This serves to emphasize their artificial character even more.
To the Mannerist architects an edifice was no longer something coherent in the old sense, no longer an overall organism dominated by the craft conception of building. Very frequently they aimed at a bold combination of the most complicated labyrinthine and self-contradictory spatial configurations. We see this very clearly in the Villa

Giulia at Rome or the villa at Caprarola. Parts of the building which are secondary in themselves, such as the outside staircase at Caprarola or the niches on the Villa Giulia, are suddenly magnified into main features. It is also significant that palaces and villas were designed together with their gardens, for example the Palazzo Pitti by Ammanati at Florence. The Mannerist architect concentrated on the ground plan, i.e. he began with a mental conception freed from the structure of the building. Owing to this procedure strangely inconsistent and tormented forms were produced when the edifice was actually built. The ground plans are often fanciful combinations of ideally conceived flattish geometrical figures and not really projections of practicable creations. The ground plan of the Escorial has the symbolical shape of a gridiron, which is the attribute of St Lawrence, the patron saint of the monastery. But iconographic motifs so to speak also blend with Mannerist architecture in another way. Thus in an ideal design for a monastery for Naples by Giovannantonio Dosio the central main building is surmounted with that symbol of sovereignty, the royal crown. It was no wonder that a lively increased interest for precisely such ideal designs of buildings, as independent ingenious pastimes, flourished. Peruzzi prepared designs for the façade of Bologna Cathedral in different styles, one contemporary, one in the Gothic manner — another example of the intractable craving for freedom of the imagination.

The preference for the artistic play of imagination explains why Giorgio Vasari the Younger wrote the treatise *Città Ideale*. In the treatises on the science of fortification which received great impetus in the sixteenth century, there were often most ingenious combinations of geometricizing elements, while something frivolous about them was still recognizable. Artists began to revel in hypothetical conceptual buildings, without paying attention to their practical realization. Painters and engravers also joined in this tendency, indulging in architectural fantasies; e.g. Martin van Heemskerck in his series of engravings the *Seven Wonders of the World* or Hans Vredeman de Vries *p. 234* with the imaginary palaces and courtyards in his architectural pictures, or Antoine Caron with representations of *p. 235* architecture in paintings where it was suitable. Jacopo da Pontormo invented especially fanciful architecture which could hardly have been erected in practice in the painting *Joseph in Egypt*.

The oval ground plan

Mannerism developed the oval ground plan, a shape which was peculiar to it. Its characteristic is the tension contained in this geometrical figure between the axes of length and breadth in contrast to the inherently restful shape of the circle. Such a hybrid shape inevitably had a special appeal for the ambivalent Mannerist way of thinking. Vincenzo Danti supplied an oval-shaped design for the Escorial. This ingenious *invenzione* was prized by his contemporaries, although everyone knew that it would never be carried out. Mannerist theory tried to attribute an anthropomorphic proportion to the oval shape, something accepted as a matter of course in the Renaissance for the centrally planned building which was widespread at the time. Lomazzo tried to show that classical elliptical ground plans too were anthropomorphic. Then Zuccari established a direct connection between the principle of the oval building and the female body. In such a process thought comes before the concrete conception. For if we ask (as we are wont to do in the characterization of other stylistic epochs) about the concept of space for example, then the answer can only be a negative one as far as Mannerist interiors are concerned. Frequently they literally deny and disorder space. The interior unity and harmony which Renaissance churches aimed at were abandoned; instead the most heterogenous spatial units were deliberately juxtaposed without transition. They thought nothing of alternating tall light spatial compartments with surprisingly low gloomy cramped sections in one and the same church interior. The sharp up and down of the height of interiors in no way disturbed the Mannerists; if anything they enjoyed the rapid change between sections normally considered incompatible and encouraged the feeling of inner strife in its spatial compositions.

JACOPO DA PONTORMO: *Joseph in Egypt*. National Gallery, London

This principle of placing conflicting spatial shapes next to each other is carried to the extreme in the churches of S. Barbara at Mantua and SS. Flora and Lucilla at Arezzo, rebuilt by Vasari in 1575. In S. Barbara, which is built into the Palazzo Ducale, soaring shaftlike rooms with bright overhead lighting alternate with low-ceilinged gloomy chapel-like compartments; in SS. Flora and Lucilla lofty rooms arched over with cupolas alternate with low ones surrounded with columns. The usual relation of nave to aisles, or of chapels to nave, as the dominant feature is debased. The cathedral at Mantua as rebuilt by Giulio Romano demonstrates this. The side views looking from the aisles toward the central nave disclose the intentions of the spatial conception far more stirringly than the normal central view down the nave. The impetus only develops from the aisles as does the intentional feeling of oppression induced by the original coffered barrel-vault which weighs heavily on the relatively slender columns. In Mannerist conglomerations of this kind the church-goer feels torn restlessly hither and thither; he loses a clear overall view. Instead of unified space he is presented with a juxtaposition of different inconsistent spatial compartments.

Vistas in perspective and suites of rooms

In some cases even the exteriors looked like a hotchpotch of projections and indentations, as in SS. Flora and Lucilla at Arezzo or again in the model which Antonio da Sangallo the Younger designed for the façade of St Peter's, Rome. It is also typical how in such a central work of Mannerist architecture in Italy as the Uffizi by Vasari at *p. 92* Florence the open space is neither conceived as such nor really disclosed by the two parallel wings which are close together and lead into the distance. It remains a narrow deep chasm. Although the organization of the façades of the two sides is carefully restrained in its details we cannot see the whole façade of either right or left wing of the building because the distance between them is far too small. Another surprising thing about this vista is that it does not lead up to anything of importance. Towards the Arno it ends in the motif of an archway borrowed from Palladio which does not allow a completely free view of the river; towards the town it culminates in the admittedly interesting but comparatively limited oblique view of the Palazzo Vecchio, the statues of *David* by Michelangelo and *Hercules and Cacus* by Bandinelli, and the tower of the Palazzo Vecchio. We have the impression that in this *p. 157* building vista and deep narrow courtyard were regarded as merits in themselves, that they did not need to lead up to some more important feature. Similar painted vistas in perspective in the pictures of Tintoretto and also the way in which street vistas were introduced into the Teatro Olimpico at Vicenza as stage motifs show to what extent Mannerists attempted to inflate such views to the level of a visual experience for the spectator.

As a result space enclosed in tunnel-like vistas is also very frequently found in Mannerism. Vasari gave a sample of it in the Gallery of the Cathedral Square at Arezzo by which he sought to confer a more grandiose and seignorial character on his native town. We may also mention the Biblioteca Vaticana, another example which does not succeed as a unified room because the big rectangular pillars dissect the whole into separate tunnel-like sections. In the north the concept of the tunnel-like room merges with Late Gothic constructional tendencies. Ducerceau and Hans Vredeman de Vries produced original solutions in their engravings, indeed de Vries designed whole series of church interiors of this kind. The maximum which could be done in the way of cutting across and chopping up unified space is conclusively shown in the grandiose Mannerist hall of the Antiquarium at Munich. A continuous *p. 93* architrave is not led along the walls of the hall as is usual in such cases; instead the vaulting of the separate bays pierces deep into the wall space and as a result they follow one another as emphatically independent spatial compartments. This impression is further heightened by the introduction of extravagant pedestals and stands on the walls between the pillars for exhibiting busts and statues. In this way the spectator is forced to keep departing from the longitudinal axis of the tunnel and turning aside from the main direction of this imposing lay-out.

The relation between exteriors and interiors

A peculiar relationship between exteriors and interiors arose owing to this attitude of ignoring space. Now it became possible to divide up the walls of interiors with features whose sculptural solidity had previously seemed exclusively suited to the outsides of buildings. The most striking example is undoubtedly Michelangelo's Biblioteca *p. 95* Laurentiana at Florence. In it the claims of the interior are disregarded; there is an almost complete lack of a cubic conception of space. The shell enclosing it is much more important than the space itself. Mannerism worked on the principle of opposing the main palace façades within a town square or the longer walls of a hall to each other making no attempt to unify the area as a whole by paying appropriate attention to the side façades and end walls. *p. 30* Consequently in the Sala Regia in the Vatican the end walls intentionally stand in formal contrast to the longer walls which are treated quite differently. Although it is a narrow room the longer walls are thrown into relief by the rich door frames with their own powerful sculptural value; consequently the end walls recede even more and the room seems even more confined than it should according to its proportions. Similar effects were sought for in the Palazzo Vecchio at Florence and the banquet hall of the Villa at Poggia a Caiano. And Michelangelo in the *p. 123* square of the Capitol at Rome sited the Conservatori Palace and its counterpart in such a way that they both seem to reject a direct relationship with the narrow sides of the square and remain in striking isolation. The Mannerist architect did not work towards consistent spatial structures which are coherent in their spatial value; like the mediaeval Gothic builders he still believed in the individual architectonic value of the building's separate components. To the Mannerist not only the columns and pilasters, but also the entablatures and windows were still self-contained independent structures which could be distorted and interpreted extravagantly at will.

The theory of the order of columns

A highly developed theory, the science of the order of columns, stands behind Mannerist architecture. It was established in a series of treatises with wide ramifications. At first these works were the exclusive preserve of Northern Italians. Between 1537 and 1551 Sebastiano Serlio published his *Regole generali di architettura…sopra le cinque maniere degli edifici*; it was in great demand and soon went through a number of editions. Pieter Coecke van Aelst translated it into French in 1554 at Antwerp and Fr. de Villalpando produced a Spanish version at Toledo in 1565. Serlio's fame as an architectural theoretician who also published his own plans became so great that he was summoned to the French court at Fontainebleau. He must be credited with expounding a practical system of architecture and not merely compiling ideas from the works of earlier writers on the subject. His most effective contribution was the lucid teaching of architecture through the illustrations to his writings. His way of specifying the five orders of columns according to definite shaft heights rising by whole numbers, as well as their corresponding bases, and so re-establishing in practice the theory of the orders, was the result of his own reflections. His theory met with the greatest response in the north, in France, the Netherlands and Germany, where it was expanded by peculiar ideas about the special ethical principle involved in using the orders: the columns were conceived of as sublime and valuable structures which had human proportions and even exhibited human characteristics. This was the re-acceptance of one of Vitruvius's basic ideas, according to which the individual orders of columns for certain architectural problems are predetermined and are meaningless if applied otherwise.

The connection of the orders of columns with specific gods

The following is a passage from Vitruvius: "As once the ancient heathens made threefold distinctions between the gods, those of the strong and the tender and those who keep the middle course in both attributes, so they built the temples of the strong gods such as Mars, Hercules and Minerva in the Doric manner because of its graver appearance. But to the tender divinities such as Venus, Proserpina and Flora they gave the Corinthinian manner, because of the more delicate and enhanced decoration or ornamentation. But to the moderate gods such as Juno, Diana and Bacchus they gave the Ionic manner, because such a manner keeps the middle way in that it is neither too gross nor too delicate." Initially these three original orders were only used on the temples of the gods; from the sixteenth century onwards there was a general extension of their use to Christian and profane works as well. For example when Philibert de l'Orme began to build the Tuileries for Catherine de' Medici in 1564 there was no question of using anything but the Ionic order to divide up the ground floor; it alone was suitable in character to the personality of the Queen Mother; neither the masculine Doric, nor the maidenly Corinthian would have been appropriate for the purpose. And in one of his two designs for the Cologne Ratshausstube produced in 1577 Cornelis Floris felt obliged to resort to the Doric order without bases for the ground floor in order to emphasize the dignity of the *Senatus populusque Coloniae*.

Northern architectural mysticism

These connections between men and columns also led the Northern Mannerist architectural theoreticians to indulge in profound speculations about them. In his series of engravings *Theatrum Vitae humanae* (1577) Hans Vredeman de Vries combined the orders of columns with the ages of man. The *Composita* for example represented childhood from the first to the sixteenth year. Since man behaves most spontaneously in his childhood, children at play also appear on the plate devoted to the composite, i.e. the freest, order of columns. In continuation the concepts of manhood and heroism were combined with the Doric order, and old age and awkwardness with the Tuscan order. Paul Vredeman de Vries proposed another less ingenious kind of combination by comparing the five orders with the five senses, apparently merely because of the number.

The last offshoot of Mannerist speculation about columns is the *Architectura* by the Strasbourg painter Wendel Dietterlin, with its artistically outstanding etchings, in which the human and mythological significance of the orders of columns was increased by a religious interpretation. In all these series of plates what we might call a columnar philosophy was advanced which had hardly any connection with the practical theory of architecture, representing instead a product of purely speculative Mannerist mental acrobatics.

Italian theoreticians

But Jacopo Barozzi, known as Barola, had an incomparably greater and more lasting success than Serlio and the Northern architectural philosophers with his *Regole delle cinque Ordini d'architettura* which came out in 1562. This treatise literally became the textbook of architecture. Owing to its concise easily remembered explanations it had a vast circulation all over Europe, even during the centuries which followed.

Palladio's theory of architecture as expounded in his book *I quattro libri dell' architettura* enjoyed even greater fame. This more classical theory had its greatest influence in France and England, the two countries where Palladianism developed in its purest form. The most comprehensive Mannerist treatise on architecture is the *Idea dell' architettura universale* by Vincenzo Scamozzi published in Venice in 1615. Both in title and contents this publication is connected with the hypersubtle didactic literary treatises of the end of Mannerism, of the type already mentioned by the painters Lomazzo and Federigo Zuccari. The architect too wanted to be a scholar; he too wanted to make contribution to the glorification of the divine idea which man imagined as dominating art.

GIORGIO VASARI: Nymphaeum. Villa Giulia, Rome. Post-1552   BALDASSARE PERUZZI: Courtyard of the Palazzo Massimo alle Colonne, Rome. Post-1532

       An example of virtuosity in architecture, illustrating arbitrary division into storeys and the diminution of structural solidity

Palace façades can be ornamented more richly by integrating decorative schemes with a comprehensive range of statues

Heidelberg Castle, façade of the Ottheinrichbau, 1553–1562

Below: Façade of the Palazzo Spada, Rome, *c* 1555

In some cases frivolous decoration may get the upper hand, while in others the regimented inflexibility of the order of columns is overemphasized

Villa Medici, Rome. The garden façade, 1572

The church of the Escorial. High altar, *c* 1590. The structure is 84 feet high and 45 feet wide

The Cathedral, Mantua. Rebuilt by Giulio Romano in 1545. View of the southern aisle

91

Architectural vistas, both interior and exterior, with their perspective effects, are very attractive just because they are self-contained

Left: GIORGIO VASARI: The long narrow courtyard of the Uffizi looking towards the Palazzo Vecchio, Florence. 1556–1680

Below left: ANDREA PALLADIO: Teatro Olimpico at Vicenza, 1580–1583. Stage wall with three street vistas

Right: The Vatican library. 1588

Far right: Vatican, Rome, Galleria delle Carte Geografiche, fresco decoration of 1580–1583

PIRRO LIGORIO: The walk with the 'hundred fountains'. Villa d'Este, Tivoli. 1563

Far right: The Antiquarium at the Residenz, Munich. 1569–1577

Extravagant playing with architectural patterns transcends reason

Left: GIULIO ROMANO: Palazzo del Tè, Mantua: the treatment of a wall. Post-1524

Left below: BARTOLOMEO AMMANATI: Courtyard of the Palazzo Pitti, Florence. 1558–1570

Right: MICHELANGELO: Anteroom of the Biblioteca Laurenziana at Florence (1524–1534), with the staircase by Giorgio Vasari (1555–1568)

BERNARDO BUONTALENTI (1536–1608): Steps leading to the choir of the Church of Santo Stefano, Florence

ANTONI KELLER (architect) and CHRISTOPH JELIN (sculptor): Gateway of Tübingen Castle, 1606

Below left: FEDERIGO ZUCCARI: Portal shaped like a gigantic mouth at the former entrance to the garden of the Palazzo Zuccari at Rome. Post-1593

Below: WENDEL DIETTERLIN: Etching of a portal from his pattern book *Architectura*, 1598

66

French and German theoreticians

The fashion for treatises also spread to France. Two architects issued magnificent works of this kind: Jacques Androuet Ducerceau in the *Livre d'architecture* (1559) and *Le second livre d'architecture* (1561), and Philibert de l'Orme with *Le premier tome de l'architecture* (1568) and *Nouvelles inventions pour bien bastir* (1578). The more provincial German publications, the so-called *Säulenbüchlein*, seem quite modest in comparison. Hans Blum's *Buch von den fünf Säulen* derives from Vitruvius and Serlio. In the Netherlands Hans Vredeman de Vries published his book *De Architectura* at Antwerp in 1565. From all this theoretical literature which was esteemed and also used by contemporaries a regimentated, calculable and inflexible element penetrated architectonic thinking.

Wall division

Knowledge of the orders of columns had previously been a subsidiary affair, its employment a useful practice; now it became a canon and a scientifically supported belief. Mannerism far surpassed former ages in the variety with which it organized and daringly combined the orders of columns. The scale is surprisingly comprehensive and far-reaching, it goes from the strictly canonical arrangement of ideal theory to the wild grotesque distortions *p. 91* of practice. The masterpiece of the high altar of the Church of the Escorial, in the form of a display wall, is the highest embodiment of the scholastic canon of the orders of columns. The Doric, Ionic, Corinthian and composite orders are superimposed on each other in precisely determined succession. But the variety of Mannerist architecture also includes quite different kinds of wall arrangements. Instead of clear proportions within the orders of columns and the wall divisions, deliberate displacements may occur. The divisions into storeys on palace façades was often peculiar; at times conspicuous mezzanine storeys were inserted which disturb the classical harmony of any building. In the coupled columns themselves entirely new rhythms, extensions and compressions were introduced; double columns and double pilasters were also used.

Mannerism does exactly what it wants with the elements of the wall organization; the old traditional system was relaxed to the borders of the tolerable and even of the admissible. Brand new combinations in the rhythms of the distance between columns and pilasters, between arches, niches and windows were thought out. Columns could be cramped together or be forced arbitrarily far apart by intervening spaces, and even the difference between genuine portals and genuine wall division was obliterated. Michelangelo made the most powerful division of *p. 95* a wall in the anteroom of the Biblioteca Laurentiana at Florence. In the first place an exaggeratedly high, indeed door-high, base carries the whole wall organization. On it, on empty white expanses of wall, hang the consoles above which rise the double columns. Next to these columns are placed blank windows with powerful sculptural frames whose pilasters are slightly broader at the top than at the bottom. The wall spaces above are filled up with ornamental fillets in delicate contrast, which should indicate a mezzanine storey. But the most striking feature is that the double columns are recessed, let into the wall. This suppression of the spatial development of the columns instinctively arouses a fellow feeling in the spectator and leads him to share their oppression. This is undoubtedly deliberate on the artist's part. As a sculptor Michelangelo had already made man's restriction, *p. 64* the limitation of his freedom of movement, the theme of his art in the famous figures of the writhing slaves originally intended for the Julius Monument. The feeling of oppression produced by columns of which the Laurentiana provides the first example could be still further heightened in Mannerism by the literal imprisonment of the shaft of the column. For that is what we might call Vignola's procedure when he bandages the columns with several square blocks piled on top of each other. Sticking human figures through the holes in strapwork was further developed in the fantastic grotesques in the ornamental engravings of the Dutch Floris school.

Mutilations, arbitrary exaggerations and abnormal combinations of the individual features — the architraves and arches with keystones, and even the wall treatment itself, with its squared stones, bosses and rustic work — were common, a phenomenon which was rare in earlier ages. Unorganic and ornamental tendencies are noticeable in the stone laying. Keystones for example could acquire exaggerated importance for no apparent reason. These bowdlerizations of individual shapes which were subject to classical rules produce a deliberately bizarre, recherché effect. Every great Italian Mannerist architect thought out original combinations. The Florentines and Romans, Michelangelo, Giulio Romano, Ammanati, Vasari and Buontalenti, particularly excelled in this. The Upper *p. 94* Italian architects, Vignola, Palladio, Sansovino and Michele Sanmicheli, were more restrained in the free play of fantasy.

One of the most inventive of all was Giulio Romano, as the Palazzo del Tè at Mantua shows. He played fast and *pp. 73, 101, 137, 141* loose with the various features on the east wall in the courtyard. Even in the sizes of the stones we can observe a striking contrast; narrow bands of stone are followed by broader ones, while the blank areas of wall are also skilfully placed. Then again smooth and sunk stonework alternate. On the bases beneath the windows the two possibilities of rough and smooth sometimes occur on one and the same block. In this way the contrast between dressed stone and the rough forms of nature is stressed; a contrast which Giulio Romano exploited on a grand scale in the frescoes in the Sala dei Giganti. There he obviously struggled to emphasize the contrast between the divine round temple of Zeus — smooth, artistically accomplished and harmonious in itself — and the earthy, rough crude, chaotic Cyclopean masonry. Reverting to the outside of the palace we find that in some cases the windows and niches of the façade have no particular framework, contrary to all the correct rules. But when a pediment which projects emphatically is suddenly placed above a window, the arrangement has a fragmentary unexpected effect and so produces an even stronger psychological shock. One of the most astonishing and ingenious conceits is that part of a triglyph in the entablature threatens to fall, so bringing the frightening effect of collapsing architecture into the actual construction. For Giulio also treated the phenomenon of collapsing architecture in the frescoes in the Sala dei Giganti, where capitals are shown falling through the air when the temple caves in. But the unprecedented thing is that Giulio Romano even included these highly exciting complicated incidents in his real architecture — incidents which one would normally imagine could only be painted, as has already been mentioned.

The Mannerist artist's concern to enliven and add interest to even a very modest façade is shown by the Villa della Magia at Tissani, province of Pistoia, whose façade was richly decorated by Buontalenti. On the façade the artist placed flat frames with little expenditure of material. Although there was no direct reason for it, he wanted to arouse a sense of the grandeur of classical columns, so he placed single columns in the niches. They have nothing to support and are purely decorative motifs. A tendency towards the dissolution of architectural features is evident in Mannerist architecture in general. The important supporting function of columns is repeatedly called in question. The columns of the arcade in the court of the Oratorium of S. Caterina at Siena by Peruzzi create an unsteady vacillating impression. They stand on disproportionately high bases which makes them seem to be balancing. Giulio Romano again provides an example. He attacked the material substance of the columns at the entrance to the Palazzo del Tè by leaving them as a kind of undressed natural stone of indefinite consistency with vague outlines. Vasari again called the supporting function of pillars in question in the long narrow courtyard of the Uffizi where he broke each one up with a niche which covered its entire width. The supporting elements in the treatment of a wall can also be effaced and dissolved by other means, such as rusticated pilasters and embossed columns. Frequently the shafts of the columns were covered with rich ornamental work or the solidity of the column was lessened by spiral-shaped rib ornaments, for example on the Palazzo Boncampagni at Bologna. In Ammanati's courtyard in the Palazzo Pitti stone bands are drawn across the engaged columns and these bands form a decisive flattish pattern which deny the architectonic stability and swamp the actual structural arrangement of the Palace seen as a whole.

Structural details and minor components as special productions assume a surprisingly important place on the tombs and monuments of Mannerist architecture. Without excessive effort the artist was able to show more ingenuity in them than in large unwieldy buildings. Details in this sense are portals, windows, fireplaces, balconies, staircases and even memorial tablets. As a prelude there was an increase in the flood of engravings which became the standard models for them. The north was particularly productive of them. Ducerceau, Cornelis Floris and Hans Vredeman de Vries are prominent again. Often the forms displayed are limited to cabinet work, the so-called *Metselereien*. A typical work is the rood-loft of St Etienne du Mont at Paris or even more so the staircase in the anteroom of the Biblioteca Laurentiana at Florence which — designed by Vasari — seems like a separate creation beside Michelangelo's treatment of the walls and to some extent has the effect of a foreign body in the rooms as a whole. One of the most eccentric works was the staircase by Buontalenti which could formerly be admired in the *p. 95* choir of S. Trinita at Florence. Its frivolous shape denied its practical function; it was almost impossible to use its steps because they were bizarrely designed with motifs like the inside of an ear. At the foot of the organ in Arezzo Cathedral Vasari allowed the architectonically subsidiary motif of the volutes to become a dominating element in the composition, by giving them bloated proportions. They easily drown all the other features; in contrast the niches between them are compressed into small shapes and even the ornaments on the organ balustrade seem deliberately finicky and angular. The general effect is based on Michelangelo's Julius Monument where he risked similar dissonances in the structure as a whole in his placing of the gigantic figure of Moses in relation to the surrounding architecture.

Portals as independent works of art

It is remarkable how often we find portals as valid works of art in themselves. The portal motif as such, as *p. 92* a gateway, as the frame for a vista in perspective, such as we can actually see in the Teatro Olimpico, must have had a special attraction for the Mannerist artist and given rise to surprising trains of thought. During his last years, in 1561, Michelangelo himself designed a grandiose portal, the free standing Porta Pia at Rome, and developed strange individual details on it which he never used elsewhere, such as the bands which hang down limply over the small circular fillets. The main entrance of the Escorial shows how far a portal can project in contrast to a long deliberately plain wall thereby creating an independent effect. For the portal which is introduced there is more than an unobtrusive emphasis of the middle of the wall, it is a separate entity standing in definite opposition. Baroque would have aimed at a smoother less abrupt transition from portal to monastery wall, whereas Mannerism thought in harsh clashing contrasts in such cases. How little value they laid on assimilation is shown by the fact that no fundamental difference was made in Mannerism between portals on exteriors and doors in interiors. There are surprisingly lavish portals in interiors as well, for example in the hall of the Hirschvogelhaus at Nuremberg. Germany in general is very rich in individual portals decorated with figures, but only a few of them are especially fine examples: the portal of the Piastenschloss at Brieg (1552), the portal *p. 96* of the Alte Hofhaltung at Bamberg (1591) and the outer town gate of Tübingen by Antoni Keller as Italian trained master-builder and Christoph Jelin as native sculptor. On this gateway strap- and scroll-work are blithely combined with the completely realistic motif of two soldiers with their weapons.

Understandably enough, writers on architecture attached extraordinary importance to the demonstration of portals *p. 81* and architraves for windows. In his architectural treatise the *Seven Books of Architecture* Sebastiano Serlio devoted the whole of the sixth out of eight chapters exclusively to portals. Fifty examples were presented and in his own words Serlio was proud of making each of the fifty portals as different as possible. Obviously he could not satisfy everybody, but he demonstrated the ones which he knew: thirty portals were in rustic work with a mixture of various orders; twenty were "more delicate pieces". The strict rules of the Renaissance as regards the orders were no longer observed; on the contrary, as many different orders as possible were used and even their details were mixed which often produced an intricate hotchpotch. Fortuitous combinations and capricious effects were deliberately sought. Serlio justifies himself by saying that there always have been, are and will be bizarre men who strive for novelty, and so he wanted *rompere e guastare la bella forma*, i.e. to break and destroy beautiful form. As he remarks elsewhere, the clever architect can omit the oddities if he considers it necessary.

For all this Serlio's portals are comparatively restrained; Wendel Dietterlin, a German painter who felt impelled to try his inventive gifts in architecture as well, proved much more fantastic and grotesque. In 1593 he brought out his *Architectura* in two volumes in which he exclusively depicted separate architectonic details. He turns pilasters and columns into roots and tree trunks. This extravagance was relished by northern and German Late Gothic which had already experimented with the transformation of small columns into treetops. Obviously such emphatic naturalism ran counter to the basic principles of architectonic thinking. But Mannerism was already intent on ridiculing the remote grandeur of the classically regulated world of forms. Portals, windows, memorial tablets, sarcophagi and designs for fountains whirl confusedly in Dietterlin's imagination and he presents them like that in his book. The last word on all this was said by Federigo Zuccari — not in an imaginary design but in an actual creation — with the gruesome misshapen masks with which he decorated the portal of the garden wall and the windows of his palace at Rome. The lofty art of architecture had become the playground for ingenious flights of fancy and disturbing apparitions to alarm the spectator.

GIULIO ROMANO: *The Temple of Heaven*. Ceiling fresco from the Palazzo del Tè, Mantua

Great Mannerist painting and decorative art

In Mannerism the most varied historical hypotheses were employed in exaggerated form. Not content with those, the style sought complication and extravagance in both formal construction and subject matter. Instead of form and content combining simply and harmoniously, which art normally strove so hard to achieve, in Mannerism there was a dichotomy between them; this is highly characteristic of the unusually disrupted mental attitude of Mannerist art and makes it doubly hard to understand. If on the one hand the greatest importance is attached to the purely aesthetic formal treatment of elegant individual figures and groups of figures, and their self-sufficiency to some extent cultivated, on the other hand our attention is claimed by the most complicated systematic combinations of themes and subject matter which are difficult to understand. Beside the theory of the *figura serpentinata* is the theory of the ingeniously thought out programme of contents. Instead of a decrease in the combinations of allegorical figures still surviving from mediaeval systematic conceptual and symbolic thought, there was on the contrary an appreciable increase. This was all the more surprising because previously in the Renaissance, especially with Raphael, fresco painting had become balanced and calm, serene and easily digested in both conceptual and visual terms.

The intellectual background and origin of the fresco schemes

In order to execute the highly complicated fresco schemes according to the new requirements the painter needed a great expenditure of artistic media of the most varied kind. The main point was not so much to create solid "eternal" works of art as to stage great improvisations with the utmost splendour and ultimately effect a rich ensemble of figurative, allegorical and architectural accessories. The best way in which we can characterize this extraordinary display is to make use of the concept of the "apparatus". The word apparatus, *apparato*, was used by contemporaries to designate *inter alia* the ephemeral festive decorations, grandstands and triumphal arches, so popular at the time, which were fabricated on the occasion of the sovereign's entry into a town, for weddings, funeral rites and other festive or solemn occasions. Since the frescoes of the period exhibit the same features as these festive decorations we can justifiably transfer the concept of the apparatus to them. Making festive decorations was one of the official duties of court artists; such work was produced by Holbein the Younger, Peruzzi, Giulio Romano, Vasari, Niccolò dell'Abbate, Stradanus, the brothers Zuccari, Spranger, Vredeman de Vries, Otto van Veen and Rubens. So we can understand why the frescoes painted on the walls of palaces and churches looked very similar to the improvised festive decorations.

When the architecture at its disposal allows, the fresco decoration often covers both walls and ceiling uniformly. The unity of the scheme is also emphasized because the treatment of walls and ceiling was specified at one and the same time in overall plans for halls. Brilliant examples of such Mannerist overall decoration are the halls in the Palazzo Ruspoli at Rome, painted by Jacopo Zucchi, in the Palazzo Capponi at Florence, painted by Bernardo *pp. 124, 127* Poccetti and the Sala Clementina in the Vatican by Cherubino Alberti. Even the arched library rooms in the *pp. 121, 93*

Vatican and the Escorial are completely covered with frescoes. A sacred interior decorated in this way is the Cappella del Giglio in S. Maria Maddelena dei Pazzi at Florence whose walls and dome were painted by Bernardo Poccetti.

One of the main features of these decorative frescoes is the striking emphasis on their framework on both walls and ceilings. The framework is so exaggerated that it even crowds out the pictorial areas, which had always dominated before, and becomes almost an end in itself. The artist does not hesitate to juxtapose different elements which normally would only have been associated against his inner conviction. But in these works emphasis was laid on just such contradictory combinations. Nudes were grouped with architectural details, medallions coupled with columns and statues in niches united with animated gesturing figures; powerful forms could be combined with elegant details and vast figures of colossi appear next to small paintings in their own frames. Moreover artists took pride in shifting the orders of reality just as they wished: apparently three-dimensional illusionist figures could be placed in competition with others which looked markedly two-dimensional, as if painted on tapestries, or the scale of objects be arbitrarily changed as the artist thought fit.

Given this view the apparatus is no longer a mere accessory and support required to turn the painting areas into clear-cut fields for the unfolding of the pictorial event; it acquires a separate existence with its own dynamism. This kind of fresco painting encouraged an entirely new way of treating interiors; out of the formerly technically balanced and normally proportioned division of walls and ceilings grew something quite different in character: an ingenious virtuoso decorative art which was eager for effect. In a real sense the representations free themselves from the surfaces of the wall and carry on a daring independent game away from them. The solid craftsmanship of painting still organized in guilds was in no way equal to such demands; it received its deathblow and its place was taken by the brilliant improvisation, the rapid painting of the intellectual virtuoso artist.

The decisive example of a fresco composition hypertrophied by apparatus, whose subsequent influence was *p. 30* irresistible, was Michelangelo's Sistine Ceiling on which figures and framework oppress each other with terrifying yet fascinating force. The painted architectonic framework of the ceiling as a whole lays no claim to stability in any verifiable sense; only individual sections have their own rational logic. The decisive feature is the individual figures. In their violent movements they overpower the architectural framework and reduce it to an ancillary function. The dynamic force of the figures tends to liberate them from their setting. Consequently it seems quite natural when they frequently appear on the most unorthodox parts of the ceiling, without an adequate reason, and create a personal domain there.

Ceiling painting

Following the unique, overpowering model of the Sistine Ceiling, Mannerism in general chose the ceiling as a particularly suitable playground for its decorative frescoes; to a great extent it recognized ceiling painting as a separate branch of art beside mural painting. Apparently the Mannerist artist was attracted by the very difficulties which were inevitably caused by the ceiling as a painting surface high above the spectator's head. On it the artist was perfectly justified in using acrobatic, equilibrist and highly virtuoso effects. In Florentine High Mannerism even the spatial oppression already discernible on the Sistine Ceiling may be surpassed on occasion and we find a spaceless crowded conglomeration of broad-framed panel pictures clustering together in which the figures *p. 127* have scarcely any room. This is the case on the ceiling painted by Poccetti in 1585 in the Palazzo Capponi at Florence.

Alternatively the ceiling may merely be covered with a thickmeshed network of small panel pictures, as in the Sala dei Venti in the Palazzo del Tè at Mantua by Giulio Romano. Such productions make us realise that great technical skill had been expended merely on the plan for dividing up the ceiling. But it must never be forgotten that although these divisions could be formed in any way the artist chose, they also had to enclose the subject matter planned for the frescoes. For this reason there were definite practices in many cases. A frequent procedure was to put the master concept of the fresco scheme in the central compartment and the subordinate scenes, whose subject matter was less important, around it. Giulio Romano followed this principle in the Sala dei Venti of the Palazzo del Tè when he put Mount Olympus in the middle and arranged the gods around this allegorical central figure, followed by the signs of the Zodiac and the appropriate symbols of the months, with mythological genre scenes on the outside edge. Domenico Beccafumi used a similar procedure on the ceiling of the Palazzo Pubblico *p. 105* at Siena. In the central field he placed the allegory of *Justitia* and framed it with fields in which *amor patriae*, love of the fatherland, and *mutua benevolentia*, mutual benevolence, appear; the practical historical examples of these allegories were displayed in the adjoining outer fields in scenes from Greek and Roman history. In the library of the Escorial, Pellegrino Tibaldi arranged the seven liberal arts in the central fields and in the adjoining lunettes pictures of the historical places where those sciences were most zealously cultivated. The scheme was further complemented by lunettes on the shorter sides of the ceiling containing allegories of religion and philosophy. Tintoretto approached the problem rather differently in the Scuola di San Rocco at Venice; he abandoned *p. 234* allegories and relied solely on biblical scenes from the Old and New Testaments to establish Christ's work of redemption systematically in accordance with a given plan.

The subject matter of the frescoes

The various subjects of the frescoes were mixed up in much the same way as the formal elements. Allegories, historical scenes and genre scenes mingle with comparatively unimportant decorative figures, geniuses, caryatids, masks, escutcheons and light grotesque work. Often the old simple personifications of higher concepts were no longer adequate and soon increasingly subtle interpretations were invented. The allusions which were attributed to things became so complicated that a special branch of literature had to be introduced to explain them: iconology, the knowledge of the meanings to be attached to pictorial representations. At the end of Mannerism a comprehensive codification of allegories was made by Cesare Ripa in his book *Iconologia overo p. 106 descrittione d'imagini delle virtu, vittii, affetti, passioni humani, corpi celesti, mondo e sue parti.* The first edition appeared in 1593. This important reference book was translated into many languages. By 1764 twelve Italian editions had been published, in addition to two German, two English, five French and one Dutch. Ripa's *Iconologia* grew out of the antiquarian leanings of the humanists, especially their interest in ancient Egyptian hieroglyphics; as a result the classical and mediaeval Christian allegories handed down in literature were increased by many new ones and reduced to a system.

Emblems and hieroglyphics were also given a powerful new impetus. By an emblem the sixteenth century understood the association of a symbol with a maxim, the so-called device. The more remote and obscure the connection between word and picture, the more fascinating an emblem was considered. Endeavours to invent a pictorial language which would be intelligible to all initiates over and above the permanence of speech go back as far as Leon Battista Alberti; nevertheless they were greatly intensified in the sixteenth century. A collection of symbols and epigrams by Andrea Alciati entitled *Liber Emblematum* appeared in 1561. It contains a mixture of history, allegory and animal fables. This book found adherents and was reprinted and enlarged in various countries, such as France, Italy and the Netherlands. The first independent Dutch books of emblems by Johannes Sambucus and Hadrianus Junius appeared in 1564 and 1565 respectively, and were followed up in specialist works by Cryspin

Domenico Beccafumi: Ceiling in
the Palazzo Pubblico, Siena

Evil Thoughts: Woodcut from CESARE RIPA's *Iconologia.* The first edition was published in 1593

de Passe. Otto van Veen illustrated the *Emblemata Horatiana*, symbolical representations and sayings from Horace, in 1607 and the *Amoris emblemata* in 1608. The *impresi*, i.e. personal emblematical insignia, which were exhibited next to the family coat of arms were also emblems; their laws were laid down by Paolo Giovio. Collections of *impresi* differ from other books of emblems because the name of the great lord who bears it is sometimes added to the emblem, so that such a volume becomes a sort of book of heraldry. Theodor de Bry wrote the most famous genealogical and heraldic book, which was published in Frankfurt am Main in 1593. The invention of ingenious allegories was virtually indulged in as a sport in late Mannerism. Every artist who was full of these artificial mental combinations was a passionate devotee of the game. The painter Cornelis Ketel in the Netherlands distinguished himself as the most adept master. As the darling of the Muses (he was simultaneously painter and poet) he "created a number of ingenious and significant allegories, like old Timanthes". Karel van Mander gave a detailed account of Ketel's allegories and also appended the verses which the painter composed to accompany his pictures of the allegories. But in his case the whole learned mental apparatus only served to demonstrate dull moralistic popular saws.

In the compilation of Mannerist fresco programmes wide use was made of traditional thinking in terms of groups of subjects. Not only separate personifications were portrayed but also whole series, such as the gods of the planets, the virtues and vices, the seven liberal arts, the four temperaments, the five senses, the four continents and the four seasons, the twelve months and the times of day.

All these groups of allegories were acceptable means for dissecting and classifying the world. In his *Iconologia* Cesare Ripa called the four elements "le parti minori della grandissima macchina universale", and went on to mention the "macchina del mondo", which conformed to the cold rational attitude of the Mannerists. All the allegories enumerated also appeared in the Middle Ages and the Renaissance, but in a more subordinate role than in Mannerism. Now they acquired a much more incisive significance because they impressed as being systematic

106

and well arranged. Mannerist art liked enquiring into the classification of the world and nature. And allegory is to some extent an offshoot of classification, an ingenious recherché neo-scholasticism. This pretentious aim of forming a world picture made great demands on the artist. He had to be well versed in every branch of technique and knowledge, he had to be a good draughtsman and painter, and also a scholar. He had to know all about emblems, hieroglyphics and heraldry, and be thoroughly conversant with mythology, with Ovid's *Metamorphoses* as well as the Bible: only then could he lay claim to the honorary title of ingenious inventor.

The theory of artistic invention

We can understand that the Mannerist artists in this critical intellectual situation made great efforts to explain the creative process behind a work of art both philosophically and aesthetically. They attacked the basic question of how it was possible for the mind to produce an artistic idea at all and speculated about how the invention of a work of art functioned. The reason why this question could arise as an urgent concern was that the purely scientific reproduction of nature which was prevalent during the Renaissance was no longer adequate to meet the new demands on the work of art. The artist was faced with the alarming and unpalatable fact that rationalism and scientific treatment break down when it comes to things artistic. In Mannerism the view that artistic activity was a higher, more creative mental accomplishment was held more firmly than ever before. A typical sign of this is that mathematics, which were still regarded as the sacrosanct foundation of the fine arts during the Renaissance, were now literally attacked with hatred. Zuccari expressly rejected the science of mathematics as the foundation of the art of painting and came to the conclusion that: "...the artist's thinking must be free as well as lucid, and his mind must be liberated and not restricted by a mechanical dependence on such rules." For the first time the human mind expressed views in opposition to nature, which people had believed they could only master in the artistic field, with the help of mechanical constructions such as perspective and proportion. The power of the imagination resisted purely external appearances, announced its rights and fought for them heroically and stubbornly. The contrast between subject and object was also reflected in this conflict.

The Mannerist artist sought his salvation in a sphere quite different from nature; he turned to higher powers. He believed in *disegno interno*, a mental image of what he was going to paint, in *forma spirituale* or the Idea. A complicated theory of ideas was developed, and expounded in several treatises on aesthetics. For all its ponderousness this literature did supply the mental superstructure considered quite indispensable for practical artistic activity. Giorgio Vasari laid the foundation for Mannerist artistic theory with his spiritualization of the concept of *disegno* in the theoretical introduction to his lives of the Italian painters. The Milanese painter Giovanni Paolo Lomazzo wrote the most comprehensive treatise on Mannerism. In his *Trattato dell' Arte della Pittura*, first printed in Milan in 1584, the most striking opinions, from the Mannerist point of view, are expressed on the most varied themes: composition, the ideal figure, the portrait, landscape and individual artists. So theory and practice were mixed in the plan of the book. The author deliberately linked his treatise with the mythical number seven by dividing it into seven books. The treatise entitled *De'veri precetti della pittura* by Giovanni Battista Armenini, a painter from Faenza, appeared only three years later in 1587. The claim that the true rules for painting were to be learnt in it demonstrates the highly propagandist aims of Mannerism. This work also aimed at outlining a theoretical structure of artistic activity. After these basic works which presented comprehensive subject matter *in extenso* came books which threw out the ballast of practice as it were and concentrated on aesthetic speculations. In his book *Idea del tempio della Pittura* (1590) the Lomazzo already mentioned continued the work begun in his earlier treatise and put forward an artistic metaphysic with idealistic and Neoplatonic tendencies. He borrowed from other fields for the construction of this mental edifice. Astrological, cosmic and mystical conceptions were called in, the temple of art was compared to the vault of heaven and speculation about the appearance of the temple was based on the number seven. The seven columns of the temple of art corresponded to the following seven great Italian painters: Michelangelo, Gaudenzio Ferrari, Polidoro da Caravaggio, Leonardo, Raphael, Mantegna and Titian. These seven painters were introduced as controlling powers in the same way as the constellations are in astrology, the theory in which every man, according to his temperament and characteristics, was understood to be under the influence of a corresponding constellation. In other words Lomazzo enlisted the help of the widespread mediaeval and Renaissance theory of children being born under the influence of the planets. In his theory of the concept of beauty Lomazzo followed Florentine Neoplatonism and transferred its ideas, which were purely philosophical originally, to his special Mannerist aesthetic. An uncompromisingly scholastic spirit is revived in the systematic conceptual structure of this book. Only here it is exclusively applied to throwing light on the nature of art, which was now the focus of interest. This would have been quite impossible in the Middle Ages when entirely different, religious problems were to the forefront.

Federigo Zuccari's theory of the idea

The zenith of the Mannerist artistic theory of ideas was reached by Federigo Zuccari in his great work *L'Idea de' Scultori, Pittori e Architetti* which came out in Turin in 1607. Zuccari's theory is that whatever is to be realised in the work of art must pre-exist in the mind of the artist. This mental image Zuccari calls *disegno interno* or *Idea*. The opposite, i.e. the practical execution, regardless of the branch of art, painting, sculpture or architecture, he calls *disegno esterno*. The "inner drawing" does not have to be directly connected with the execution of the work of art. Man received the ability to see this "inner drawing" from God, consequently the idea is a spark of the divine mind, a *scintilla della divinità*. Zuccari's concept of the Idea is based on the Platonic Idea as well as that of Thomas Aquinas. "The Idea exists in God and the *disegno interno* also exists in his divine majesty." God possesses the immanent archetype after whose pattern he created the world and, in that he created it, "drew" it internally and externally. But God also gave man the divine ability "to produce an intelligible cosmos" and "compete with Nature". This profound motivation for art turns artistic creation into an exacting activity. We can see this in the best works of Mannerism. Zuccari writes: "I say then that God...after he had created man in his own image, in his goodness...also wanted to endow him with the ability to picture an inner mental image within himself so that with its help he could apprehend all creatures and form a new world inside himself, and so that, by virtue of this inner image, he could, imitating God and competing with Nature, produce unlimited things which are artistic yet resemble Nature and through the medium of painting and sculpture place new paradises on earth before our eyes." Naturally man must settle for an inadequate realisation of the Idea. God possesses a "unique image which is perfect in accordance with its essence and comprises all things in it". But man forms various images for himself depending on the difference between the objects imagined by him; consequently these images have an inferior origin, in the senses.

According to Zuccari, man is a being bound to his body who can only form his inner images on the basis of his sensuous experience. On the other hand Zuccari tries to defend himself against the objection that perceptions by the senses rank before inner images and he expressly emphasizes the primacy of the *disegno interno*, the Idea. Although he does not deny the necessity of sensuous perception he affirms that the origin of the idea is more metaphysical and *a priori*. Artistic creation is conceived of as the emanation of divine grace. The artistic man who is affected by this grace is a genius. In the field of art this places the genius on the same plane of reverence as the saint, the man

JACOPO DA PONTORMO: *Autumn.* From the frescoes in the Villa Medici at Poggio a Caiano

especially affected by divine grace in the field of religion. In no other century was the evaluation of the saint and the artistic genius so close as in the sixteenth. The honorary title of *divino* was rightly applied to the greatest artists, such as Michelangelo; an artist like El Greco was on the same plane as St Teresa. Whether artist or saint, all these men were visionaries, recipients of the piercing ray of supernatural knowledge.

We should also mention the artist's special difficulty when faced with the question whether or not he also had to be completely responsible for the theme of the fresco with its learned allusions and profound train of thought in every case. Mannerist thinking was not so strict about the work of art being a unified original invention such as we demand of the artist today. Artists did not think it was beneath their dignity to enlist the help of literary scholars. We must not forget that the *invenzione* were divided into two separate parts in contemporary artistic theory. According to Lodovico Dolce's treatise *Aretino or dialogue about painting* there is on the one hand "the fable or historical event which the painter either chooses himself or which is specified by others as the object to be executed" and on the other hand "the attitudes and diversity and so to speak the expression of the figures", which were entirely of his own invention.

Artists and their intellectual advisers

It was honourable for artists, in accordance with their important social standing, to cultivate the closest possible relations with scholars and indeed to belong to their learned circles. Artists mixed with poets, theologists, philologists, historians, archaeologists and musicians, and were conversant with their problems. The Roman circle of scholars was under the protection of Cardinal Hippolytus Medici and had combined to form the Accademia delle Virtu. Paolo Giovio, Annibal Caro, Claudio Tolomei and Cesane were among its members. Linguistic and stylistic studies were pursued and Vitruvius's technical terms were investigated. Vasari too felt completely at home in this circle. The result of all this activity was the founding of the Accademia del Disegno by Vasari and Federigo Zuccari. Rather typically this academy had its model in a philological association, the Accademia della Crusca, a society for promoting the native tongue, at Florence. Tintoretto frequented the first noblemen and scholars of Venice; his friends were Daniele Barbaro, who was patriarch of Aquileja, expounded the writings of Vitruvius and wrote a famous book on perspective, as well as Maffeo and Domenico Venier, and the Secretaries of State Vincenzo Riccio and Paolo Ramusio.

Michelangelo and the Neoplatonist circle at Rome

Michelangelo, who also occupied a striking position in social life, belonged to the Neoplatonic circle formed in Rome around Vittoria Colonna, the widow of the Marquis of Pescara. He exchanged letters and poems with that devout and cultured lady. In her circle there were among others Cardinal Pole, the learned Cardinal Quirini, who was Bishop of Brescia, the erudite writer Claudio Tolomei, who commented on Vitruvius, and the antiquarian and philologist Raffael Maffei. Besides Michelangelo the artist, the painter, sculptor and architect, there was yet another Michelangelo: Michelangelo the poet, thinker and humanist. More than three hundred poems and fragments of his are preserved, madrigals and sonnets predominating, followed by epigrams, *capitoli* and *canzoni*. In many respects his poetic production and his work as a practitioner of the fine arts belong together. A superficial example of this is that Michelangelo frequently chose to draft his poems on drawings. The themes around which his poetry revolved were love, art, especially sculpture, and lastly politics. Philosophical and religious themes, and thoughts about death took a large part in his reflections. Michelangelo was one of the greatest Dante experts of his time and in certain circles enjoyed just as much fame and authority in that capacity as he did as a painter elsewhere. Thus he dealt with the question which was important for contemporary Dante scholarship: "About the days on which Dante wandered through Hell and Purgatory." It contains an excursus "On tyrannicide", in which the question was asked whether Dante had erred when he banished Brutus and Cassius to Lucifer's abyss. Michelangelo also made use of his literary knowledge as an artist. It benefited his paintings, yet it is not easy to understand its full effect: with its help Michelangelo set to work to operate, so to speak, on the foundations of the traditionally accepted subject matter. Until his arrival this had been handed down to artists as an immutable heritage of knowledge of the world around them. It was not customary for a practising artist consciously to interfere with the ideological conceptual background of the representations, or even wilfully alter it. All this changed with the advent of Michelangelo. This intellectual hero became an independent self-willed cultural power. He interfered authoritatively with the *concetto*, the mental programme. His personality practised its own mental politics, as it were, on the strength of its philosophical humanistic culture. We can estimate how daringly Michelangelo went to work in his *Last Judgment*, in which the sad universal tragedy of mankind is proclaimed with tremendous force. Besides his own personal ideology Michelangelo was burdened with images from Dante's *Inferno*. He lived and thought in Dante's world; consequently he transferred a great deal from it to the mighty theme which inherently made certain clear-cut demands and could claim that they be adhered to. In Michelangelo's work there is scarcely a trace of Christ judging in imperturbable calm. There is nothing to be seen of the traditional hierarchical orders of saints and angels, nothing of the heavenly host admitted to eternal bliss, or of the twelve apostles majestically gathered around Christ. Instead of all that we have a chaotic juxtaposition of individual figures, quite uncomposed in the ecclesiastical sense. Arbitrary changes in the sizes of the figures prevail; they are not matched against each other to scale. But Michelangelo did not only push to one side the traditional construction of the theme of the Last Judgment, one of the mightiest central themes of Christian iconography; the location for mounting his composition is also exceptional, although admittedly he did not choose it. Customarily the Last Judgment belongs on the west wall, so that it becomes visible on leaving the church, and not behind the altar as the main view during the celebration of Mass.

Conflicts between artists and patrons

Once artists began to behave so untraditionally as to allow inner artistic problems to come first, it is not surprising that they came into conflict with the wishes of their patrons. Hans Fugger complained about the composition of a Resurrection which he had commissioned for the Church of St Moritz at Augsburg in 1568, although he recognized its artistic merit: "…But the Resurrection is not fashioned as it should be, for our Lord God should rise from the tomb and not be depicted flying…so I do not know whether he (the painter) will serve me or not, from out here one might think it was an angel and not Christ himself, who soars on high." "…so this altar-cloth or *quadro* seems unsuitable to me (for it is too much *a la italiana*, audacious and such that anyone who stands in front of the altar does not know it is meant)." Afterwards an altar-painting of the Trinity was commissioned instead of this picture of the Resurrection: "I would much prefer it to be devout and beautiful, and not so that the artist shows only his art and there is nothing more to it…but first of all I would like to see a small sketch in any case, so that it shows no Matthew on Shrove-Tuesday." The same Hans Fugger sent a *disegno* to Italy with the remark: "…yet I want it to have not only great art but also much devotion. Your Italian painters are too *vagi*", i.e. too superficial, too indefinite.

The artist's intimacy with scholars

Undoubtedly the artist's authoritativeness was connected with his cultural aspirations, which increased his self-assurance. This tendency was by no means confined to Italy. We even have proof that Pieter Bruegel the Elder, the great portrayer of Dutch popular life, mixed with many cultured men on an intimate footing and was esteemed in their circles. During his stay in Italy he had friendly relations with the famous miniaturist of the day Giulio Clovio, and the latter was one of the most important members of the artistic circle which had formed in Rome around that mighty patron of the arts Cardinal Alessandro Farnese. In Antwerp Bruegel had a close friendship with the famous geographer and engraver Ortelius who belonged to a circle of politically and religiously radical progressive humanists, among them the politician, moral philosopher and illustrator Dirck Volckertsz. Coornhert and the publisher Christopher Plantin. Two other Dutch painters, Karel van Mander and Cornelis Ketel, had connections with the associations for studying popular national literature, the *Rederijker*. Otto van Veen and his great pupil Peter Paul Rubens were completely bound up with the universal humanistic cultural ideal. The same thing happened in Germany. Hans Baldung Grien mixed with the humanists of Strasbourg. The two Cranachs, father and son, were at home in the circle of the reformers and were on the closest terms with them. They produced their "reformation" altars in direct exchange of ideas and consultation with them. Testimonials to this marriage of minds are the group portraits of the German reformers on the Wittenberg and Dessau altars. In 1544 Melancthon tells of the dogmatic pictures Cranach the Elder produced. Hans Mielich self-assuredly put his own likeness next to that Orlando di Lasso in the last volume of miniatures for the composer's Psalms, and Hans von Aachen married the daughter of Orlando "the highly renowned musical Orpheus of our day".

"ut pictura poesis"

Painting and poetry were closely connected in the sixteenth century. The old saying about the equality of painting and poetry, "ut pictura poesis", was even truer than before. In the picture of *St Luke painting the Madonna* painted *p. 159* by Martin van Heemskerck in 1532, the poet, who is of one mind with the painter, stands behind him at his easel. Many artists practised poetry and painting simultaneously, examples being Michelangelo, Bronzino and the sculptors Danese Cattaneo and Vincenzo Danti. The painter and art theoretician Lomazzo published two collections of his own poetry in 1587 and 1589. Among the Dutch Dirck Volckertsz. Coornhert, Lukas de Heere, Cornelis Ketel and Karel van Mander wrote poetry. The Swiss Tobias Stimmer and Hans Mielich of Munich tried their hands at writing plays. Artistic theory saw poetry and painting united in the same struggle. So Armenini could write: "Poetry and painting have striven to feed the souls of mortals with the highest pleasures and delights, they wish to comfort and stimulate the human spirit." That declaration expresses both the extremely didactic goal and the moralistic ethical character of Mannerist art. The true connoisseur wanted to read the contents of a picture like the contents of a book; looking at art should also give intellectual pleasure. Significantly enough Cesare Ripa says in his *Iconologia* that pictures are like puzzles: "in forma d'enigma".

Writers and scholars plan painting programmes

Given this intimate connection between the fine arts and literature it is only too understandable that cultured advisers frequently supplied painters with the programmes for fresco decorations with their complicated subject

ABRAHAM BLOEMAERT: *Banquet of the Gods*. Alte Pinakothek, Munich

matter. This was necessary, because the frescoes also had to underline the identity of the patrons. In their palaces, castles and churches people were supposed to find themselves in the highest spheres of the cultured virtuosity so esteemed at the time and also to share in the extraordinary inventive gifts of the human mind. They were supposed to feel the united impact of the noble and important ecclesiastical patrons, the scholars and the artists. In many cases we still know the names of the writers who collaborated. Lucas Gauricus, who published astrological works, may well have supplied the ingeniously thought out astrological scheme for the ceiling of the Sala dei Venti by Giulio Romano in the Palazzo del Tè at Mantua. The plan for the decoration of the walls and ceiling of the hall of Pope Clement in the Vatican stems partly from Vasari and partly from Cosimo Bartoli, as a letter of 1556 proves. Apart from this, Vasari, at the wish of Cosimo dei Medici, also conferred with his friend Vincenzo Borghini about the scheme for painting the Sala grande of the Palazzo Vecchio at Florence. There the problem was a wide range of historical pictures. Annibale Caro was responsible for the contents of the frescoes by the brothers Zuccari at Caprarola. And it is assumed as a matter of course that in the particularly comprehensive painting cycle in the Scuola di San Rocco at Venice, where a concordance of the Old and New Testaments was displayed, Tintoretto relied for the compilation of the contents on a member of the brotherhood who was especially well versed in biblical studies.

There are similar examples in Germany too. The humanist Johann Stabius supplied the subject matter for the triumphal gateway of Emperor Maximilian, that monster work of genealogical knowledge, which Dürer put together from many woodcuts. For the lavish woodcut of the "Imperial eagle with the emblems of the Celtis society" by Hans Burgkmair "the learned Viennese writer Celtis himself wove the beautiful history", as the caption says. The historiographer Dr Johann Pistorius supplied the historical and genealogical substrata for the family portrait gallery of the Margrave of Baden in the Neues Schloss at Baden-Baden which Tobias Stimmer was commissioned to paint in 1580. The Swiss mathematician Conrad Dasypodius and Tobias Stimmer collaborated to work out the highly complicated scheme for painting the astronomical clock in Strasbourg Cathedral. As *p. 115* the scientist remarked in his account of the origin of what was then a world-famous work: "Tobias Stimmer the painter showed great industry and helped us a great deal in our mutual consultations." The Dutch doctor Samuel Quickelberg probably advised Hans Mielich on the arrangement of the subject matter for the High Altar in the Frauenkirche at Ingolstadt, which was completed to celebrate the centenary of the University in 1572. This altar consists of a hundred separate panels, a number which obviously alluded to the jubilee year. The Rostock theologian David Chytraeus supplied the biblical plan for the ceiling paintings compiled in accordance with the Protestant doctrine in the Burgkapelle at Strechau in the Steiermark in 1579.

We know from a contemporary source the exalted spheres in which such counselling took place; it is a drawing by Federigo Zuccari which depicts the consultation on the programme for painting the dome of Florence *p. 157* Cathedral. On the right is Vasari who was already dead by then and whose unfinished work Zuccari was to complete. Borghini, the literary adviser, is talking to Zuccari; the figure in the middle is presumably to be interpreted as Wisdom. Evidently it helped the fame of the Mannerist artist if such great frescoes were planned in a refined conceptual style. It was not intended that the content of any of these works of art could be deciphered at first glance by any casual spectator. In some ways they recorded a secret language which could only be interpreted by the humanistically trained classes of the nobility and the church. These paintings are the product of an emphatically literary cultural world; the exclusive knowledge and understanding of them was a class privilege. Paolo Giovo claimed that the invention should not be so obscure that no one understood it, but obscure enough not to be intelligible to every plebeian. It was no argument against this art that even an experienced connoisseur like Vasari could sometimes be mistaken when analysing the contents; Vasari wrongly interpreted the classical scenes painted by Beccafumi on the ceiling of the Palazzo Bindi-Segardi at Siena — he confused Zaleucus of Locri

The clock in Strasbourg Cathedral. A woodcut
after the design by Tobias Stimmer

115

with Torquatus among other things. In the sixteenth century people even had enough sense of humour to enjoy it when a representative of the lower classes misinterpreted mythological themes in his own way. In his life of Cornelis Ketel Karel van Mander relates that a farmer mistook Cupid and Diana for the Annunciation — "and with his boorish intelligence the man went on no wiser than he was before", remarked the painter grandiosely from the ivory tower of the intellectual. It was an essential characteristic of the highly intelligent Mannerist artist to show great sympathy for the attitude of simple uneducated people, apparently in compensation for his flights of fancy. This polarity can even be confirmed in Michelangelo of whom Vasari tells the following story: "For all that, he took pleasure in certain people to his fancy, such as the hack painter Menighella from the Upper Arno, a stupid but very droll fellow who sometimes came to him so that he could make the drawing of St Rochus or St Antonius whom Menighella had to paint for the peasants. Michelangelo, who only worked for a king with reluctance, let everything drop and made simple drawings suiting Menighella's manner, taste and way of expressing himself. Among other things the fellow had a very beautiful model for a crucifix prepared by Michelangelo, made a mould of it, shaped crucifixes of paste and other substances and went round the countryside selling them. It made Michelangelo split his sides with laughter when funny things happened to Menighella, like the time when a peasant who had had a St Francis painted by him complained when he saw the saint in a grey habit, because he would have liked it a more beautiful colour; upon which Menighella painted a brocade pluvial over it and made the peasant quite content."

Essays in explanation of the fresco cycles

It is admittedly instructive to learn that regardless of all the work they did for the upper classes, with their over-subtle cerebral requirements, artists still remained aware of the primitive iconographical outlook of the simple people and took it into account — at least according to anecdote. But on the whole it is quite understandable that literary glosses were often needed to decipher the frescoes accurately. Artists published their own essays to elucidate and illustrate the involved trains of thought with all their recondite allusions and intricacies. The best known of these writings is by Vasari and describes his own frescoes in the Palazzo Vecchio at Florence. Vasari had produced it ready for the press in 1567, but it was not published until 1588 by his nephew under the title "Ragionamenti del sig. cavaliere Giorgio Vasari pittore et architetto sopra le inventioni da lui dipinte in Firenze nel Palazzo di loro Altezze Serenissime" (Explanations of the inventions which were painted by him in the palace of their Serene Highnesses at Florence). Seven dialogues, each corresponding to a hall in the palace, were held between Prince Francesco Medici and Vasari himself. The mythology of the gods was called in to design an allegory of the whole cosmos. The four elements and the gods appear in the upper storey, while the genealogy of the *dei terrestri*, the earthly gods, i.e. the Medici family, was represented in the rooms below. In this way a certain analogy between the two storeys was supposed to be reached. This literary gloss by the painter is undoubtedly necessary for an understanding of the profound allusions, although the author openly admits that even he could not decipher all the hidden references.

From a slightly different point of view Jacopo Zucchi wrote his *Discorso sopra li Dei de' Gentili e loro imprese; Con un breve trattato delle attioni de li dodici Cesari con le dichiarationi delle loro Medaglie antiche*, about the gods which he had painted on the ceiling of the Palazzo Ruspoli at Rome. This work came out in 1602 after Zucchi's death. It is more about philology than aesthetics and attempts to place the literary key in the spectator's hand. We should also mention that immediately after the completion of the Biblioteca Vaticana in 1590 the work *Della Libreria Vaticana Ragionamenti* by Mutio Pansa came out in Rome. In it the historical background of the fresco

One of the brothers ZUCCARI: Fresco in the Villa d'Este, Tivoli

programme was explained and the programme itself learnedly commented on. It enumerated the councils depicted in the frescoes up to the Council of Trent, as well as the famous libraries of the world and the men who helped to invent printing. After the completion of the painting of the astronomical clock in Strasbourg Cathedral by Tobias Stimmer the already well known mathematician Dasypodius published the small volume *Wahrhafftige Auslegung und Beschreibung des astronomischen Uhrwerkes zu Strassburg.*

Conversation between King François I and Cellini

From Benvenuto Cellini's autobiography we know the mental climate in which a conversation between a princely patron and an artist developed. On the occasion of a visit to François I he explained a project for a fountain with a central figure and four allegories: "The central one is intended to represent the god of war; the other four figures represent the arts in which Your Majesty takes delight and which find every support from Your Majesty. This one on the right is science, here is the symbol by which one recognizes philosophy and all the characteristics which accompany it; the second figure portrays the fine arts, namely sculpture, painting and architecture; the third is music which associates well with those arts and sciences; but the last, which looks so pleasant and gracious, represents generosity, because without it none of these wonderful talents can be exercised. The figure in the middle is supposed to portray Your Majesty, for you are the god of war and the one brave man in the world and you use valour justly and piously for the preservation of your fame." The King had scarcely the patience to let me finish my speech before he said in a loud voice: "Truly, in thee I have found a man after my own heart!" He called for his treasurers and ordered them to give me what I wanted. The expense might be what it may. Then he slapped me on the shoulder with his hand: "Mon ami (i.e. my friend), I do not know who has the greatest pleasure, a prince who has found a man after his own heart or an artist who finds a prince from whom he can expect every facility in order to carry out his great and beautiful thoughts." To this I replied: "If I am the man you mean, then my luck is surely the greatest." Then he answered: "Let us say they are equal."

The appropriate use of fresco schemes

However ingeniously thought out the schemes for the Mannerist fresco decorations might be, they still had to conform to the traditions governing their suitability for the immediate practical task and fit rationally into their background. To that extent nothing had fundamentally changed since the rules laid down in the Renaissance. In his great treatise on architecture Leon Battista Alberti used a new rationalism to make precise distinctions between the different problems. He demonstrated cogently what purpose a dwelling house for example serves and advised on the design and interior fittings best suited to that purpose. The sixteenth century was still dominated by the same attitude; artists adhered to clear-cut rules and customs. These were treated in detail in a treatise by Giovanni Battista Armenini, *De' veri precetti della pittura*, published in 1587. In the last of the three books into which the work is divided the subject is exclusively *Della distintione e convenienza della pittura secondo i luoghi e le qualita delle persone*, in other words how painting should be adapted to the place for which it is intended or to the rank of the patron commissioning it. A codification of the conventional *decoro* is put forward. The tenor of the contents of a decoration, and its character, had to conform to quite definite rules. Fixed spheres can be distinguished within which specific ranges of themes can and must be used. The plan for the frescoes would always state in advance whether they were to decorate a town palace or a country villa. Town and country were still considered as separate domains in the sixteenth century and consequently the frescoes had to match the general atmosphere and fit into the environment in each particular case. A distinction was also made between the decoration of an official building and the commission for painting the interior of his town palace given by some minor nobleman. Precise class distinctions were accepted and they were followed when taking into account the rank and dignity of the patron.

The municipal schemes

The frescoes of the town palaces are distinguished by a note of heroism and monumentality. The monumental ceremonious style would not have been possible elsewhere and would have been held inappropriate. We find p. 122 such monumental frescoes in the battle scenes in the Sala di Costantino by Giulio Romano in the Vatican, in p. 123 those in the Salone dei Cinquecento by Giorgio Vasari in the Palazzo Vecchio at Florence, in the scenes and battles from Roman history by Cesari d'Arpino in the Salone of the Conservatori Palace at Rome, in the *Fall of the Giants* by Perino del Vaga in the Palazzo Doria-Pamphili at Genoa and in the ceiling pictures with battle scenes from the Trojan War, and the battle between Hercules and the Amazons, by Luca Cambiaso in the Palazzo of Andrea Doria, also at Genoa. In these places for official display the gigantic heroic style broke through on the most imposing scale. The artist refrained from every kind of trivial decoration; even the sentimental landscape idyll was proscribed. Not even the architecture determining the spatial division of the room gets a chance to say a significant word. Mannerism employed the highest subjects it possessed: Herculean nudes and the dynamic body of the noblest animal, the horse. Here we find the biggest agglomerations of masses, great piles of bodies. Even the illusion of space was subdued as far as possible, because other more elemental powers and forces were concerned.

Even in the case of the illusionist painting of a view the artist's thinking is confined to the appropriate sphere and the basic principle of *decoro* operates. Even the *quadratura* painting of Cherubino Alberti at the end of the sixteenth century preserves the calculated, urban, intellectual, non-scenic, chill a-natural element. Although he had acquired the ability to portray the space of the sky and nature, he had absolutely no desire to give the impression p. 121 of real panoramic space with mountains, trees and clouds in the Sala Clementina in the Vatican. Such space as is disclosed is confined to the painted columns which recede to give a view of the sky. Only artifical text-book type architecture was chosen as a theme. Landscape, the depiction of idylls, was out of the question as a subject. The historical scene of *St Clement on the Stormy Sea*, which was a landscape, was immediately confined in a frame, turned into a gigantic panel picture, removed to the sphere of the artificial picture. It is excluded from the chill apparatus of the columns in perspective, but at the same time it is not narrated profanely and bluntly as a naturalistic illusion. In spite of the fact that the open space of the heavens is captured by illusionist means, it remains an ideal intellectual space free of ornamentation in which columns and allegories stand out, where emblems can be symmetrically and neatly established. The artist knows what his duty is to the lofty ecclesiastical milieu of the Vatican with its premium on ideas.

The mirror of princes

When individual royal households were glorified by specific historical scenes there was a relaxation of the pictorial structure; the artist could use a somewhat lighter and more frivolous touch. Painted architecture and illusionist effects played a greater part. Now and then artists even turned to stage scenery which was more limiting. A special range of iconographical themes was developed to record the virtues of rulers. Over and over again variations on the theme of good and virtuous government were treated. The relevant programmes were conceived as a challenge and reminder; they were supposed to glorify the rulers' moral responsibility and at the same time to exalt their actions. Rulers had to be shown conquering evil and weakness, and establishing a strong and benevolent government. Brilliant examples of the basic maxims of sovereignty were demonstrated to their subjects in schematic works of various kinds. The following main works or groups of works of this type are worthy of mention: the frescoes and murals by Rosso il Fiorentino in the Gallery of François I at Fontainebleau; the façade of the Ottheinrichbau of Heidelberg Castle; a scheme for a palace façade composed by Vincenzo Borghini which is only preserved in literary form; the no longer extant canvases in the banquet hall of Baden-Baden Castle painted by Tobias Stimmer for Margrave Philip II; and lastly the panel pictures and engravings with the representation of *Hercules at the Crossroads*.

The Gallery of François I at Fontainebleau

In the Gallery of François I at Fontainebleau the decoration achieves more than the mere customary glorification *pp. 121, 124* of sovereignty in general. The scheme is under the sign of the personal virtues of the French king. The qualities which qualified François I to be a good ruler were extolled in twelve pictorial compartments. But there was nothing straightforward about the way they were presented. Consequently it was only possible for the most skilled scientific expert in iconography to unravel the profound allusions and understand them in their right contexts: Erwin Panofsky made a detailed analysis of them. He says that these allusions resembled a *roman à clef* and laments the lack of a contemporary commentary. In its absence the meaning has to be reconstructed from the somewhat exceptional setting of the themes. The main pictures were always complemented by small subsidiary pictures called *inquadraturae* which were inset into the scroll-work frames. With their help a continuous cross-check on the interpretation of the main paintings can be made. The pictures in the first four bays are to be considered as the opening chapter, as it were, of the story told in the Gallery. At first François I is depicted as the heaven-sent successor to the throne; then as protector and furtherer of artistic and scientific culture; next as guarantor of the nation's unity and lastly as Cosmocrator who is so outstanding in wisdom and virtue that he becomes a second Alexander the Great. In the fifth bay the theme changes. The allegory turns from the mystique of kingship and takes the King's life and character as the subject for portrayal. The King no longer manifests the dignity "which never dies", he appears as a human being who shares with other mortals the weaknesses and shortcomings as well as the virtues. Some incidents illustrate such weaknesses and this may be why the artist did not portray François I in them in person. For example the stories of *Cleobis and Biton* and the *Twins of Catania, Amphinomus and Aenapius* were chosen, both of which embody *pietas*, or piety, or more strictly construed the *voluntas grata*, which Cicero demanded vis-à-vis parents and relations. The classical example of piety is Aeneas who drags his aged father Anchises out of the ruins of Troy and saves him. The story of Cleobis and Biton tells how they pulled their mother, the priestess Cydippe, to the Temple of Juno in an ox-cart to which they were harnessed like draught animals in the fields. This was supposed to intimate that François I had always cherished an extraordinary esteem for his mother Louise of Savoy. The artist reproduced contemporary history in skilful humanistic camouflage and so made it exclusively accessible to the few initiates; simultaneously he glorified the history of the day and removed the present to a higher plane. In the last four bays yet another tone was adopted, the manner of narration becomes rather more meditative and reflective than dramatic or exaggeratedly panegyrical.

Monumental frescoes in the vast halls of the official government palaces at Rome and Florence

Sala di Costantino in the Vatican. Post-1520

Salone dei Cento Giorni, 1546. Palazzo della Cancelleria, Rome

Right above: Salone in the Conservatori Palace, Rome. 1596–1636

Right below: Salone dei Cinquecento, Palazzo Vecchio, Florence, from 1565

122

Naturalism in a nobleman's country-house and a remarkable variation on the method of dividing up the Sistine ceiling which Mannerists considered to be heroic

CRISTOFANO GHERARDI (1508–1556): Ceiling fresco in the Palazzo Vitelli a S. Egidio, Città di Castello, near Florence

Right : BERNARDINO POCCETTI: Ceiling fresco in the Palazzo Capponi, Florence. 1583–1590

126

Sala dei Cavalli in the Palazzo del
Tè, Mantua. Horse and landscape

Right: The Rittersaal in Trausnitz Castle near Lands-
hut: a group of troopers storming into the hall

The interior can be completely cut off from the outside world

Palazzo Vecchio, Florence. Studiolo of Francesco dei Medici. 1570–1571

PIETER BRUEGEL THE ELDER (c 1525–1569): *The Death of Mary*. Grisaille. Upton House, Edgehill, National Trust

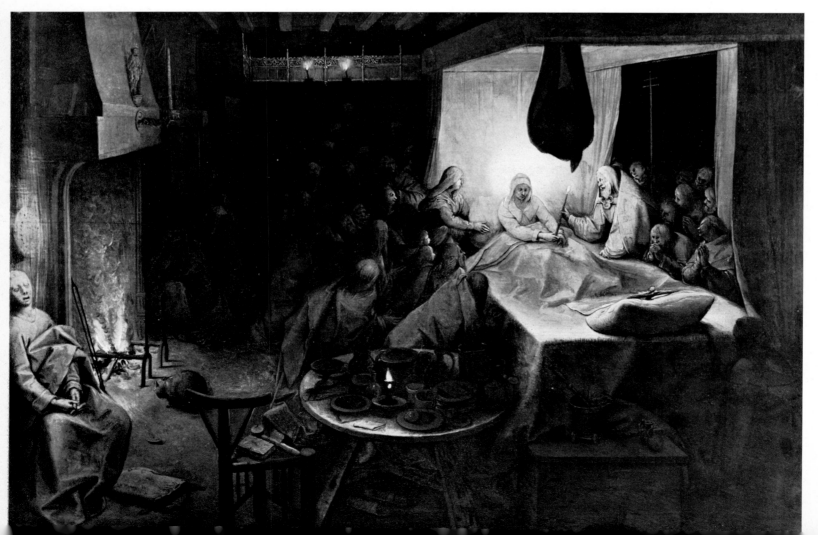

130

A group of animals above a drinking trough becomes a zoological exhibition

GIOVANNI DA BOLOGNA: Grotto in the garden of the Villa Medici at Città di Castello. Post-1565

132

The last pictures, such as the *Vengeance of Nauplius*, the *Fountain of Youth*, the *Education of Achilles* and *Venus Deceived*, are almost imbued with resignation; a remarkable final stanza for the epic poem which began on a note of greatness and brilliance.

The Gallery of François I, arranged by Rosso il Fiorentino, provides a genuinely Mannerist solution to the problem involved. No attention was paid to the whole fitting together into a harmonious unity such as the Renaissance aimed at. The separate divisions of the total space are left as detached compartments, consequently the Gallery as a whole seems chopped up and disintegrated. The strongly emphasized frames also spoil the impression of a self-contained whole. Their plastic accessories are often so striking that they confuse the spatial organization. The corners of the fields have been loaded with caryatids or scrolls with small inset pictures and made vague as a result. So it is not surprising that the unfolding of the subject matter only proceeds haltingly and even independently from bay to bay. The coherence of the whole has no compulsive inevitability and the general treatment of the room leaves it open; it has really neither a true beginning nor a true end. It would not come as surprise if the Gallery were a few bays longer. In this Panofsky sees a certain relationship with the elongated Mannerist figure where a little more or less elongation is also comparatively unimportant. The total sequence is inherently involved and complicated. To understand such a lay-out properly we have to struggle through many twist and turns, cross-references and comparisons. Admittedly this wealth of variation, these manifold tensions and interpenetrations of the contents have their own attraction. We need to use much more brainwork, almost mental acrobatics, in order to do justice to a Mannerist total work of art than we do with a Renaissance work which is harmonious in itself, or a Baroque work of concentrated energy.

The Ottheinrichbau at Heidelberg

pp. 26, 90 Various levels and spheres are interwoven in the scheme for the façade of the Ottheinrichbau of Heidelberg Castle. A different conception is stressed on each separate storey, but Ottheinrich's horoscope is interpreted in all the storeys taken together. The aim was to portray the astrological powers which stamped his personality. On the ground floor the telluric zone dominates, the kingdom of the four elements, which are conceived of as associated with the four temperaments. The Christian virtues which appear on the middle storey make it possible for these earthly powers to be placed in a higher order. They are *Fortitudo*, *Fides*, *Prudentia*, *Justitia* and *Spes*. In other words those virtues which particularly become a ruler, but which through their introduction on the palace façade turn into symbols guiding the ruler's actions and decisions. But in the case of Ottheinrich the Christian virtues were not considered as the highest instances of the attributes of the ruler; for above them are the gods of the planets and they are the ones which influence men from the hour of their birth.

A scheme with an original moral aim which Vincenzo Borghini conceived for a *sgraffito* painting on the façade of the Palazzo Montalvo at Florence was not actually executed, but it has at least been handed down as a literary project. In this case the figurative decoration of the storeys would have extolled the qualities of a good Christian servant and the agreeable results of a "noble, honourable serving relationship". The representation takes the following course: on the base appear *le Virtu dell'Animo*, those virtues and mental gifts which are particularly important in the service of princes, such as modesty, cleverness, honesty, sympathy and love, bravery and tenacity; on the lower part of the first storey appear the *Effetti ed escercitamento delle prime Virtu*, in other words those qualities which result from good gifts in a loyal servant: readiness, discretion, obedience, speed, taking pains and perseverance; on the upper part of the first storey is the *Persona del Duca*, the Duke himself, as guarantor

133

that the man who serves him faithfully will receive the rewards for his good behaviour; this reward, *Effetti dei A e B: Premio e Corona*, was depicted on the second storey; it consists in winning goodwill, satisfaction, esteem, wealth, repose and honour.

The Palazzo della Cancellaria at Rome

One of the great Mannerist fresco programmes was carried out in the Palazzo della Cancellaria at Rome. In 1546 *p. 122* Vasari was commissioned by Cardinal Alessandro Farnese, the nepotist and grandson of Pope Paul III, to paint the magnificent council hall of the famous palace built by Raffaele Riario. The idea was to glorify the rule of the still living Pope Paul III of the house of Farnese. In the pictures the narrative impetus was severly curtailed in favour of a more rigid conception which makes use of every possibility to glorify the Pope. Paul III is introduced as the exalted ruler in the midst of numerous allegorical figures. It is significant that specific historical events were scarcely used for the purpose. Vasari limited himself to portraying the general attitudes of a man who is bestowing his grace on the world. In the first picture Paul III receives the homage of the nations; a great display of attendant figures, envoys and courtiers from the different countries in their national dress is introduced: Greeks, Latins, Dutch and Italians. Many presents are brought and exotic animals depicted: apes, camels, giraffes and elephants. The pictorial area is framed by two tabernacles conataining the allegories of Eloquence and Justice. High above them the busts of Caesar and Alexander the Great can be seen; all of which are naturally to be related to the person of the Pope. Below on the steps reclines the river god Tiber who is crowned by the founders of Rome, the boys Romulus and Remus. In the second picture Paul III orders the continuation of the building of St Peter's. The Pope appears in a new historical dimension as Jewish High Priest. The arts (architecture, sculpture, geometry and painting) kneel before him and a plan of St Peter's is spread out. With a forceful gesture of command the Pope points to the view of the unfinished church in the background. On the steps in front rests the allegorical figure of the Vatican with the emblem of the Church. Michelangelo once said: "The image of the prince is reflected in his buildings." In the third picture Paul III distributes honours and dignities. This ceremony takes place in a hall with magnificently ornamented twisted columns. A vast number of deserving men have thrown themselves at the feet of His Holiness. We recognize portraits of Cardinal Bembo, Cardinal Pole of England and Cardinal Sadolet, as well as those of Michelangelo, Antonio da San Gallo and the historian Paolo Giovio. This event is installed between the figures of *Virtus* and *Labor* as the basic qualities of men worthy of honour. Grovelling on the steps in the foreground we see Envy, an important figure in connection with the distribution of offices and dignities. Lastly, in the fourth picture, Paul III is glorified as the Prince of Peace for he himself considered the ten years' truce concluded between François I and Charles V in the spring of 1538 at Nice as one of his greatest political successes. This is the covenant which is celebrated in the picture. We see Paul III carried in in triumph by the allegories of *Vittoria*, *Autorita*, *Fermezza* and *Pace*. All the princes of Christendom are present to experience this glorious moment. *Amor* and *Constantia* appear in the niches to left and right.

The value attached to working fast

Patrons attached great importance to the frescoes being completed as quickly as possible. Vasari actually worked to meet a dead-line which was almost too close; he wanted to produce a bravura piece of rapid decoration and he succeeded. But the shortcomings of such excessive haste are noticeable. Artists were used to executing ephemeral festival decorations in a hurry and still calling on a wealth of ingenious ideas. Karel van Mander relates of Hans Vredeman de Vries that in 1570 when the Emperor's daughter Anne of Austria came through Antwerp on her way to Spain he produced a triumphal arch with great industry in five days at the German's command. So an artistic steeplechase such as Vasari undertook in the Cancellaria is not over-remarkable; it was the product of virtuoso ability and more or less formed one of the obligations of a dutiful Court Painter. Vasari had a sufficiently large group of collaborators at his disposal and so he succeeded in completing the work in a hundred days. Under normal conditions he would have taken years over it. Vasari mentions his helpers by name: "The Spaniards Bizzera and Roviale, Battista Bagnacavallo from Bologna, Bastian Flori from Arezzo, Giovan Paolo from Borgho, Fra Salvatore Foschi from Arezzo and many other of my young helpers". Around 1800 the Italian art historian Luigi Lanzi remarked sarcastically that Vasari had even more hack workers as a painter than as an architect.

In those days people went from one extreme to the other. Michelangelo felt compelled to do without collaborators on his giant fresco compositions because they did not satisfy his extremely high standards of work. He wanted the most sensitive personal idiom to be visible everywhere, whereas previously trained assistants would have been called in to execute the parts which merely required the labour of a craftsman. Thus two poles were opposed to each other in Mannerism, the eccentric genius and the highly skilled experienced painter. The latter was also entrusted with the execution of frescoes which hitherto had counted among the most painstaking and difficult achievements of the artist. Now it was even possible to carry out such tasks as a masterly piece of virtuosity and consider them as light-weight, almost frivolous works of art. A solid foundation as a craftsman was no longer the first commandment in this new virtuoso work. Later Vasari regretted with commendable frankness that he had only produced rough sketches for the Cancellaria frescoes. Personally he set great store by scrupulously executed cartoons as the foundations of a composition. In other words he definitely did not like relying on inadequate sketches and schematic designs when he went to work and wrote: "The whole work can be judged by the cartoon."

Although the question of the tempo of work really concerns the field of pure technique and does not affect the basic principles of art, it often formed the subject of discussions in artistic circles. For Mannerism also set a certain value on clever feats. Working fast was praised in the letters written to Tintoretto in 1545 and 1546 by the famous Venetian writer on art Pietro Aretino, and Armenini was astounded by the unbelievable speed with which Luca Cambiaso put his frescoes on the wall; he used both hands and painted more than ten painters put together. Even in Germany Lucas Cranach the Elder was praised as a very rapid painter, *pictor celerrimus*, on his tombstone in the Stadtkirche at Weimar. In Francisco de Hollanda's dialogues about painting the question is directly put to Michelangelo: "Which is better; to finish a work quickly or slowly?" Michelangelo answered at some length:

"To fashion something with great facility and skill in a few hours which would take someone else several days is useful and good. It is to be accepted as a gift received from the immortal god... Consequently the man who works quickly without neglecting to paint as well as the slow artist deserves greater praise. If on the other hand, led astray by the facility of his hand, he disregards the limits of his art, which should not be exceeded, then he had better paint more slowly and conscientiously. For even the esteemed and skilful artist must not be enticed by his inclination for speed and his deft hand to neglect or even to forget the great duty to achieve perfection; that is the goal which every artist must have in view. Hence it appears that it is no fault to work somewhat more slowly if necessary or even to expend much time and care on his work if it will be more perfect as a result. Only a bad result will bring him censure.

"What I would also like to say to you, Francisco de Hollanda, is the highest law of our art, which you certainly know and likewise consider as fundamental: the painter should strive by the sweat of his brow to fashion his work with zeal and effort so that it appears as if it was designed rapidly and easily and almost effortlessly, although the opposite is true. Most works of art are only produced after endless labours and still have the distinction of seeming easy. If it came to the point of working carelessly or slowly, I would prefer speed to slowness. I would prefer a painter to paint eagerly and slightly less well than laboriously and possibly better, but not much better."

In other words Michelangelo positively valued speed of execution as long as it was not at the expense of perfection. To what extent Vasari overdid fast painting in the Cancellaria frescoes would be a question for the artist himself; yet his procedure was basically recognized, in theory at least. Paolo Giovio supplied the scheme for the frescoes in the Cancellaria and also wrote the captions for the cycle. He reported to Cardinal Farnese on the progress of the frescoes: "It is really a wonderful thing to see at one glance a group of three hundred people painted from life." Vasari was paid a fee of 1,000 florins for the work and it is noteworthy that he was satisfied with the amount.

Influence of the stage on the organization of frescoes

In his fresco cycle in the Cancellaria Vasari attached the main importance to the grandiose treatment of the whole room; the pictorial and figurative elements took a secondary place. A method such as Giulio Romano had already used in the Sala di Costantino in the Vatican was continued and extended. Compositions of niches with pronounced frames, beneath which are large scrolls with luxuriant garlands—also painted—, serve to demarcate the edges of both the longer and end walls. This effected a grandiose and more especially an emphatic architectonic division of the hall as such; for the pictorial areas were limited to the space between these independent motifs of niches which put so much stress on the corners of the hall. But Vasari stripped even those areas of their autonomous existence. He did not isolate the fields of the historical scenes with the normal surrounding frames; the columns dividing up the wall, the niche frameworks, also have a function connected with the actual picture and belong to it as its lateral conclusion. The proportioning of the painted architecture in the pictorial areas and that of the framing niche architecture is the same. Vasari used a similar method in the foreground of the pictures of the different scenes. He allowed it to pass obviously into the painted architecture at the base of the picture, without a division. For this purpose he placed painted steps in front of the "stages" of historical scenes and thus introduced elements of theatrical construction into mural decoration. This brilliant notion is wholly in terms of a stage set, and that was how he must have conceived the pictorial areas. How closely such a wall resembles a theatre wall is shown by comparing it with the outstanding example of stage wall treatment, the Teatro Olimpico at Vicenza by p. 92
Andrea Palladio: there too niches form frames; there too are portals which allow a free view of the stage scenery; there too a similar limiting wall is included under a flat ceiling, and there too architecture and scenery are mixed in a similar relationship.

Vasari's Cancellaria frescoes mark the invasion of painting by the theatrical world, especially scenography. This is not surprising because the stage also received a powerful stimulus from the Florentine Mannerists. Vasari and Salviati not only devoted great attention to it, they were also celebrated *maestri scenografi*. During his visit to Venice in 1541 Vasari erected a theatre for a play by Pietro Aretino with the help of Christofano Gherardi and Battista Cungi in a house of the Company della Calza. At the same time Sebastiano Serlio published his architectural treatise *Septem libri della architettura* and presented the famous examples of decor, the *Scena tragica*, the *Scena satirica* p. 138

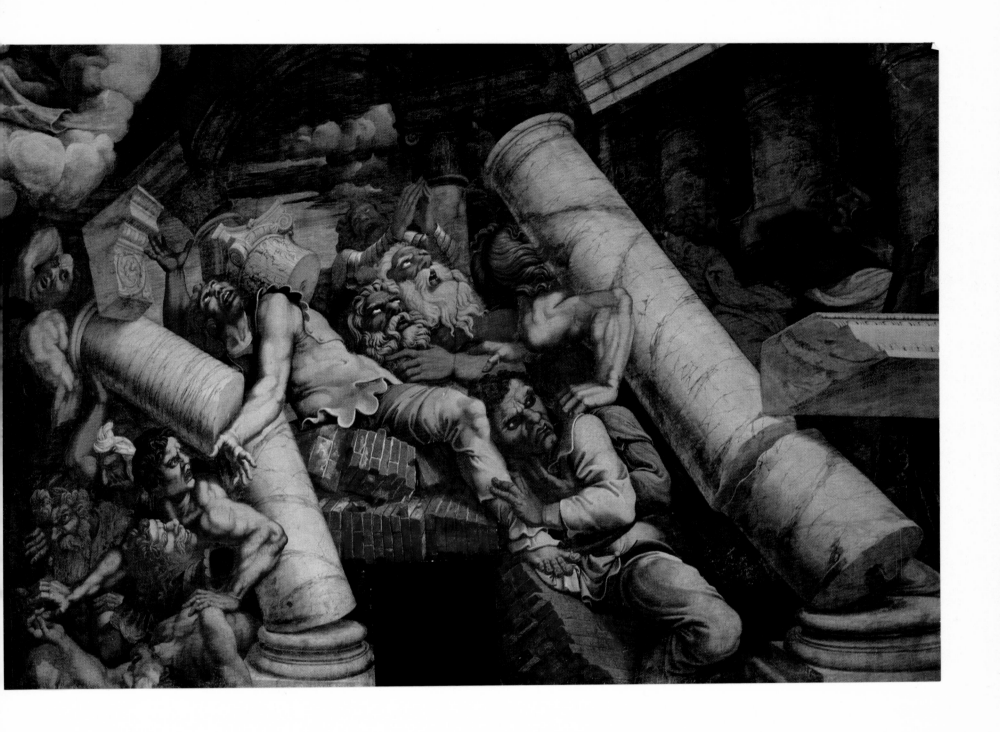

GIULIO ROMANO: *Collapsing columns*. From the frescoes in the Sala dei Giganti, Palazzo del Tè, Mantua

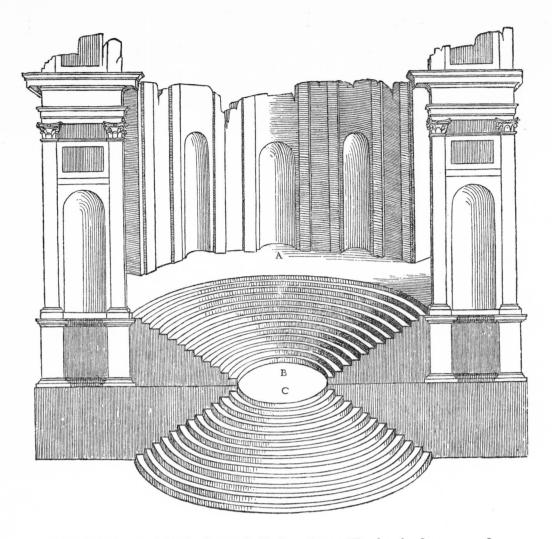

Exedra of the Cortile del Belvedere in the Vatican, Rome. Woodcut by Sebastiano Serlio
from *Tutte l'opere d'architettura*. The first edition was published in Venice from 1537 onwards

and others in the chapter on perspective. If we keep an eye open for special examples of this staircase motif, we realise that its use for various purposes was very widespread. For example it is portrayed by Sebastiano Serlio in his woodcut of the Exedra of the Cortile del Belvedere and it occurs again with Giulio Romano. In the work surrounding the windows of the Sala di Costantino a nymphaeum is represented whose fountain is in the shape of a staircase, with the upper concave steps transformed into convex steps below, via the intermediary of a circular landing. Giulio Romano had already used round steps in a monumental fresco of the baptism of Constantine. So it was only a short step to extend such steps into the spectator's space as Vasari actually did.

The relation between picture and spectator

By allowing the pictorial space to project into the spectator's space Vasari released tendencies which had long been latent in the picture. The Mannerists aimed at intensifying the relation between picture and spectator, and where-ever possible at swamping the contrast between the two spheres. Vasari's procedure made the relation between picture and spectator rationally intelligible; instead of causing a break in the relationship between the latter and the picture, he lulled the spectator into a feeling of security by illusion and skilful obliteration of the boundaries between them. In his fresco of the *Massacre of the Innocents*, in the Ospedale degli Innocenti, the Foundling Hospital *p. 125*
at Florence, Bernardino Poccetti, following Vasari's example, intensified the illusionist staircase motif as the prelude

138

to historical scenes even more. There the two circular landings literally invite the spectator to set foot on the steps and climb up them so that he can witness the historical event. Two small rectangular panels form a minor obstruction to the eager spectator's impetuous ascent; situated on the two top steps they demonstrate almost symbolically the border between the real space of the spectator and the painted space of the picture proper. The picture itself is divided into two sections with events from different periods. On the left hand side is the horrible biblical scene of the massacre of the children of Bethlehem, on the right hand side are the blessed charitable works of that beneficial institution the Hospital. Mary is enthroned with the infant Jesus surrounded by an angelic host in the centre between the two widely different sections of the picture. This composition becomes even more many-layered and tense in its construction just because of the radical inclusion of the steps in the event portrayed.

These flights of steps in the frescoes of Vasari and Pocetti introduced an innovation which deserves attention. With them the boundary line which had previously separated the world of the fresco from the spectator was obliterated. The spectator had indeed been able to look into the picture, but the illusion that he could also step into it did not exist. The space and event in the pictures were never continued down to the floor level of the spectator and they never began from it; there was always a separating base. Raphael's *School of Athens* for example still has a base just like the mediaeval frescoes. Even in the fresco by Andrea Mantegna in the Camera degli Sposi in the Palazzo Ducale at Mantua the members of the Gonzaga family do not quite belong to the spectator's level, although they are realistically portrayed in themselves. If these figures were to step from their relatively low base into the real space of the spectator they would be ghostlike awkward genre figures who could only move laboriously and clumsily in reality. But Mannerism sees the disappearance of the base, the last threshold separating picture from spectator. Now he believes that he can set foot on the staircase directly and mount step by step into the space of the allegorical event. He is even eager to see the figures in the pictorial space walk about at floor level, in his (the spectator's) actual space.

And this actually happens in Mannerist painting; with Salviati in Castel Sant'Angelo, with Veronese in the Villa Maser and lastly in the Rittersaal of Trausnitz Castle. There a swarm of troopers brandishing their halberds storm out into the hall from a trompe l'œil anteroom. But in the case of the Trausnitz Castle frescoes, we must remember that for all their trick illusionist effects these extremely naturalistic men are only the links and lowest steps in a greater context, that they come from outside into a room on whose walls allegorical figures stand in niches and remote historical deeds are recorded. Their panopticon-like figures are only the lowest section — that identified with our everyday environment — in these paintings which are graduated in significance and lead to higher spheres. But even the banal soldiers conceal a yet higher meaning. In their gestures, in the artificiality of their movements, they contribute in their own way to the ghostly atmosphere of the Rittersaal. The contemporary group portraits

p. 203 of 1581 and 1588 by Cornelis Ketel only show the stormy and violent effects of stepping out of a picture. We even find the remarkable phenomenon of the floor itself, normally the unquestioned sure support of the spectator, becoming unstable and precarious. In the Sala dei Giganti in the Palazzo del Tè at Mantua the spectator stands on a floor with a wave-like pattern which continues the agitated surface of the water painted on the lower sectors of the walls. In this way the spectator is ruthlessly placed in the middle of the stretch of water in which the Cyclops are floundering or even on the point of drowning, before our very eyes as it were. The gigantic heads of the Cyclops sinking into the water look as if they were placed some way below the spectator's eye level. Thus the scale of levels in Mannerist fresco painting also included the extreme realistic possibility of undercutting the spectator's normal level.

Mannerist works of art had become level-conscious so to speak. Particular importance was attached to the relationship between the objects portrayed and the spectator. As already mentioned, the persons and figures in the picture make direct contact with the spectator. This invasion of the spectator's actual space could even be brought home to him in the most emphatic way. In Michelangelo's Medici Chapel the statues of the times of day on the lid of the sarcophagus placed in front of the wall no longer remain in their ideal sphere, their space as part of a work of art; they force their way into the space of the visitor. This effect would have been even stronger if the river gods originally intended to lie on the ground in front of the sarcophagus had been executed. A purely practical result of this effect is that one is tempted to touch the figures with the hands or stir them with one's feet. Their immediate proximity literally challenges the visitor to this disrespectful reaction. The same thing is true of the mourning allegorical figures of the fine arts which sit in front of Michelangelo's tomb in Santa Croce at Florence or the guardians of Christ's tomb by Adriaen de Vries in the mausoleum of the church at Stadthagen. The awaking *p. 80* guardian, who sits lower on the edge of the base than his companions, allows his legs to dangle down very close indeed to the zone of the visitor to the mausoleum. Moreover this almost tortured *figura serpentinata* shows him the direction in which he should look; the spectator's goal is the slim figure of the resurrected Christ with one delicate hand raised in blessing and the other holding the standard of victory.

In a similar attempt to remove the distance between picture and spectator Bruegel made the scythe and heel of the drinking farmer project over the actual edge of the picture into the real space of the spectator in his design for an engraving, the drawing of *Summer*. By this trick the transition from the reality of the spectator to that of the *p. 131* picture is indicated; a transition which the spectator makes mentally in any case every time he looks at a picture. Passignano then raised projection into the spectator's space to a noteworthy main problem in his frescoes in the Cappella di Sant'Antonio in St Mark's at Florence. Above and between the pediments of the doors he placed Herculean male nudes whose legs reach out into the visitor's own space. The fact that people were first led into the pictorial space by such artificial crouching figures is peculiar in so far as the event in the pictorial space itself is dowright banal, in spite of the historical happenings narrated. The Mannerist artist has used idealistic figures as a kind of filter for the spectator. He did not want us to penetrate into the fictitious world of the picture.

In the Middle Ages and even in the Renaissance it was taken for granted that the event in the picture personified a "higher" existence. In Mannerist naturalism of the sixteenth century there was a danger of the fundamental distinction between the pictorial event and the reality of the spectator being obliterated as the two levels approached each other. The Mannerist artist protected himself and us from the levels actually coinciding by figurative or other accents, for example by interpolating idealistic nudes, as in the work already mentioned. Tibaldi also used original changes of level and sudden transitions between the orders of reality in his frescoes of the life of Mary and Christ in the cloisters of the Escorial. The grey colour of the painted architecture is exactly synchronized with the grey granite of the real architecture. The arches of the vaulting form the frames of the pictures. The frescoes begin exactly at the spectator's breast height. At the height of the visitor's head life-size half-length portraits of figures are frequently introduced to make the transition from the spectator's space to the pictorial space, for example in the Visitation and Christ crowned with thorns. In the scenes of Christ appearing to Mary Magdalene and the three women at the grave the half-length portraits making the transition are replaced by a staircase or a piece of ground on the lower edge. But there also scenes which are excluded from the sphere of this direct relation with the spectator because of the higher significance of their contents. Thus double scenes painted as panel pictures on wood are inserted at the four corners of the covered walks. They show the birth and adoration of Christ; the transfiguration and the institution of the Lord's Supper; the crucifixion and the resurrection, and the ascension and Pentecost. The change from fresco to wooden panel is exactly equivalent to a change in the orders of reality. The interpolation of a flight of steps breaks up the regular unfolding of the frescoes. Tibaldi made use of the difference in level so created by placing the following scenes one storey higher: the disciples at the tomb; Christ as gardener; Christ and the three Marys; the procession to Emmaus and Christ appearing to the disciples. The scene of "doubting Thomas" is once again flush with the ground on the normal level.

GIULIO ROMANO: *Stricken Giants.* From the frescoes in the Sala dei Giganti, Palazzo del Tè, Mantua

The sixteenth century was faced with a different type of knowledge from that faced by the Middle Ages. The world picture had widened immeasurably as a result of great discoveries and general scientific research. Now man was faced with factual knowledge which had swollen in size until it was scarcely possible to take it all in. Zoology, botany, geography and archaeology had to be mastered in their entirety. This was primarily attempted by making long catalogues of individual species. This also had its effect on the world of painting. In a library such as the Vatican for example every ecclesiastical council was portrayed regardless of its importance. In a hunting hall such as that of Weickersheim Castle different kinds of hunting scenes from all over the world were depicted. Nor should we forget the paintings of Bruegel which juxtapose individual cases as if they were a series, the *Proverbs*, for example, which give a pictorial compendium of such sayings, or his *Childrens' Games*. Not to mention the genealogical series of portraits with their wealth of figures of the type found in Ambras Castle. The sequence, the series, the conjugation of individual cases became a favourite way of thinking. Men systematized general knowledge and thought highly of it. Consequently people also wanted to enable art to profit by the new thought, and the new subjects of knowledge were admitted to the conceptions of comprehensive fresco schemes.

The most magnificent examples come from the science of geography which was very much on the ascendant. Only the new attitude to knowledge enables us to understand why actual maps which completely exclude free pictorial composition appear in the great fresco schemes, in spite of their fixed subject matter, on the same footing as the pretentious historical pictures. In the Sala di Mappa Mondo at Caprarola maps are freely included in the overall programme of painted decoration and are as lavishly framed as pictures. They too have Michelangelesque seated figures placed above them at the corners, while large scrolls are introduced over the doors with the framed portraits of the great discoverers of the earth, such as Magellan. For the latter had actually charted and experienced the greatness of the world for the first time by his circumnavigation of the globe. Scientific knowledge was prized above everything and was ultimately used in the decoration of less important parts of palaces as well. In 1565 the outer entrance courtyard of the Palazzo Vecchio at Florence was decorated with views of Austrian towns in honour of the marriage of Francesco Medici to Joan of Austria and now it looks as if part of an ephemeral festival decoration had been perpetuated.

This kind of representation was better suited to printed illustrations such as appeared in the large contemporary atlases and cosmographical works than to monumental painting, except that people were not satisfied with the former. Expert knowledge was granted a brand-new place. The best example of the new power of knowledge is the alteration made in the ground-plan of the Vatican. The long wing which separates the Belvedere Court from the papal garden was, as already mentioned, transformed into the Galleria delle Carte Geografiche. In it a singular *p. 93* mixture of religion and geography was attempted. Miracles and saints are depicted in numerous small fields on the barrel-vault of the ceiling. An inscription of 1581 says that these saints are supposed to have consecrated the regions which appear on the walls below by their presence. In this way the naturalistically conceived landscape is conceded a more exalted idealistic value and factual data are raised to a higher sphere. The broad expanses on these walls between the windows are painted with panoramas seen cartographically; the spectator can take in wide tracts of land at a glance. The seas, plains and mountains as well as the courses of the rivers are drawn in and even the woods are pictorially represented. The lighthouses on the coasts are denoted too. The whole of Italy which is extolled as "the most eminent region on the earth", is spread out in this way in 32 large maps. The corridor with its many windows is light and friendly, and the painting further heightens this clear rather technical atmosphere by the colours of the blue sky, the yellow earth, the blue sea and the green woods and meadows. The landscapes have stucco frames of white and gold. The barrel-vaulting was painted by Girolamo Muziano, who in his

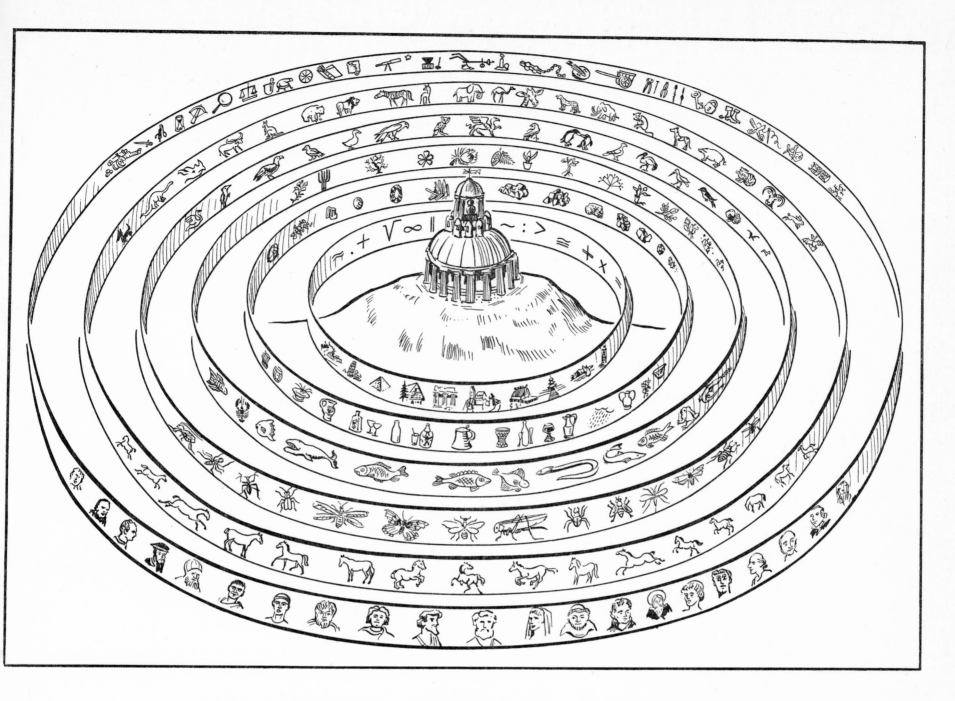

The design for painting the six concentric rings of the capital of the *Civitas Solis*, drawn by Franzsepp Würtenberger after Campanella's account

other works specialized in depicting hermits in their solitudes; Cesare Nebbia and his assistants painted the maps, which are among the most beautiful of their kind.

The fresco scheme in the "Civitas Solis" by Tommaso Campanella

The absolute zenith, the peak of scientific, encyclopaedic and systematic Mannerist schemes was not carried out in practice; it remained a product of the imagination. In 1602 the philosopher and Dominican monk Tommaso Campanella (1568–1639), who was revolutionary for his age and permeated by Communistic ideas during his life, wrote a book about the republic of the sun entitled *Civitas solis*. This book was revised from 1612 to 1620 and

143

appeared in Frankfurt am Main in 1623. As an imitation of Plato's *Republic*, it belongs with the great Utopias of the modern times which were beginning, in the same class with Thomas More's *Utopia* and Francis Bacon's *New Atlantis*. In Campanella's republic of the sun deified nature was exalted in the typical modern systematical Mannerist way. In it we find a scheme drawn up for painting the walls of the six rings which encircle the capital of the republic of the sun. An integral *orbus pictus* was produced. First comes mathematics, then follow geography, geology, meteorology, botany, zoology and finally the science of men. The intention was to portray all the actual conditions of our earth as in a text-book.

In the following descriptions, the subject matter which was intended for each of the rings is enumerated, with occasional reference to how closely the fresco scheme of the republic of the sun matches in its details the related range of themes of contemporary art, whether in frescoes, panel pictures, miniatures or sculpture. In the process we shall realize that Campanella passed in review the essential ranges of themes of the sixteenth century in brilliantly systematic form.

I. The inner side of the wall of the first ring contains all the mathematical figures, "more by far than Archimedes and Euclid invented". On the outside of this wall was firstly an exact and complete description of the whole earth. Afterwards followed specific pictures of each individual region. In other words the subject matter, which had already been used in practice in the frescoes in the Vatican, the Palazzo Vecchio and Caprarola already mentioned, was called on again. An attempt was made to establish a synthesis of the inherently separate fields of the scientific quest for knowledge and artistic creation. The reality of the cartographical site of the localities was raised to an artistic and scientific object in the so-called "true counterfeit", with which great efforts were made to do justice to the new sense of reality. In the second half of the sixteenth century topography had been raised to a very high level in the urban atlas embracing the whole of Europe by Braun and Hogenberg. Work on this book went on for four decades from 1572—1618. It bears the proud title *Civitates orbis terrarum*, the towns of the terrestrial globe, i.e. the most important towns in the world were supposed to be collected in it. Shortly before Braun and Hogenberg a similar world-embracing work by the Flemish cartographer Abraham Ortelius came out in 1570. All the regions of the earth are displayed in 53 engraved maps; the title is *Theatrum orbis terrarum*. The resultant tremendous success of the publisher first induced Braun, a canon from Cologne, to get in direct touch with Ortelius. But although Braun did so, his enterprise was of a different nature. He was able to win for it the famous Antwerp miniaturist Georg Hoefnagel, a widely travelled man who collected the material for his pictures of customs and costumes from all over Europe and visited Spain, France, Italy and England, as well as living for a long time in Germany where he painted a great deal for the Duke of Bavaria and the Emperor Rudolf II. In Braun's book of towns the new feeling for factual specific cases was given convincing expression. The work became equally important for the geographer, the historian, the folklorist, the traveller and the collector and dilettante, and it went far beyond Hartmann Schedel's world chronicle of 1493, and the Cosmography of Sebastian Muster (1544).

II. On the inside of the wall of the second ring one sees all kinds of precious stones, minerals and metals. At the same time a typically Mannerist plan is developed, a leap from one order of reality to another; for apart from the paintings the exhibition of actual fragments of the objects named as specimens was planned, accompanied in each case by an explanation in two verses. On the outside of the wall the fluids were portrayed. All the seas and rivers, lakes and springs on the earth were included, and also the wines and oils. In the walls-niches stand vessels with 100—300 year-old liquids for the healing of various diseases; in other words a pharmacy. Here it should be remarked that the first so-called independent still-lifes by Lutger tom Ring (1562), which represent flower vases in niches, were introduced in a pharmacy. The next subject is meteorology; hail, snow, thunderbolts and other phenomena which take place in the air are portrayed. But all this was to be demonstrated practically as well as visually in closed rooms where the phenomena of wind, thunder, rain and rainbows could be experimentally

Tɪɴᴛᴏʀᴇᴛᴛᴏ: *The Origin of the Milky Way.* National Gallery, London

produced. So the corresponding laboratories are present besides the subject shown in the paintings. In this connection it is perhaps relevant to remark that the covered way which leads from the Uffizi across the Arno to the Palazzo Pitti also has something of this laboratory-like atmosphere; people can move from one interior to the other over a long distance protected from the inclemency of the weather; perhaps there is also a reminiscence here of the covered ways in the Castle at Prague.

III. On the inside of the third ring all kinds of trees and plants are depicted, but once again in a typical combination with reality. Some living plants are placed in pots on the curve of the outer wall. They are accompanied by inscriptions and explanations of their use in medicine and other fields. Here we may think of the publication of herbals in the sixteenth century, especially the one by the German doctor Joachim Camerarius; moreover since Dürer the art of scientific botanical drawing had made great progress. Jacopo Ligozzi for example produced a series of large drawings of plants which are close to Dürer's water colours. They strike us by their painstaking observation of nature.

IV. On the fourth wall fishes, birds, reptiles and insects can be seen. These are creatures which were modelled by Bernard Palissy and Giovanni da Bologna in Mannerist sculpture. Among the birds the phoenix was explained to the citizens of the republic of the sun as perfectly genuine. People still believed in the existence of fabulous animals, as at Castello where the unicorn appears among the animals of the fountain decorations by Tribolo and p. 132 Giovanni da Bologna. Georg Hoefnagel undertook a survey of animals in water colour in four books for the Emperor Rudolf II: it included all the quadrupeds, reptiles, flying animals and birds.

V. On the fifth wall are the highly developed land animals in astonishing numbers, many more than were normally known. Because they are so numerous and of such great size they are also painted on the outside of the wall. "My goodness!" Campanella exclaims, "How many kinds of horses there are alone. What beautiful pictures one sees there and how beautifully they are reproduced." We think at once of the magnificent horses which Giulio Romano painted in the Sala dei Cavalli of the Palazzo del Tè. In these painted horses the reality of the animal p. 128 has undoubtedly been transferred to art, just as reality and illusion, nature and painting are continually changing with Campanella. We know life-size horse portraits capturing nature painted by Jacques de Gheyn in 1603.

VI. After the noble animals an ascent was made to the highest being in nature, man. On the inside of the sixth wall all the mechanical arts were represented, the implements needed for them and their use by various peoples arranged in order of importance and explained, together with an acknowledgement of their inventors. Lastly the greatness and power of men was portrayed. On the outer wall we see likenesses of all the discoverers and inventors of scientific and technical things, as well as the law-givers, among them Moses, Osiris, Jupiter, Mercury, Lycurgus and Solon. Then, almost casually, follows the remark: "However in the place of honour I saw the likeness of Jesus Christ and the twelve apostles whom the inhabitants of the republic of the sun held for supermen." In addition famous heroes in war and peace were enumerated, especially Romans, who were painted on the lower walls below the colonnades.

As far as the practical didactic side of this Utopia was concerned, Campanella conceived of teachers, "Who explain all these pictures and without great labour teach the children all the sciences before they are ten, as if in play and yet in a historical manner (i.e. by observation)". Only the rational belief in nature is glorified in the *Civitas solis*, but the form conceived by Campanella, e.g. the specific schema of division, belongs wholly to the Mannerist neo-scholastic way of thinking. In this he is just as closely bound up with and committed to the great scheme as Giulio Romano was to the programme for the Palazzo del Tè. As regards the contents Campanella was wholly on the side of rationalism. Whereas previously schemes of this kind had descended from the primal point of departure, the Divine, to earthly things, Campanella trod the opposite path. For him the first and highest things are the mathematical figures and the description of the whole earth, then he descends to mineralogy and meteorology, botany and zoology. The famous men with their culture-creating insights and deeds come last. We are forced to ask who is God for Campanella. The writer of the republic of the sun leaves us in no doubt about this: for him God is physical nature and nothing else. The surmounting and crowning of the frescoes on the rings of the town walls ensues in a temple which is sited on a hill and deifies the idea of nature. "The temple is distinguished by being completely round. ...On the altar all one sees is a large sphere on which the firmament is portrayed and another sphere on which the world is painted." In other words purely cosmic and geographical realities are displayed, devoid of any religious symbolism. "Furthermore one sees on the curved surface of the great dome all the stars of heaven from the first to the seventh magnitude labelled with their names and the powers by which they influence earthly things in three verses. ...seven golden lamps with everlasting lights hang down; they bear the names of the seven planets."

We are struck by the systematic cold reasoning in Campanella's artistic visions. But we also find this elsewhere; *p. 27* we can confirm it in that great realisation of an architectural Utopia, the Escorial. There all the proportions and shapes were calculated and rationally related to each other. There the last word in cathedrals was built and simultaneously — something new and entirely unmediaeval — a rational interrelated organism for the most various purposes was brought into being: a monastery, a royal residence and mausoleum, a palace with a college and a laboratory. The marked emphasis on the scientific practical element was at the expense of the genuinely religious, devout element. Regular rational planning steps forward as the guiding principle. There is much that is didactic in it, indeed at times it verges on propaganda. Instead of a building which has grown up organically, we are presented with a calculated organized edifice.

We can give credit to Mannerist art for having a delicately developed and sympathetic understanding as to which range of themes best suited various localities. A suitable scheme had to be invented anew for every new environment and every new purpose. It was even able to find a solution to quite unusual problems. The Mint at Venice wanted to display allegories connected with the production of money and to honour the various metals in the form of personifications. Three statues were ordered from Danese Cattaneo, the Tuscan sculptor and pupil of Sansovino, symbolic of the silver of the moon, the gold of Apollo and the copper of Venus respectively. It is especially noteworthy, and a typical Mannerist conception, that such essentially banal and profane objects as metals were now identified with the figures of the gods. In the Netherlands there are cycles of paintings which glorify the industrial activity of towns. Such a programme, which is firmly rooted in everyday practical life, is *p. 131* contained in the cycle of six canvases by Izaac Nicolai van Swanenburgh which he painted for the Regents' Chamber of the Cloth-hall at Leyden between 1594 and 1612; today this sequence is in the Leyden Town Museum. In it the artist descends from the lofty allegory of the Goddess of the Town with *Past and Present Trade* via the *staalmeesters* and regents to the lavish portrayal of the various processes involved in making cloth: sheep shearing, wool sorting and washing, carding and combing, fulling and dyeing, spinning and weaving. Yet these genre scenes are by no means without an ideological foundation, for all the realism with which their workaday world is portrayed. They are always dependent on the allegorical master concept. Mannerist thought did not surrender this "ideal" mental safeguard. It was always conscious of the conceptual and divine origin of reality and represented it as well.

Schemes for the country

Attention was paid to assimilating villas standing in the open country to their cheerful spacious surroundings. This could be effected by very harsh contrasts, in a clash between the two domains of town and country. The border between urban restraint and the freedom of nature can pass through the middle of a building so to speak. We can see this in the Villa Medici on the Pincio at Rome. Its town façade, facing the street, is inhospitable, cold, *p. 91* consistent, austere and simple in its shapes. The garden façade is invitingly opened by a loggia and relaxed with rich exuberant decoration. The connection between rustic surroundings and the building can deliberately be closely knit. The Florentine architect Dosio once wrote of a design for a villa that he wanted to make a substratum of artificial rocks and create the illusion "that they were taken from their surroundings". In his theory of architecture Sebastiano Serlio is of the opinion that liberties are permissible in the country which one dare not take in a *luogo civile e noble*. The architect should be as inventive as possible in the lay-out of the ground-plan. Symmetry can be abandoned and villas may have circular or oval courtyards with pillared halls. Serlio even goes so far in his quest for naturalism that he suggests a villa in the shape of a windmill.

In the same way as the overall architecture, the fresco designs also harmonize with the friendly melody of the landscape. The choice of themes and the tenor of the decorations could be less pretentious and more charming. The preference for the lofty world of the gods diminishes and lighter themes appear. Even Leon Battista Alberti recommended landscapes with bucolic or genre *staffage*. In Mannerism the deities of nature were given absolute priority; they were the embodiments of the general background. The appropriate theme for painting garden pavilions was the story of Pomona and Vertumnus from Ovid's *Metamorphoses*. Rosso il Fiorentino designed the scene for a garden pavilion at Fontainebleau showing how Vertumnus, the god of autumn, turns himself into an old woman so as to be able to approach Pomona, the virgin goddess of fruit-bearing trees. A joyous crowd of cupids flutter round the group. Even if the composition of the figures shows considerable severity in its structure, a gayer lighter note is struck by the fragile garden architecture of the pergola, the wooden fence and the luxuriant heavy festoons of fruit in the framework. In such an environment the painter was able to portray artistically in the frescoes the atmosphere which prevailed outside in the open, in the gardens in the immediate neighbourhood of the castle.

Pontormo gives the gods of nature an idyllic habitation in the Medici Villa at Poggio a Caiano near Florence. *p. 109* The figures adapt themselves happily to the rhythm of the vegetation and the contours of the landscape. This is the place for repose, calm and the carefree immortal life. At Fontenallata Parmigianino depicts Diana bathing *p. 125* and hunting. Giulio Romano's horse paintings in the Palazzo del Tè outside the gates of Mantua create the *pp. 121, 128* impression of a stud in a naturalistic way and this idea fits in well with the rest of the programme of divinities, although that too is considerably relaxed. For example we find the Olympians at a rural banquet in the Sala di Psiche. The natural motif of the grotto also occurs, in the Sala dei Giganti, a motif which would have been out of place in a town palace, for it would not be re-echoed in the real natural environment. A similar sensitivity to the background can also be observed in Germany. In Weickersheim Castle hunting scenes from all over the world appear on the coffered ceiling which was completed in 1602. The theme of hunting is clearly in the right place there because it was possible to hunt in reality in the woods surrounding the castle.

In the pictorial decoration of a town palace "Nature" was allowed to appear once at the most, in the form of a fountain such as might actually stand in the Cortile of the palace. Thus in the frescoes in the Palazzo Capponi *p. 124* at Florence Poccetti put such a courtyard fountain on the end wall as the lowest step in an otherwise very serious scheme. Vasari made a particularly original contribution to assimilating the fresco scheme to its natural environment with the Terrazzo di Saturno on the second floor of the Palazzo Vecchio at Florence. There a loggia with a wooden ceiling was built out into space and afforded a beautiful view of San Miniato al Monte. Vasari used the ceiling to create a monument to the god Saturn and the movement of the heavens, i.e. time. It was a particularly deft environmental invention to insert it in the airy loggia open to the sky. The Mannerist artist who perceived such connections was able, through his work of art, to refer the actual surroundings to higher spheres and confer

GIUSEPPE ARCIMBOLDO: *Autumn*. Pinacoteca Tosio e Martinengo, Brescia. The features resemble those of Emperor Rudolf II, depicted in the same manner as the artist portrayed him as Vertumnus on another occasion

on them something of the divine spark. Just as Vasari turned the actual heavens into the kingdom of the god Saturn, Adriaen de Vries in 1598—1599 turned the market square of Augsburg into the dominion of the god of trade and commerce through his Mercury fountain. According to this way of thinking it was perfectly natural for the Mannerist artist to imagine that his own house or studio belonged to the kingdom of Minerva or Mercury. Giulio Romano put a statue of Mercury on the façade of his house at Mantua by which the sphere of the artist's life was elevated to a higher, divine sphere.

Then in later Mannerism there are programmes which increasingly discard the world of the gods and place greater emphasis on the concept of nature. Hans Fugger commissioned such a scheme for his newly-built Castle at Kirchheim in Schwabia from Paul Franck, known as Paolo Fiammingo, and he received the following twelve large canvases: the four continents, the activities of man and four pictures of two lake divinities, a wooded district and a pastoral scene. Peter Candid produced a ceiling design very appropriate to its rural character for the dining hall of the old castle at Schleissheim c. 1617. First comes the central conception under whose protectorate the hall stands: a thank-offering to Pan and a roundelay in honour of *Magna Pales*; then the herdsmen in the service of the divinity, at a festive banquet and singing a serenade in honour of *Pales*. Lastly the practical activity of the country people and herdsmen was portrayed — dairy farming and its products, including cheese making.

The oddest intermixtures with naturalistic accessories, which often completely swamped the mythological scenes, were also produced. In the Palazzo Vitelli a S. Egidio in Città di Castello Cristofano Gherardi used a pergola *p. 126* supported by four caryatids as the central motif; it is so thickly entwined with vine tendrils that scarcely a patch of sky can show through. From this lush foliage the rich treasures of nature hang down: fruits, pears, apples, even cucumbers and root vegetables, as well as fish, fowl and animals of all kinds: mice, rabbits, cats and birds. Everything which would normally have been seen in the most luxuriant of still-lifes appears there as decoration on the ceiling. In this way a monumental still-life of the most peculiar kind is presented; the central zone with the mythological scene of Jupiter and Neptune has to struggle to make an impact in comparison with the exuberance of the naturalistic portrayal of the accessories. We pass without transition from the world of the gods to the world of fruit, vegetables and the rearing of small livestock, although the two are essentially different. In country palaces the actual environment, the exterior, the landscape, was logically drawn into their interiors much more naturalistically and illusionistically by means of frescoes than in town houses. The enclosed character of the buildings in relation to the real space of nature was counteracted as far as possible. Now artists took up themes which unfolded in the immediate vicinity of the palace and in a broader sense belonged to it. For example they portrayed garden scenes. In the frescoes by the brothers Zuccari in the Villa d'Este at Tivoli we see men coming *p. 117* in from outside accompanied by their dogs or apes. Decorative birds (peacocks, ducks and turkeys) saunter between the illusionist columns. Spacious views of isolated trees and the whole lay-out of the gardens unfold above the low wall joining the bases of the columns. In this way the view the visitor to the interior expects to see when he looks out of the window, or opens the door and steps out into the landscape, was represented pictorially. But in spite of this naturalism, the artist does not forget that here too the world remains under the supervision of the gods: a banquet of the gods and the council of the gods with the Labours of Hercules appear on the arches of the Sala principale. The animal world, which Zuccari meant to be the lowest stage in the fresco scheme for the interior, is taken up again and extended in the garden sculpture.

When it came to gardens the animal world fitted perfectly into the Mannerist planning of programmes with its sensitivity to environment. Rich sculptured animal groups appear on sarcophagus-like fountain basins in the garden grotto of the Villa Medici at Castello. Giovanni da Bologna finished these animal groups after the death *p. 132* in 1550 of Niccolo Tribolo who had left the grotto uncompleted. Here we should take note how intensively the interior decoration of country villas was influenced by garden lay-outs. In Mannerism the leap from architecture, from the painted interior, to the exterior is completed with peculiar logic. The small garden, especially, which adjoins the building, is very closely associated with the architecture of the house in the general artistic conception. To some extent it still counts as architecture and its ground plan is designed with fixed forms. The ground plan of a casino can be continued without a break in the garden lay-out, as the plans of the Florentine architect Dosio show. After Raphael's Villa Madama the garden was included in the overall planning of a villa. Often approximately equal proportions were adhered to for both, for example equal squares, as can be seen in the Villa Monte Imperiale near Pesaro by Girolamo Genga, c. 1530.

Garden lay-outs

The transitions from architecture proper to the garden are also smooth in the larger garden lay-outs; the same architectural motifs as were used in the interior may also appear in the gardens; busts, for example. They were placed beside fireplaces, but were now also set up in rows in the open, as at Caprarola and the Villa Farnese near the Fontana dei Cavalli Marini. On the other hand features which only appear in nature were also drawn into the interior; this was even done with the motif of the grotto. Grottoes and various kinds of rusticated walls were used for the ground floors of villas; fountains in the form of grottoes were introduced into the basements. As far as the buildings were concerned, what we might call intermediate structures between interior and exterior were often situated in the garden. The best name for them would be semi-rooms. In the Fontana della Civetta of the Villa d'Este at Tivoli the walls indicate an interior room, but its ceiling is missing. The actual sky and the trees look down into it. A similar intermediate function between exterior and interior is performed by the

p. 89 Nymphaeum of Pope Julius III in the Villa di Papa Giulio at Rome designed by Vasari. We must continually bear in mind that Mannerist architecture frequently interchanges motifs from interior and exterior architecture;

p. 95 the best known example, which has already been mentioned, is the Biblioteca Laurentiana by Michelangelo.

The themes of the frescoes in the villas concentrated on rural diversions and were enlarged by their more trivial motifs. When this carefree world was continued in the garden, a kind of garden sculpture developed, striking a burlesque witty popular note which would have been out of place in "high" sculpture. In addition to Giovanni

p. 204 da Bologna there was a whole group of sculptors in Florence, among them Valerio Cioli, Orazio Mochi and Giovanni Battista Caccini, who more or less specialised in this genre. By the same Valerio Cioli who produced the group of the dwarf Barbino riding on a turtle, the group of a woman washing the head of a child has been preserved, as well as that of a vine-dresser emptying a small barrel while a boy watches him. Orazio Mochi executed the group of boys fighting. All these minor genre scenes are distinguished by the dexterous drama of the movements. In these figures we can identify an incongruity between idealistic rhythms of movement and naturalistic observations of men in action which is matched in the contemporary Dutch genre scenes painted

pp. 131, 229 by Pieter Aertsen, Joachim Bueckelaer or even Pieter Bruegel the Elder. But great didactic allegorical schemes of garden sculpture which are self-contained and develop a theme were also invented. We could characterize

p. 153 the Park of Bomarzo near Viterbo as one of them. This extraordinary park was commissioned by Vicino Orsini c. 1560 and situated on a hill within sight of the Orsini Castle. The varying heights of the ground were exploited iconographically. On top of the hill lies a temple which obviously embodies a citadel of virtue. Below it appear the most varied motifs which are not yet explicable in detail: an elephant, a group of giants, a house which is built lopsidedly and throws the visitor off balance when he enters it, and a monstrous dragon. Undoubtedly daemonic powers were unleashed. We know from inscriptions in the Park that it was meant to be a *Sacro Bosco*.

In a comprehensive survey of the total subject matter of Mannerist fresco works it is noticeable that the various contents are not of equal value. They are manifold and intellectually speaking lie poles apart. This surprisingly widespread difference in the subject matter distinguishes Mannerist fresco painting from the range of fresco themes of other epochs. Its span ranges from the world of gods and heroes via historical events to depiction of the present. Idealistic remoteness and tangible proximity were both mastered; a whole repertoire of fields was covered and at times the individual fresco schemes were on several levels. To understand these schemes in their proper sense the spectator has to traverse these levels himself and yield to their inherent tensions. If he does not or cannot do this, the basic intentions of Mannerist art will remain inexplicable and foreign to him. Mannerist thought fluctuated between abrupt contrasts in a way which has never happened before or since and at times it is not always easy to bear the tension.

The change of atmosphere in suites of rooms

The change of levels and switching of atmosphere can also make itself very consciously felt in the sequence of the rooms in palaces. We can experience the most impressive Mannerist achievement of this kind in the sequence of the rooms in the Palazzo del Tè. In it Giulio Romano's inventive genius was fortunately unhampered by any consideration for an existing building. In this completely new creation he could draw on every single technique at his command as architect, painter and decorator, and indeed he made full use of the opportunity. A fairy-tale atmosphere prevails in the rooms; as he walks through the apartments the visitor is surrounded by inexhaustible splendour and variety. It should be explained that the creation of the Palazzo del Tè took place in an atmosphere of imaginative freedom quite different from that surrounding similar Renaissance projects and that the overall plan lacked consistency to a degree unknown before. A certain habitual traditional restraint had always existed in such undertakings; we sense the official, painstaking, limited point of view. Artists could not rise to jokes and flourishes, and frequent changes of atmosphere, indeed they did not even envisage such possibilities. In the Palazzo del Tè it was no longer a question of the balanced organization of a single room, nor of the normal sequence of rooms with similar proportions such as Raphael's Stanze. The artist particularly sought the ebb and flow of the atmospheric content of the separate rooms. The range of moods is quite astonishing, heaviness can follow lightness, and gaiety melancholy; brightness and gloom can succeed each other, the relaxed and beautiful find its partner in the gloomy and oppressive. The psychological contrast between spacious pleasant well-lit banquet halls and small cramped almost windowless private apartments was also exploited. The spectator's ability to experience his surroundings is tried higher when walking through these rooms than it is in any suite of apartments built earlier. The visitor's receptivity is ruthlessly, heedlessly and violently handled by the artist. Well-being and happiness change suddenly to oppression and anxiety. The extremely varied techniques and materials which were used also help to increase the diversity of effects. Easily worked white or coloured stucco appeared next to the fresco. Reliefs could be played off against sculptures in the round. Often surprising variations in the system of dividing the pictorial areas occur. The classical division of walls into large areas by pilasters is combined with tightly woven small fields. Inside the room itself walls and ceilings can be treated in an entirely different way. This happens in the Sala dei Giganti where walls and ceiling are completely negated *pp. 101, 141* in their architectonic function. But the accent of the room can really only lie in the ceiling zone, which makes the walls insignificant. In the same way the contrast between a rather simple wooden ceiling and a pretentious division of the walls can be fully exploited, as in the Sala dei Cavalli, and indeed cause a sudden change in the *p. 121* atmosphere in one and the same hall. In the Sala di Psiche all is bright sunshine and joyful activity on the walls;

One of the monsters in the Orsini garden at Bomarzo, near Viterbo

the ceiling on the other hand is in small sections and dark clouds gather; the happy light note gives way to a gloomier mood. All these tricks and atmospheric effects were completely at the disposal of Giulio Romano's inventive talent; he strains every nerve and yet in the end everything meets in an indivisible whole. Combining almost hostile contrasts to create atmospheric effects is one of the most typical characteristics of an exceptionally talented Mannerist artist, as Giulio Romano undoubtedly was.

But the contradiction between types of rooms could be even more blatant. In castles, palaces and monasteries the artist aimed at the basic contrast between huge wide state halls and small narrow intimate private rooms. A striking example of this procedure is the plan for the rooms of the Palazzo Vecchio at Florence composed by Vasari.

The Salone dei Cinquecento and the Studiolo of Francesco dei Medici

There we find the Salone dei Cinquecento where so many people can foregather that the individual looks lost, *p. 123* and where we are astounded by the mere dimensions of the room. In addition the frescoes on the walls drag us into a violent event of monumental weight, the steaming and stamping of the milling horses on the battlefield. Then we step abruptly into a diminutive room which is scrupulously fashioned as a work of art in its own right: the Studiolo of Francesco I dei Medici. The room is windowless and dark, forcibly cut off from all contact with *p. 130* the outside world: a cell for study. It is intended for the private concentration of a single man and with its many small framed sections it has the character of a large piece of furniture. We could easily be inside a cabinet. The cabinet went through a peak period during Mannerism; cabinet makers strove to express large architectonic conceptions in little and they found the appropriate art form in the cabinet. Undoubtedly something of this attitude survives in the Studiolo of the Palazzo Vecchio. But it is very typical of the range of room design in Mannerism that both rooms, the vast assembly room, the Salone dei Cinquecento, and the small Studiolo were designed by one and the same artist, Vasari. The Mannerist man felt at home in such fluctuating dimensions.

Church interior, royal apartments and landscape in the Escorial

The Escorial stands as an example of how a change in dimensions was included *a priori* in the conception of a great architectural plan and not subsequently as with the Palazzo Vecchio at Florence. In the Escorial the modest dimensions of one man's living rooms clash directly with the mighty dimensions of the church interior devoted to God. Philip II had the royal apartments built on to the choir of the church as an appendix. Previously rooms *p. 91* in which normal secular life went on had never been brought into such close contact with the sanctuary of a monastery. Wherever possible the abbot's house had been situated outside the monastery proper like a small ecclesiastical court, but in any case never joined to the actual church. Philip II on the other hand wanted to be perpetually in the protection of the Almighty; for this reason alone he had his living room and bed room built directly on to the choir. But what ambiguities this symbiosis leads to! In his private rooms Philip II merely wanted to be himself without excessive pomp and circumstance. The ruler was a simple human being in the small rooms built on the human scale in which he spent his earthly days. On leaving these intimate private apartments the sovereign had to face the enormous dimensions of the divine. This divine quality was evident in the imposing vast interior of the church, in its choir, in the gigantic altar, in the overwhelming pilasters of the crossing and the enormous dome.

p.27 Looking at this strikingly tense combination of rooms one is instinctively driven to ask with regard to the dimensions: what is paltry mortal man against the greatness of God which is superior to time and space? These reflections are not purely mental, as they were in the Middle Ages; here profane corporeal man in his everyday appearance contrasts with the ideal and divine. As a result the orders of magnitude of human and divine no longer rest on the same mental hypotheses and man is made to realise his forlorness in the world, and even to embody it in a work of art. But when one is in the small private apartments of King Philip II, one is stimulated to put yet another question about the dimensions. Not only are the apartments "in the shadow" of the church, they also have a special relationship to the real earthly environment, the landscape: they are built like a look-out. An imposing panorama unfolds, the visitor looks far out over the spreading Spanish tableland. From the point to which the small rooms of the royal apartments contract, we find ourselves facing the sheer endless extent of the real landscape, that region of the earth which the King in his wisdom tried to rule with a righteous government which was pleasing to God. So the King as a small unassuming man found himself facing two different categories of large space: the divine ideal monumental sacred space of the church interior fashioned by architects and the unfashioned (from the artistic point of view) actual space of the landscape. The new man of the Mannerist epoch was placed between these two polarities and had to orientate himself within them.

It was an entirely new phenomenon that such fundamentally different conceptual spaces and actual spaces could compete in this way at all. In the Middle Ages actual proportions and dimensions were never placed in relation to ideal dimensions; they were never judged from a comparative point of view and consequently contrast could not become a problem. This opposition of different kinds of dimension first broke out with full force in the sixteenth century when the difference between the spiritual scale of the divine world and the actual scale of the profane world were recognized with uncompromising acuteness. The description of the Abbey of Thelema in Rabelais' *Gargantua* also illuminates how harshly and consciously these contrasts clashed with each other. There everything was supposed to take place in exactly the opposite way to what had happened before. If abbeys had previously been surrounded with walls in accordance with the walls of their order, then the new Abbey of Thelema would not have any walls. The walls, the feeling of being hemmed in, would only create discord, boredom and disobedience. We can interpret this downfall of the monastery walls as symptomatic of the fact that man wanted to live in direct intercourse with the world and felt that seclusion was unnatural and therefore harmful.

Pieter Bruegel the Elder

What happened in architecture can also be observed in the new-style composition of paintings. In this connection we may well call to mind the entirely new dimensions which Pieter Bruegel the Elder had to master. On the one hand there are the broadly conceived universal and panoramic landscapes in which the actual surface of the earth lies at our feet in all its superabundance; but on the other hand there are works which depict the opposite: *p.130* the intimate seclusion of man in a cramped interior, as for example in the room in the painting of the death of Mary. She is saying farewell to the great world around her, there is no outside world left, no seasons, no more land and sea, plains and mountains and clouds, only the oppression of the small interior. Instead of the light of the sun or moon, the stump of a candle glimmers. St John has withdrawn to a corner near the fireplace, to an ultimate refuge where he can give himself up to his own thoughts. Man's existence shrinks to a crumpled piece of material — and this happened at the same historical moment when the colossal landscape was discovered.

The Ages of Woman, fifth woodcut by TOBIAS STIMMER

The Ages of Man, fifth woodcut by TOBIAS STIMMER

FEDERIGO ZUCCARI (1540–1609): Zuccari and Vincenzo Borghini working out the plan for the dome of Florence Cathedral. Vasari, who had begun the project and was already dead at the time, is also present, asleep at the table. A drawing in the Uffizi, Florence

BACCIO BANDINELLI: *Hercules and Cacus*. A marble group in front of the Palazzo Vecchio, Florence. 1534

Both private and official works-of-art reflect the emotional state of the man who created them; they do not shrink from the most distressing situations

BARTHOLOMEUS SPRANGER: *Allegory on the death of his wife.* Engraving by Egidius Sadeler, 1600

Far left: FEDERIGO ZUCCARI: The so-called Porta Virtutis, 1581. Sketch for a painting intended to pillory the artist's critics. Städelsches Kunstinstitut, Frankfurt

JACOPO DA PONTORMO: Design for the frescoes in the choir of San Lorenzo, Florence, 1548–1557

158

Works-of-art painted for the artist's own pleasure

PARMIGIANINO (1503–1540): Self-portrait in a convex mirror. The diameter is only 9 ⁵/₈ inches. Kunsthistorisches Museum, Vienna

MARTIN VAN HEEMSKERCK: *St Luke painting the Madonna*. According to the inscription, the picture was completed on 23 May 1532. Frans Hals Museum, Haarlem

Artistic creation and material want

MARCUS GEERAERTS: *The painter torn between Olympus and everyday life.* A drawing dated 1577. Bibliothèque Nationale, Paris

The work-of-art as a record of pleasant moments in the artist's own life

OTTO VAN VEEN: *Self-portrait with parents, brothers and sisters.* A painting dated 1584. Louvre, Paris

Right: Extravagances of a painter-cum-architect in adorning his own house

FEDERIGO ZUCCARI: Façade of the Palazzo Zuccari, Florence. 1579

160

FEDERIGO ZUCCARI: *Scenes from the life of his brother Taddeo Zuccari. c* 1600. A series of drawings (five copies and one original of the Laocoon study). Uffizi, Florence

FEDERIGO ZUCCARI: *The artist's marriage to Francesca Genga*, *c* 1598. Central panel of the ceiling frescoes in the Camera dei Sposi, Palazzo Zuccari, Rome

FEDERIGO ZUCCARI: *Apotheosis of the art of drawing*, *c* 1598. Palazzo Zuccari, Rome. Ceiling fresco in the Sala del Disegno

Decoration of the rooms and halls of artists' palaces

GIORGIO VASARI: Grandiose studio room, 1548. Palazzo Vasari, Arezzo

Baccio Bandinelli: *Pietà* on his tomb. 1560.
SS Annunziata, Florence

Above right: Michelangelo: *Pietà*. He worked
on it between 1550 and 1553, and it was
intended for his own tomb which was to
have been placed in Santa Maria Maggiore
at Rome. The height of the group is just
over 7$\frac{1}{2}$ feet. Florence Cathedral

*The tombs of artists as monuments to preserve
their fame*

Michelangelo's tomb in Santa Croce, Florence,
c 1570

Mannerist art as a medium for the glorification of artistic creation

During the Middle Ages and the Renaissance almost the only works of art were those produced by painters and sculptors for other people, i.e. they were commissioned by patrons. The artists were governed in their work by the requirements and taste of their patrons and they said goodbye to their works once they were completed. But the sixteenth century saw the rise of a new phenomenon: in addition to the normal patrons another party interested in works of art appeared, the artist himself. Artists began to work for themselves in a way which had never happened before. Consequently side by side with the normal commissioned art there arose what we might call an artists' art, those works of art which artists created for themselves. Often the two types could blend with each other. When the Swiss stained-glass-window designer Christoph Murer issued a magnificent series of drawings of Christ's Passion between 1600 und 1610, he himself appeared as a donor on the last plate, the Last Judgment, and thereby the draughtsman included himself on an equal footing with the various ecclesiastical patrons, the bishops and monasteries, who had commissioned the other plates. Christoph Murer proudly added his own coat of arms to the arms of his patrons.

This new possibility of artists themselves laying claim to works of art was connected with their higher social status. In proud consciousness of their own dignity they placed themselves on a level with the great and mighty men of their time and attained to a power which was capable of playing a new autonomous role in cultural life. The new cultured artists led an exalted life in society and belonged to the scholarly, and often to the noble, classes. A whole series of Mannerist artists were elevated to the nobility: Michelangelo, Bandinelli, Arcimboldi, Giovanni da Bologna, Bartholomeus Spranger, Hans von Aachen and Jacques Bellange.

The artist's creative work and environment as a subject for artistic representation

Artists could turn their work to serve their own interests and needs in the most varied ways. This was sometimes done conventionally but could also be carried to eccentric lengths of subjective self-admiration. There is a group of works of art which take art as such, and with it the activity of the artist, as their theme. In them the field of the fine arts appears as a self-contained special domain and as worthy of representation as religion, the state or trade — all themes which play an influential part in the sixteenth century.

Paintings and engravings were conceived using the fine arts and their allied activities as subject matter. A large p. 236 engraving executed by Giovanni Stradanus in 1578 shows a veritable compendium of art and artistic activity. The following branches of creative work are represented: *Statuaria, Sculptura, Pictura, Incisoria, Anatomia and Architectura*, and the activities take place simultaneously in a confined space. A workroom for academic and craft activities is depicted which is exclusively devoted to the production of works of art. The uncertain semi-craft semi-scholarly character of the subject is well suited to the ambivalent situation in which the practice of the arts found itself at the time. As a general symptom of the situation we should remember that the painter's Guild of St Luke at Rome, an old institution dating from the Middle Ages, was only turned into the higher more intellectually exacting form of an Academy one year before, in 1577, thanks to the tireless efforts of Federigo Zuccari. Pope Gregory XIII expressly confirmed its foundation by a papal bull. Thereby a decisive step for the history of art's status, and one of unique importance, was taken. After the foundation of this Academy there was an officially recognized special mental domain of the fine arts which was separated from all the other arts and sciences. No longer had the fine arts to be bundled together with grammar, rhetoric, music or cookery, they no longer needed to take refuge with *Temperantia* as in Bruegel's sequence of engravings of the virtues and vices (1560). The fine arts, with their problems, potentialities, different forms and representatives, had emerged from the association in a general hierarchy of all human creation and thought which had previously sheltered them; they stood on their own feet and from then on could choose their own setting. Bartholomeus Spranger's *Allegory of the Fine Arts*, an engraving executed in 1600 after the painting in Grenoble Museum, can be considered as the best illustration of this historical achievement. The fame of the three fine arts, which had been included in the concept of *disegno* since Vasari, is trumpeted to the four corners of the earth by *Fama*. The allegorical figures of architecture, sculpture and painting rise on a cloud freeing itself from the earth to Olympus where Pallas Athene prepares to receive them. These *artes* soar above the tiny swarming earth far below where men are busy at their tasks. Corresponding to the three arts, we see a painter working on a picture, a sculptor carving a statue and an architect supervising the erection of a building. The sphere of influence of the fine arts is so comprehensive that, like the field of theology, it spans heaven and earth and at the same time is completely self-contained, recognized and legitimized as independent. The work already mentioned by Lomazzo, published in 1590 with the significant title *Idea del Tempio della Pittura*, forms the literary aesthetic parallel to the idea that art exists side by side with theology as a separate field and embodies a mental structure of its own.

Artists were soon so much at home in their own field that they could also indulge in reflections and investigations concerning the difficulties of their own working conditions. Here the drawing of a painter's studio made in 1577 by the Dutch painter and engraver Marcus Geeraerts is an informative document. It gives a clear unvarnished *p. 160* picture of the peculiarly critical situation of the Mannerist artist. The painter finds himself between two spheres which lie poles apart mentally, yet he has to come to terms with both of them. On one side, in the left of the drawing, the world of ideas and the ideal predominates. Mercury, the god of the arts and sciences, appears behind the easel; a genius in the figure of a boy has approached the painter and holds his mahlstick because the artist is being dragged roughly away from his work. The world of higher consciousness and ideas is further characterized by the allegorical figure of Truth or Wisdom sitting at a table. But the artist cannot devote himself exclusively to this lofty world of the mind. He also has to cope with the everyday world of harsh reality. It appears on the right of the picture: the family makes its claims and the mother who is breast feeding her youngest child clutches the arm of the painter and father while he tears his hair in despair. The other children are playing with the cradle and the toy on wheels. Mother Care spreads her arms above the family. From this family scene a door opens into a workroom where a colour-grinder is at work; he embodies the more menial work involved in the craft of painting as opposed to lofty flights of thought. This picture of the Mannerist artist's tragic conflict goes to the root of the matter; for the artist's problem is to take into account or even unite in his work the domains of Olympus and everyday, of idea and reality, a daring undertaking with the ever present threat of succumbing to melancholia in the process. It is symptomatic of the new attitude to art that an artist often wishes one of his fellow painters to treat and depict themes which are only intended for their private circle and special interests. In a small allegory by Cornelis Ketel, which according to Karel van Mander he drew at the request of the engraver Raphael Sadeler, Love was depicted with a burning heart sitting near a fountain in the midst of Music, Painting and Poetry. By this Ketel meant to say that Love was the source of all the arts. In the rest of the picture the necessary qualities of the good artist are shown, namely industry, zeal and patience; the story of Daedalus and Icarus which is also introduced into the composition is intended to warn against the dangers of hubris. Artists even designed whole programmes of pictures whose subject matter was aimed not at the general public but exclusively at their own fellow *p. 162* artists. One of the best examples of this is the cycle of scenes in which Federigo Zuccari portrays the life of his brother Taddeo, who died young. He transferred the preliminary sketches, most of which have been preserved, to paintings on leather to decorate the room which was kept at the disposal of foreign colleagues in his palace at Rome. There he wanted to show his apprentice colleagues the life of his brother as an encouraging, morally great example, just as in the contemporary churches and cloisters of monasteries the virtuous lives of the saints were exhibited as a model for the faithful.

The artist his own patron

On occasion painters also paid homage to their own class or their own organization. A large altar painting which Martin van Heemskerck presented to the painter's Guild of St Luke at Haarlem before he went to Italy in *p. 159* 1532 is an example of such a dedication. The painting represents the painter's patron saint, St Luke, in the act of painting the Madonna. Heemskerck overloaded the composition with all sorts of details and he placed the figures in the most ingenious postures imaginable, as if to show everything he could do in the way of daring feats. Consequently the picture is to be evaluated as a testimonial to his high artistic talent. We sense the artist's committedness, as it were, to the artistic sphere and that the work was only painted for connoisseurs of the inside business of painting, without regard to the general intelligibility of the details. In some circumstances an artist could use an uncommissioned painting in a personal way and even as propaganda for his own art. Federigo Zuccari attracted attention in a memorable case. When he had to paint an altar painting for Paolo Ghiselli, Pope Gregory XIII, in an important site, his work was not found satisfactory and was severely criticised in many quarters. Annoyed by this, Zuccari, ingenious even in this precarious situation, was not at a loss for a revenge. In the autumn of 1581 *p. 158* he designed an allegorical satirical composition, the so-called *porta virtutis*, and put his critics in it, recognizable by everybody because of their accurate portrayal, and thus exposed them to ridicule. When this tendentious painting was exhibited in Rome, it caused an unprecedented scandal. The Pope was so incensed at the artist's presumption that he banished Zuccari and his colaborator Passignano from the country.

We must also consider it a personal commission of a conventional kind when Benvenuto Cellini, after a splinter of the finest steel had got into his eye while he was working and endangered his sight, made a golden eye in gratitude for his recovery and devoted it *ex voto* to St Lucia on her Saint's Day in the church. It appears to have been a personal whim when Hans von Aachen made himself an extra copy of his portrait of the brilliant Florentine poetess Donna Laura. It is recorded of Titian in his old age that he painted many paintings purely for his own enjoyment and not to give them away to others. He expressly admitted this in a painting of Lucretia to which he gave the inscription: *Sibi Titianus pinxit*. When Tintoretto visited the aged Titian one day and saw the picture of Christ being crowned with thorns in his studio, he was so carried away that he called it a model of how people ought to paint. Upon which Titian presented him with the precious painting which is now in the Alte Pinakothek in Munich.

Events in the artist's family as subject matter

In their new higher social environment artists could naturally do more work for their own personal requirements than before. So the portrayal of family events became more frequent. During his second stay in Basle between

1528 and 1532, before he returned to London, Hans Holbein the Younger portrayed his wife and two children in a painting now in the Basle Art Gallery. It almost looks as if, when he was leaving the nearest members of his family and would no longer be able to number them among his immediate circle, he wanted at least to record them pictorially and include them in his artistic *œuvre*. This picture is filled with an atmosphere of solemn piety as if it were a picture of Mary with Jesus and the boy John, so lovingly does the mother watch over and protect her two children. Bartolommeo Passarotti also painted his own family in a group portrait of several figures. In such paintings the members of the family were often drawn directly into the background of the studio showing how they shared in the working atmosphere. In 1596 Josef Heintz painted a singular family trio; it shows him with his brother and he himself is in the act of painting a portrait of their sister, who as a result is close to the brothers *in effigie* at least. Luca Cambiaso depicted himself painting a portrait of his father. In a painting done in 1594 Jakob Willemsz. Delff (c. 1550—1601) shows himself working at the easel, presumably on a portrait of his wife. In this activity he is accompanied by his three sons who have collected behind his back. Artists felt that family scenes were especially worthy of portrayal. In 1571 Frans Pourbus reproduced the wedding celebrations of the painter Georg Hoefnagel in a painting. It is said of Karel van Mander that he put his literary talent at the service of family events; on the occasion of his sister's wedding he wrote a "Braut-Christi-Spiel" (a bride of Christ play). Hendrik Goltzius also carried his family pride into the field of his art. We know drawings from the time of his marriage which he furnished with the warning annotation: "My children, learn the lesson that God must be honoured with all your strength. The man who observes this commandment will be raised above his fellow men."
In memory of his visit to his elderly brothers and sisters in Leyden in 1584 Otto van Veen painted a large family *p. 160* portrait with the inscription: "D. memoriae sacrae hanc tabulam sibi suisque pinxit et dedicavit Otho Venius. Anno 1584": in other words the painter of this work dedicated himself and his near ones expressly to the holy memory. The painter sits at his easel among the crowd of relatives as if he were a court painter, although he is only reproducing his own family.

Now events in the artist's family could be celebrated in works of art painted by himself to meet his own requirements, which had previously only been possible for the rich and mighty. In the fresco decoration of Vasari's studio at Arezzo and Zuccari's house at Rome both artists introduced portraits of their relations as if they came from *p. 163* families which ought to be particularly proud of their origins. In the bedroom of his palace at Rome Zuccari celebrated his engagement to Francesca Genga with the full-scale allegorical apparatus. By the introduction of *putti* with swords and weapons he alluded to Venus and Mars, the mythological marriage theme. On the four ovals of the ceiling he shows the pre-requisites for a happy marriage in the form of allegorical female figures: *Concordia*, *Continentia*, *Castitas* and *Felicitas*, in other words harmony, moderation, purity and a fortunate destiny. When Bartholomeus Spranger's wife died the artist immortalized the event, which was so tragic for his personal *p. 158* life, in a most impressive engraving. He made use of an extensive allegorical apparatus in order to give his grief the necessary emphasis. The apparatus used on the occasion of private family events is almost as complicated and intellectually demanding as that used for the great state activities of princes, except that in this case it is employed for a special theme.

Portraits of colleagues

Now artists honoured each other much more frequently than before and also expressed their awareness of their new status by painting portraits of each other. For example we know Michelangelo's appearance from the bronze bust by Daniele da Volterra and the painting by Francesco Salviati. El Greco painted the portrait of his friend,

BARTHOLOMEUS SPRANGER: *Minerva victorious over Ignorance*. Kunsthistorisches Museum, Vienna

the Croatian miniaturist Giulio Clovio. During his stay in Italy Hendrik Goltzius portrayed a series of his colleagues in particularly fine drawings: in 1590 Palma il Giovane and his friend the painter Dirck de Vries, who worked in Venice, and in 1603 Giovanni da Bologna. He devoted one of his early copper engravings to a portrait of his teacher Coornhert. Hans von Aachen produced a modest but characteristic memorial of his friendship with the Dutch goldsmith Paul van Vianen and Adriaen de Vries in the form of a small round picture. For now it mattered who an artist's friends were; his acquaintanceships to some extent determined his personal style; circles, clubs and like-minded groups were formed. Artists who had reached the same cultural and social level came together and they were proud of this companionship. Hans von Aachen was alluding to it in his portrait of the three artists.

Self-portraits

The Mannerists often acted as willing guinea pigs when they wanted to experiment with daring self-portraits. When Parmigianino painted his famous *Self-portrait* (in which he saw himself in a convex mirror) he used a section *p. 159* of a sphere made of poplar as the painting surface, instead of a flat panel. Vasari cautiously stated that the purpose of the picture was "per investigare le sottigliezze dell'arte", to investigate the subtleties of art. The extraordinary thing about it is that the artist portrays the distortions of his own body produced by the convex mirror. It needed a marked detachment from the self, standing at a distance from the normal I, to undertake such an experiment, as it does to appreciate this picture. Parmigianino has been perfectly successful in this self-sacrifice and made a genuine work of art in the process. In Holbein's London portrait of the two ambassadors the reflection of a skull in a distorting mirror can be seen. There is no trace of such striving for effect in Parmigianino's work; he looks at the spectator with surprisingly natural pride. He sees his youthful face as smooth and glossy; it looks quite normal in the middle of the picture for the strong distortions only begin towards the edges. They primarily affect the artist's hand and the wall with the window. This self-portrait enjoyed lasting fame. Vasari saw it in Arezzo at the house of Aretino to whom Pope Clement VII had given it as a present. It was shown to foreigners passing through Arezzo as a rarity. From Pietro Aretino it passed into the hands of Valerio Vicentino Belli, a glass-cutter, and from him to the Venetian sculptor Alessandro Vittoria. In 1608 in accordance with Vittoria's testamentary dispositions the picture passed to Emperor Rudolf II in whose Chamber of Wonders and art collection it fitted perfectly. In addition to this self-portrait by Parmigianino we should also mention the very relaxed self-portrait (physiognomically speaking) of Hans von Aachen laughing. Here too the artist used his own person for an experiment. In this connection it is very typical that Cornelis Ketel first used his own person as a model for the experiments which he undertook from 1599 onwards of painting with his fingers instead of a brush; in the process he painted himself in various poses. Only after he had made these solitary experiments did Ketel create for the general public such extravagant feats as for example the Democrites and the Heraclitus executed for Hendrik van Os in Amsterdam, in which the painter "at the wish of the art lover painted himself as Democrites". Even the circle of patrons accepted pure art for the artist's sake; indeed it even encouraged it with suggestions for daring and wilful jokes.

Artists as eccentrics

It was an essential feature of Mannerist art that the artist liked to disregard the practical purpose of a commission and traditional ways of handling it. Art became a private personal artistic activity. Such features crystallized at the very beginning of the Mannerist epoch in Italy; we have only to think of Giulio Romano, Parmigianino, Pontormo or even of Michelangelo. There was no slackening of the tendency with the later masters; we can also observe freedom of this kind in Tibaldi, Passignano, Tintoretto, El Greco, Zuccari and Cherubino Alberti. Painting for the artist's personal pleasure and whims could descend into the sphere of empty experimental work.

Cornelis Ketel

The Dutch painter Cornelis Ketel, at the end of Mannerism, once again provides the most sensational example. Karel van Mander sensed that a new type of artist was concerned in his biography of the painter. He noticed especially that Ketel's inventive fertile brain left him no peace, that it was always following different inclinations and desires to satisfy its inner impulses; to this he added in alleviation "to no one's disadvantage". It almost sounds as if he suspected that this art, which was produced solely for personal pleasure, was not morally and socially justified. But Karel van Mander had some sensational details to tell us about Ketel. There is nothing particularly unusual about the fact that in addition to drawing he modelled in wax and clay for his own pleasure in 1595. It was more exciting when Ketel, as already mentioned, suddenly took it into his head in 1599 to paint with his bare hands instead of brushes and apply the paint with his fingers. In this process the outlines had to be more or less dispensed with; it was only possible to put patch of paint on patch of paint. Seen from a distance the mosaic of patches combined to form a more or less normal composition. This almost pointilliste manner depending on an optical illusion had its predecessors in certain wash drawings or perhaps in a sketch of the *Last Judgment* by Palma il Giovane in the Venice Academy, or again in the painting of the *Last Judgment* by Beccafumi in the Siena Art Gallery. But in 1600 Ketel hit upon an even more abstruse painting technique: he painted with his feet. Van Mander showed benevolent understanding even for this circus act of human dexterity: "We should not take amiss what anyone invents out of his own inclination, nor misunderstand when he shows that things which appear impossible are nevertheless possible... Yet there are many who only produce such unusual things to show their facility. Some people shoot with the gun on their backs or holding it the wrong way round and still hit what they are aiming at, quite apart from those who walk the tightrope when the earth is better suited for the purpose."

Overemphasis of their own ideal plans by Michelangelo and Tintoretto

If Ketel is an exception, nevertheless the conception of art as a personal affair went so far that artists could even consider official commissions as a private artistic concern. It sometimes happened that a commission was undertaken without payment because a problem particularly attracted them or they felt drawn to it by inner obligation. *p. 121* For example Tintoretto executed the gigantic work in the Scuola di San Rocco at Venice without payment, out of pure idealism. He only accepted reimbursement for the cost of the materials. Or again Michelangelo who took over the building of St Peter's, Rome, in 1546 "per Amor di Dio e per la Riverenza al Principe degli Apostoli", and in 1554 offered to take charge of the work on the new church Il Gesù without payment out of piety, as we know from a letter to Ignatius de Loyola. The greatest artists were the ones who could be so engrossed by enormous tasks that they neglected every material advantage and applied all their personal powers to the realisation of their ideas. Francisco de Hollanda mentions this in his dialogues about painting. He quotes a fundamental remark by Michelangelo about the artist's estimation of his own worth: "For we know of some old masters who generously and liberally made presents of works on which they had expended much time, mental energy and ability merely because they knew that their fatherland was short of money to pay for their works. Zeuxis of Heraclea, Polygnotus of Thasos and others acted in this way. There were also some impatient spirits among them who simply destroyed the work which they had painstakingly and zealously created as soon as they learnt that people did not place the value on them that they deserved. A painter whom Caesar had commissioned to paint a panel picture behaved like this. He demanded such a considerable sum that Caesar refused to pay it, possibly hoping that the the artist would do his work even better. But the painter seized the picture in order to destroy it; women and children surrounded him and lamented the imminent loss. But Caesar won him over again in a way which suited a man of his stature, in that he gave him twice the amount asked for and said to him that it was foolish to hope to conquer a Caesar."

We find the most extraordinary phenomena connected with pure art for the artist's sake in Florentine circles. Artistic activity became quite independent of commissions; it was only used to live out personal psychological states and seems so self-centred that often it can only be explained as the manifestation of abnormal or even pathological states of mind.

Baccio Bandinelli

The case of Baccio Bandinelli is most peculiar. This Florentine sculptor had a very difficult character. All his life he felt threatened by the enormous dimensions of Michelangelo's personality and he gave free rein to the feelings of envy and hate oppressing him. For long periods of his creative activity the production of his works was dictated by these negative characteristics; he literally suffered from a kind of persecution mania. When the tumult of the coup d'état of 1512 offered him the opportunity of laying his hands on Michelangelo's cartoon for the painting of the *Battle of Cascina*, he was seized with such rage that he cut it to pieces. Vasari, who tells us about this, tried to adduce many reasons for this drastic action: possibly Bandinelli had been led to it because he wanted to spare budding artists the trouble of having to digest this work; or perhaps he wanted to prove his loyalty to Michelangelo's competitor, Leonardo da Vinci; possibly it happened out of sheer hatred of Michelangelo. For a long time Michelangelo had cherished the plan of putting a second mythological giant, Hercules (together with Cacus), next to his *David*, but Bandinelli was given the monumental commission. He was particularly glad that he was able to accomplish a task which had originally been intended for Michelangelo. But owing to his persecution mania he fell still deeper into the inner power of the rival he hated so passionately and had chosen personally; for artistically he had very little original to say. Michelangelo was annoyed when he saw what a weak botched work emerged from the handsome block of marble. In any case Bandinelli's work is a testimonial to *p. 157* a failure which was bound to happen to this mediocre artist as soon as he ventured to use materials and proportions which he was unequal to. Although the group has the advantage of an effective site in front of the Palazzo Vecchio at Florence it creates an awkward dead impression; the drama of the theme of victor and vanquished has not been captured at all. In other works where Bandinelli stayed within the limits of his ability, he produced passable results, good average achievements.

Until his last breath Bandinelli saw himself as being in competition with his great rival. When he heard that Michelangelo was working in Rome on a *Pietà* for his tomb in S. Maria Maggiore, he could not resist starting work *p. 164* immediately on a very similar design for his own tomb. He hit upon the group of Nicodemus supporting the body of Christ. The behaviour of this artist who had lost healthy self-control enables us to see the unexpected possibilities which could lie hidden in the new-style subjective cult of the personality. The personal freedom in artistic pro-

ANGELO BRONZINO:
Allegory on Venus,
Cupid, Time and Folly.
Nat. Gallery, London

duction which had only just been won was irresponsibly misused by Bandinelli. Admittedly painters had always been jealous of each other, but it was new for such feelings to be allowed concrete expression in large expensive works. New dimensions of a purely imaginary subjective quality appeared which could not stand up to objective criticism by the rest of the world. Under the flag of a misguided cult of genius an inherently commonplace mediocre talent laid claim to a titanic manner to which it was quite unentitled by nature. In addition to many other peculiarities Mannerism could also show that superhuman ability like Michelangelo's and limitation distinguished by hubris like Bandinelli's are very close to each other.

Jacopo Pontormo

But there are also cases where creative difficulties occur which are referrable to the artist's psychological make-up rather than his character, so that friction with the world around him becomes second nature. The bizarre way of life and the creative work, which was in some respects dependent on it, of the painter and draughtsman Jacopo Pontormo form a good example of this. He lived as a self-appointed prisoner, having withdrawn from the outside world. Vasari tells us that he built a hut, a small *casuccia*, near S. Maria degli Angeli at Florence, which was exactly suited to such a "fantastic and solitary man". He slept and worked in the same room. He used a wooden ladder to reach it and once he was up there he had a device for pulling it up behind him, so that no one could reach him without his knowledge and consent. A document with precise details of the condition of this man and artist provides evidence of Pontormo's private life. It is his diary, the *diario* for the years 1554—1556. It contains a painfully accurate account of the minutest and most personal details of a man who was not in full control of his powers owing to sickness. All his meals are enumerated, his few visitors (always the same) are noted down, the weather plays a great part and he also describes when he plucked up the courage for artistic works. Particulars of them are not noted down separately from the other data, but placed right in the middle of entries about weather, food and the state of his health, and for this reason they impress us as intimate observations. But the account refrains from any penetrating psychological essay in self-expression. What we have is more an account of actual facts in the mediaeval manner, written in a purely objective style rather like that of Albrecht Dürer's diary of his journey in the Netherlands. Except that the events noted by Pontormo are much more banal and petty than those picked out by Dürer, who gave an account of his expenses, where he stayed and what he saw there, whom he visited and whom he drew.

What do we learn about creative activity in Pontormo's Diary? In one breath we can read: "On Monday I did that head of the child with the hat, ate two small birds. On Tuesday I got up an hour before daybreak and did the trunk of the child with the goblet; and in the evening I ate goat but I had a sore throat so that I could not spit as would have been proper. On Sunday I went to Certosa and ate in the evening." A striking feature in the accounts of the drawings is the frequency with which Pontormo only drew separate parts of his figures. He also drew the figures over several days, piece by piece; one day the trunk or perhaps only the bust, and the next day the head, on yet another the arms and then the legs. If we look at such drawings by Pontormo we can easily spot this procedure. We realise that the draughtsman felt the pure line or the pure volume of a muscle or a skull to be so valid in itself that it gave him pleasure to dwell on the small preparatory sketches detached from the whole motif. Typically enough Pontormo's accounts never speak of whole compositions. Apparently it no longer mattered very much where the various preliminary sketches were placed in the final large composition. It was a question of indulging in round shapes for the artist's own pleasure, more or less severed from their anatomical context. This explains the fact that in many drawings individual parts such as ears, head, arms or legs are suddenly emphasized as if they wanted to assert their independence and did not belong to the body at all. Consequently it was possible for a tiny head to be attached to an enormous body. Pontormo became the pathological drawer of separate parts of the human body.

The lofty art of painting was narrowed down to trifling with shapes, although with the refined technique and the great, almost uncanny, sensibility of which this kind of monomaniac artist was capable. Pontormo used painting to utter soliloquies and make personal proclamations. To that extent it is characteristic of the fate of his creative work that the last big public commission on which he had to work was more or less a catastrophe. For ten whole *p. 158* years, 1546—1556, the painter had devoted himself to a single task, painting the choir of San Lorenzo at Florence. This was completed in absolute secrecy: the paintings in production there were never even shown to a friend. The creative work was entirely dissociated from the idea that it could exist for other people and not just the artist. Pontormo died during the execution of these frescoes. There was great disappointment when they were unveiled; the spectators stood shaking their heads in front of the incomprehensible series of nudes, although Michelangelo's *Last Judgment* had already accustomed them to many surprises. Finally the frescoes were whitewashed over in the eighteenth century; we can only reconstruct them from the vast number of preliminary studies in the Uffizi.

Parmigianino

Something similar seems to have happened to Parmigianino. In the last years of his life (he died at the age of thirty-seven in 1540) the artist must have suffered from mental unbalance. Like Pontormo he was no longer equal to his work, did not fulfil his obligations and did not even finish the frescoes commissioned from him. Ultimately he was put into a debtor's prison by the trustees of S. Maria della Steccata at Parma when their patience was exhausted. This measure wounded him so deeply that he lapsed into a state of melancholia and according to Vasari devoted himself to alchemy. With a small group of followers he withdrew to the solitude of Casalmaggiore in Lombardy, fell out with the world, became an eccentric who let his beard grow, neglected his appearance and behaved strangely in public. He only worked on rare occasions, until finally his failing powers were completely exhausted. Parmigianino was one of those artists for whom the demands of art and ideas ranked far above material wants in life.

In a sense the Mannerist artist had no need of the real world around him, in contrast to the artist who merely aimed at imitating nature. As the champion of the *Idea*, of complete concentration on the conception dominating his inner thoughts, his outward appearance was a matter of indifference to him. In his drawing of the artist and the connoisseur, Pieter Bruegel the Elder portrays the typical artist as unkempt and untidy. We find all these features in Michelangelo as well, but in his case they do not appear in an extravagant or morbidly pathological form. Condivi tells us that Michelangelo was so passionately occupied with his ideas and work, "that for a time he turned almost completely from intercourse with mankind and only mixed with a few people as an exception. As a result he was considered proud by some and strangely fantastic by others, whereas he had neither the one fault nor the other; as has happened to many excellent men, love of work and the constant practice of his art made him solitary and he found such happiness and satisfaction in it that company not only gave him no pleasure but actually irritated him because it took him away from his work and (as people used to say of the great Scipio) he was never less alone than when he was alone." It is the fate of the true Mannerist for whom idea and reality are poles apart in life as well as in art that he is finally defeated in the battle for existence. This was the case with Parmigianino, Pontormo and to some extent with Michelangelo too. The conflict in Mannerist ideology is based on the tense relation between idea and reality.

The artist's palace

At the beginning of modern times we hear more and more about artists being addicted to greater luxury in their living quarters. But we can already observe this trend at the end of the fifteenth century in Italy. Thus Vasari writes of Andrea Mantegna that he built a magnificent house for his own use in Mantua and took pleasure in it as long as he lived. Today all that can be seen of the rich decorations are the faded remains of painted ornaments. The inscription *Ab Olympo* in the courtyard alludes to the fact that Mantegna had once set up his fine collection of classical statuary there, perhaps in the way in which classical statues and reliefs were later exhibited in the Vatican Belvedere, or Rubens installed a pantheon in his house at Antwerp. Vasari tells us about several other artists' houses from the early period. In his old age Andrea Sansovino erected a comfortable summer villa in his home town of Monte Sansovino. In 1540 Benvenuto Cellini arranged an old castle, Petit Nezle, at Paris as a place to carry out his work for the court of François I and also as a residence. On 5 December 1585 Bartholomeus Spranger moved into an imposing house in the Thurmgasse at Prague which he further extended by two adjoining houses bought for the purpose. Presumably he decorated this house with those façade paintings which Karel van Mander describes in detail. It was the artist's first great work in Prague, probably an advertisment for his art, but in any case one of the significant examples of the early great projects executed by an artist for himself. In the middle of the sixteenth century accounts of presents given by princes to artists increase. The painter Lorenzo Costa was given a house with a sizeable piece of ground on Mantuan territory by his protector, the Marquis Francesco Gonzaga. From 1565 onwards the Aretine sculptor Leone Leoni rebuilt the palace in Milan given him by Charles V *p. 63* in magnificent style and like Zuccari gave full reign to his *capricciose invenzioni*. The whole palace and the street in which it lies were named after the massive busts, the *Omenoni*, on the façade. Inside it this Aretine sculptor displayed his valuable collection of paintings, drawings and especially his plaster casts.

It was not unknown for artists to be exaggerated and almost pathological about the number of workrooms and living rooms they occupied. El Greco inhabited twenty-four rooms in the Palace of the Marques de la Villena, in the former Jewish quarter of Toledo, but according to the inventory of his effects he scarcely owned enough furniture for two. El Greco moved there in 1585 when he began to paint the *Burial of Count Orgaz*. His rent was four times as much as his neighbours'. There were debts and lawsuits.

Giulio Romano's palace at Mantua

To the present day the palace of Giulio Romano at Mantua still testifies to the magnificence of an artist's home. Entering it after visiting the royal Palazzo del Tè the spectator is astonished to rediscover the pretentious feudal and heavy style of building considered appropriate to the official princely commission in the palace used by the artist as his private house. In any case Giulio Romano created a lavish ambiance for himself in the interior and on both street and garden façades. On the wall of the Salone in the second storey he painted those immortal classical divinities who are especially connected with beauty, art and knowledge: Zeus, Neptune, Venus, Minerva, Mercury and Apollo. However the mythological programme was simplified in comparison to the Palazzo del Tè and the gods only appear as separate figures, not in scenes. Zeus, who was supposed to be painted from the famous sculpture by Pheidias, was given the special honour of sitting in the niche on one of the long walls as the mighty central figure. Perhaps this figure should be considered as a substitute for a large collection of classical statuary; the statue of the god ought at least to appear pictorially in the decorative scheme for his house.

Ideologically and sociologically Mannerist painters had reached the position where they could create for themselves the background for their life and work. They were the feudal lords and patricians controlling both their

MARTIN VAN HEEMSKERCK: *Mars and Venus caught in the net, and shown by Vulcan to the Gods.* Kunsthistorisches Museum, Vienna

private ideas and those realised in practice, as the main representatives of mature and decadent Mannerism showed. For these masters turned their own actual living space into an ideal, completely self-contained mental edifice. Their home had to serve two purposes: acting as the domain over which the artist was absolute monarch and embodying his most personal idea of art, while still remaining his actual living quarters and workshop. These artists dared to weld together here on earth two spheres which are normally entirely separate. Thus one of the most stiking phenomena in the history of ideas emerged: painters imagined themselves able to live actually, in person, in their own conceived and painted idea, to look round in it and breathe its special hyper-artistic atmosphere. These artists did not produce works for specific projects. They no longer worked for outside patrons; they themselves were the Maecenases who satisfied their dearest wishes. But they were no longer able to escape their artistically realised ego; throughout their lives they had to stay in their own mental edifice. They no longer passed on their work and gave of their egos to meet the needs of their fellow men, but declared that their philosophy of life was the artistic idea for its own sake. The reality of existence was not elevated to the ideal by art, but vice versa: the idea was stripped of its ideality and identified with the visible, inhabitable, actual features of a house and palace. The goal of obliterating the borders between ideality and reality which was so deeply rooted in the essence of Mannerism was responsible for this phenomenon.

Vasari's palace at Florence

Obviously only the most active Mannerists could venture into such a network of personal reflections. The most typical embodiments of such self-reflecting labyrinths of ideas are the studio palaces of Giorgio Vasari, at Florence and Arezzo, and Federigo Zuccari, at Florence and Rome. In 1548 Duke Cosimo Medici gave his court painter Vasari the still extant house at Borgo Santa Croce 8 close to the church of the same name at Florence. Vasari's whim was to decorate the great hall of the Piano nobile with episodes from the life of the famous classical painter Apelles. At first the learned Vincenzo Borghini worked out a precise scheme which has come down to us in writing, but was not followed by Vasari. It is interesting to note that at first the usual adviser prepared the scheme for the most intimate task which could ever come into the artist's hands, as if it had been a commission for some princely room and not the artist's most personal concern. But in the end Vasari painted the house according to his own ideas. The four walls of the studio were divided up by caryatids in between which allegories of poetry, painting, music, sculpture and architecture were portrayed. The house of the painter was supposed to be a house of the arts. On the upper frieze are medallions containing the portraits of great artists of ancient and more recent times. We are again astonished, especially in such an intimate personal task, that Vasari saw his work from such a remote objective viewpoint that he made a sort of memorial bust of himself and put it over the fireplace. He saw his work as a painter through the spectacles of classical anecdotes, almost as if some historical painting which had nothing to do with his own activity and existence was concerned.

Vasari's house at Arezzo

Vasari's house at Arezzo, now called Casa Mantauti, is still standing. In the decoration of his second house *p. 163* Vasari was also able to give the programme an impersonal note. Its painting in 1542 was a summer pastime for him. In a somewhat schematic chain of ideas he painted on the wall of the room facing the garden the places and provinces in which he had worked. This procedure was very similar to that of the rulers who comissioned *vedute* of the towns they governed. In addition there was *Fama* on a globe, with architecture, painting and poetry. Later oval portraits of Aretine artists were added, while the inclusion of Michelangelo and Andrea del Sarto overcame the local patriotism of Arezzo. In the summer of 1548 followed the further decoration of three rooms, a larger hall and the façade. The façade facing the street shows a central picture of God the Father blessing Abraham surrounded by four allegories of *Pace*, *Concordia*, *Virtù* and *Modestia*. After Vasari's marriage the figure of a woman going to her husband with a rake and a lighted candle was added; personal family events also appear as allegories. From the end of July to the end of August, Vasari painted the pictures on the ceiling of the hall in the first storey. In the octagonal central field are Virtù fighting with Happiness, then Envy, as well as the four ages of man and the four seasons and finally four fields with *putti* and eight classical divinities. Later allegories of virtues appeared on the walls, among them some stories which draw on Pliny and refer to classical painters, portrayed in small pictures. From 30 August 1548 onwards, twelve pictures on the ceiling of the hall in the upper storey were in hand representing the signs of the Zodiac.

Zuccari's house at Florence

Zuccari's studio projects conformed to Vasari's model and outdid it. They are the product of a Mannerism which is one shade more extreme. The artist first tried his hand on the preparation of his Florentine home. During his work on the dome of Florence Cathedral in 1577 he acquired the premises of Andrea del Sarto at Via Gino Capponi 24. They consisted of a residence and a studio which were separated from each other by a garden and a courtyard. Such a dichotomy was not unpleasing to Zuccari's philosophy of art, for it made possible the factual separation of the *Esercizio dell'intelletto* from the *Esercizio della mano*. For this reason Zuccari made himself a Casa grande or studio and a Casino, the residence proper. For him the studio was a kind of spiritual kingdom which as the place of art, the kingdom of Minerva, the preserve of intellectual work and leisure, remained cut off from the agitation of everyday life. This isolation of a place for inner contemplation is found everywhere in the second half of the sixteenth century, for example in the Studiolo of Francesco Medici in the Palazzo Vecchio at Florence. Zuccari scarcely altered the dwelling house, but gave free rein to his imagination in the studio. So that people could see at once that something extraordinary was going on behind its walls, he rebuilt it into a lofty tower to which he gave a strange deliberately bizarre façade. For artists' workplaces were supposed to contrast as clearly as possible with the fronts of normal town houses. A glimpse of conditions in Germany shows how far Italy had progressed in this respect. In 1600 the German artist was not yet fighting for the recognition of his special status; this struggle had only just been undertaken by the patrician, who in Italy had long, indeed since the Quattrocento, emphasized his right to display in the form of palaces. We have only to think of the lawsuits which the Peller had to bring in Nuremberg in order to finish building their abnormally large feudal palace in face of the opposition of their jealous petty minded neighbouring citizens. The personal emphasis which Zuccari gave his house would have been impossible in Germany. He revelled in an architecturally romantic use of stone; he left fragments of bosses incomplete as if he wanted to demonstrate the evolution of the façade. Zuccari once said of the architect's method of work: "His individual work comes into being in that he takes matter away from matter rather like the sculptor." Obviously the artist could only permit himself to leave the incomplete work, the first sketch so to speak, and esteem it a valid piece of architecture, in the case of his own house. Apparently Zuccari could not resist enjoying this piquant freedom to the full. He obviously fancied himself very ingenious in the process, in fact pretending that he was an inventor who had got stuck during the execution of his project.

p. 161

Zuccari could do exactly as he liked with the plan for his studio in Rome, the Palazzo Zuccari, and there were no bounds to his flights of imagination. The choice of site alone was raised *stravagantissimo* above the metropolis where he felt far removed from all the city bustle, could enjoy the most magnificent view of Rome and see the dome of St Peter's in the distance. In 1590 Zuccari acquired the copyhold of a plot on the edge of the Pincio, although it was conceded on the condition that all the classical statues, gold, silver, pearls and lead which were found there should belong to the former owner. However the choice of site also had practical advantages. For Pope Sixtus V had promised anyone who built up there privileges and tax reductions, because he wanted to see the Via Sistina constructed. Later many artists followed this example of settling on the Pincio: Salvator Rosa, Giovanni Battista Piranesi, Anton Raphael Mengs and Bertel Thorvaldsen. The district on the Pincio near S. Trinità was the artists' favourite quarter. When Winckelmann took rooms in the Palazzo Zuccari in 1755 he found the house full to the attics with painters. Zuccari's palace was intended to provide accomodation for homeless artists of all countries; but as the future home of the Accademia del Disegno it mainly exhibited supra-personal, art propagandist features. Zuccari again stressed the division of the premises into the studio or Casa grande as it was always referred to in documents, and the dwelling house or Casino. The most noteworthy thing about the whole lay-out was that in the architecture of this studio and its decoration, both designed by himself, Zuccari wanted to create an image of his scholastic systematic aesthetic. On a walk through the rooms the entry into the mental architecture of the temple of art is already made awesome for the visitor. He is warned that he is now treading on different, supernatural ground. The realm of ideas cherishes and defends its treasures: the new arrival is received by the terrible jaws of hell; the gateway to the kingdom of art is a gigantic mouth, a bizarre monster which terrifies him and threatens to swallow him up. Zuccari did not shrink from actually building the gates of hell taken from his illustrations of Dante. These mouths and masks on doors and windows *p. 96* take over the same apotropaic function as the gargoyles on Gothic cathedrals. Thus prepared we proceed through corridors and rooms. We ascend from step to step of an ingeniously thought out system; from room to room, from fresco to fresco, we have to complete the artist's complicated path and ascent to the original kernel of his thought. Via the corridor leading to the Sala terrena to the hall itself, then on to the Camera degli sposi, the hall *p. 163* of Ganymede and lastly to the Sala del Disegno. A series of painted busts of bearded philosophers bears the names of Aristotle, Plato, Diogenes, Euripides and Socrates, and forms the basis for everything to come. They are the same men as appear in Raphael's *School of Athens*. In other words Raphael's programme is only just good enough to serve as the prelude to further ideas and allegories! The artist as virtuoso begins to erect his kingdom on this basis of great thinkers and poets. He must acquire and persist in *virtus* as the highest quality. Zuccari makes use of the symbolism of mythology; consequently Hercules performing his labours appears as the prototype of the virtuoso artist. So he begins in the anteroom with the Labours of Hercules. The main picture is Hercules' vital choice between *Virtus* and *Voluptas*. The steep ascent can only begin after surmounting this obstacle. Now in the Sala terrena he produces allegories of those qualities which must distinguish the artist if his activities are to prosper: wisdom, perseverance, intellect, work, zeal and sincerity. The Three Graces also appear, the sense of beauty, and earthly and heavenly love. The good qualities portrayed are common to all men and in no way especially characteristic of the artist alone. They could be transferred to other professions without hesitation.

Artistic creation reflected in allegories

The form of the allegory as the mirror of virtues was current at the time. It is possibly connected with the allegories accompanying the historical scenes in Vasari's frescoes in the Cancellaria at Rome or later those in the

School of Joos van Winghe:
Herod's Banquet. Alte Pinakothek, Munich

Medici cycle by Rubens. However we must re-emphasize that even if these allegorical explanations in the Palazzo Zuccari were kept on a rather general level, it was still a notable fact that the activity of the artist was considered worthy of such extensive allegory at all. Until then there had not even such general information available about the functioning of the artist's work, imagination and technique. The programme in the Sala terrena therefore marks a by no means negligible advance and also a subtle insight. It would be unfair to apply present day ideas and demand that when the artist's activity came into his own field of vision analytically for the first time, he should immediately have held in readiness the most specific finely graded shades of judgement like a modern psycho-analyst. Even Zuccari, one of the most avid Mannerists when it came to invention, adhered to the nearest sources of ideas already prepared in other fields, for example mediaeval moral theory. We cannot blame him if, when giving a personal interpretation of his own activity, he drew on the same basic ideas by which he normally used to judge and explain other human activities.

But if we look at the allegory of Wisdom today, which may perhaps seem to have been chosen mistakenly, we must not forget that, inserted as it is at this particular point, it does contain attributes which are especially appropriate to painting. We can see how closely attempts to solve the enigma of the world and artistic mastery in portraying the world had begun to merge with each other in Albrecht Dürer's *Melancholia*, which refers to his own creative activity as well, and not merely to general despair over the lack of knowledge of the world. The many failures and difficulties of his personal experiences as an artist were translated by Dürer into a general outburst of despair over the limitations of human knowledge, research and creation. From purely personal artistic distress he arrived at a pessimistic view of the insight of the human mind. Zuccari is less heavily burdened in this respect; he provides the optimistic counterpart to Dürer's *Melancholia* in his allegory of Wisdom, *Sapientia*. In his conception all the arts and sciences were completely at the disposal of the wise artist: astrology and music, philosophy, medicine and others, as the precept of Vitruvius required of the complete artist. The cheerful allegory of Perseverance has its moody German counterpart, expressed with more human sensitivity, in a plate from an album by Caspar Freysinger dated 1582. But Freysinger also remarked in inscriptions on the plate that zeal, pain, work, rest and lastly God's mercy belong to artistic activity, qualities which the self-confident Zuccari as a *divino artista* thought less of.

The full allegorical apparatus was introduced so that the glorification and transfiguration of the artist's virtuoso could be acknowledged with the greatest magnificence. As a reward for his virtues the artist soars up into heaven like an Ascension of the type found in Christian iconography. Bamboo pen and crayon are his weapons, and as a defence against envious calumniators Athena has lent him her Aegis. It is purposely left uncertain whether this departure is for the heathen Olympus or the Christian heaven. Lastly, in the Sala del Disegno the artistic idea, the *disegno*, celebrates its highest fulfilment. It is demonstrated that the fine arts alone have the ability to transform the *disegno interno* directly into reality, i.e. drawing. All other human activities have to be content with something less concrete, for example *Militia*, the art of war, music, medicine and even theological knowledge itself. In the form of a demonstration by God, which alludes to the concept of the Trinity, the central field indicates that the idea of *disegno* develops in the three fine arts, painting, sculpture and architecture. Both before and after, Zuccari undertook to describe the concept of *disegno* in ingenious treatises on aesthetics, calling on all kinds of philosophical insights and a lively knowledge of Plato's theory of ideas such as were not always at the disposal of an artist. It must have filled him with pride and inner satisfaction when he was also able to realize the idea of *disegno* in architecture and frescoes.

The painter's palace as the cathedral of genius

Zuccari's mental edifice was so fundamental and seminal for the origin of aesthetics that even Winckelmann felt that he could derive stimulus from it. The Palazzo Zuccari itself, in which Winckelmann later lived, is a cathedral built, painted and conceived to glorify the genius of an artist who was very conscious he possessed it. It is the birthplace of an aesthetic view of the world and also a tangible visible realization of that aesthetic. After it was built, there was visible proof that art too had its sacred halls side by side with the churches of theology and the alchemist's cells of science. The sacredness of art consisted in the fact that like a theological system it consciously claimed to be an entire world in itself, independent of any other. The profane artistic profession placed itself on an equal footing with things sacred as another but equally sacred domain. But the Palazzo Zuccari cannot yet be counted as one of what we might call the aesthetic churches which the nineteenth century first felt impelled to erect, the reason being that the occupant — not spectator, as in the modern aesthetic church, by which I mean the museum — was exclusively a practising artist and not an art-loving layman. The descent from active creation to passive experience is not yet complete. At first it was enough that art had renounced its position as the servant of theology; the artistic idea, the *disegno*, stood so firmly on its own feet that art could achieve its own autonomous realization. If we regard the history of art from this point of view then the Palazzo Zuccari as a unified creation is the embodiment of the new total work of art dependent solely on an aesthetic philosophy. The Middle Ages had the theological total work of art of the cathedral, the Palazzo Zuccari on the other hand, as an equally self-contained theory of shaping the world picture, marks a decisive step on the way to the artist's self-knowledge and it lays the foundation of all future practice of art for art's sake.

Provision for posthumous fame

During the Mannerist period the great and mighty of the world saw to it that their memory, or *memoria*, and dignity were appropriately recognized. The dynasties felt that they owed this to their consciousness of their ancestry, which was highly developed, and their claim to dominion. Throughout Europe lavish monumental tombs were produced for the various families. The most famous are the Medici Chapel attached to San Lorenzo p. 78 at Florence and the Julius Monument in San Pietro in Vincoli at Rome, both by Michelangelo. The magnificent tombs of François I by Pierre Bontemps and of Henri II and Catherine de Medici by Germain Pilon were erected in Saint Denis. Late Mannerism produced three exceptionally grandiose monumental tombs: the princely choir of the House of Wettin in Freiberg Cathedral in Saxony, the Capilla mayor in the Escorial with the statues of Charles V and Philip II together with their nearest relatives and the Cappella del Presepe in S. Maria Maggiore at Rome with the statues of Pope Sixtus V and Pius V. After the princes' tombs came the surprisingly lavish and expensive tombs of scholars.

Vasari establishes the artists' posthumous fame

It is typical of the Mannerist artists' estimation of their own worth that in this field too they were no longer content merely to provide for the fame of their noble patrons; they claimed the right to posthumous fame for themselves and their achievements. As a result a new phenomenon in art history appeared: artists took an incomparably larger and more energetic part than before in the production of their own burial places. The

Mannerist artist bluntly admits that his whole effort and activity is directed at achieving fame and being remembered as long as possible by posterity. In his introduction to his lives of the painters Vasari says that the outstanding minds, in all their actions, out of a burning desire for fame shrank from no effort however great to bring their works to a perfection which was astonishing and wonderful to the whole world. Consequently personal motives are also linked with art and from them in favourable cases even eternal *Fama* could arise. In their lifetime the outstanding minds had been highly honoured for their praiseworthy endeavours by the generosity of princes and the efforts of republics; after death those honours were continued by statues, tombs, medals and other tokens of esteem which were dedicated to them. Vasari also considered it his duty to make a contribution in his *Lives* to supporting and cherishing the memory of the artist. This kind of attitude gave artists the energy and personal stimulus to provide for their memorials toward the end of their earthly days.

Artists' work for their own tombs

Here again as in so many other respects Michelangelo was the example to emulate. Some time between 1550 and 1553 he began work on a *Pietà*. Vasari relates that Michelangelo wanted to be buried at the foot of this group *p. 164* in S. Maria Maggiore at Rome. We also know that he tried to crystallize his thoughts about death in this work. The artist was able to clarify his hope for salvation in the creation of the group and make ready for his blessed end in the work itself. Michelangelo portrayed himself in the figure of Nicodemus who helps to support the body of Christ. He wanted to be as near to Christ as that in his own death. The plan for erecting it in S. Maria Maggiore came to nothing, because faults appeared in the marble and it was no longer suitable for finishing the composition. Today the group is in a chapel in the choir of Florence Cathedral.

Baccio Bandinelli at once took over from Michelangelo the noble idea of an artist honouring his last resting place with a work by his own hands. As we have already mentioned he chose an almost identical design, a variety of *pietà*, the group of Nicodemus holding the body of Christ. According to Vasari he took great pains to achieve *accuratezza* in this group. When he had finished it he looked for a place in the main church of Florence where he could set it up and erect his tomb. He found it in a chapel in the right transept of the de'Servi Church, today SS. Annunziata, and he was buried there. The inscription on the tomb reads: "Baccio Bandinelli, Knight of St James, rests here with his wife Jacoba Donia beneath the picture of Our Saviour which was fashioned by him. In the year of grace 1559." Michelangelo's desire to honour his own tomb with one of his own works was not fulfilled, yet his unscrupulous jealous rival managed to do so.

Benvenuto Cellini made a crucifix for his tomb, but it did not reach its destination; it passed to the Escorial and served King Philip II for the performance of his devotions. When the Venetian sculptor Alessandro Vittoria executed his own tomb between 1600 and 1605 for the Church of S. Zaccaria at Venice where it still is today, he called on the whole pomp of Mannerist allegory to transmit to posterity a suitable conception of his cultured humanity and intellectuality. The bust of the artist draped in classical robes is surrounded by three elegant allegorical female figures. *Pictura* and *Architectura* stand to right and left in the form of caryatids. On the pediment of the framing sits the allegorical figure of the branch of art in which Vittoria particularly distinguished himself, *Sculptura*, accompanied by two geniuses with T-squares in their hands. When the Dutch engraver Jakob Matham engraved a portrait in 1617 of his late father-in-law Hendrik Goltzius, he introduced the trinity of the three arts of *disegno* on the pediment of the tomb and, below, the allegorical figures, of *spirito* and *disegno*.

It was much the same with the painters. When the elderly Titian felt that his end was near he also wanted to secure himself a burial-place which would be worthy of the importance of his personality. He ordered his last

184

ALBRECHT ALTDORFER: *Sodom burning*. Detail from the picture of *Lot and his Daughters*. Kunsthistorisches Museum, Vienna

resting place from the monks of the Frari Church at Venice and came to an agreement with them that he should paint a picture to decorate the tomb. The painter began the *Entombment*, today in the Accademia in Venice, for *p. 78* this purpose. The scene is full of deep pathos. A garden niche in the Mannerist architectural style serves as an effective foil for the group of mourners round Christ's body. To the left and right of the niche stand the figures of Moses and St Helena like stone statues; a small votive tablet leans against the base of her figure. This work of Titian's which remained uncompleted in his studio at his death was finished by his assistant Parma il Giovane. With this memorial work the artist Titian claimed for his own person the same honour he had already expressed in the two large official pictures in the Frari Church; his *Entombment* is quite comparable, simply in its dimensions of 11′ 4$^1/_2$″ by 11′ 7″, with the high altar picture of the *Assumption* and the *Madonna from the House of Pesaro* intended for the tomb of Bishop Jacopo Pesaro.

We also find painters in Germany executing works for themselves which are equivalent to the patrician method of display on monumental tombs. In 1548 Lutger tom Ring the Elder donated a votive tablet to his family in the Überwasserkirche at Münster in Westphalia. His son Hermann tom Ring repeated the process in 1592 with a large votive tablet in the same church. The frame bears a detailed inscription giving particulars of the family. Christ and the twelve disciples stand behind a stone rampart which separates the holy realm from the present earthly one; in the latter the members of the painter's family can be seen. The painter himself stands on the far left, his wife on the far right. Lucas Cranach the Elder gave himself an extraordinarily significant memorial, in slightly different form, on the high altar of the Stadtkirche at Weimar, which was erected in 1555. He introduced his own person in the most important place in the altar ensemble, iconographically speaking: he is standing beneath the cross with John the Baptist and Luther. He appears in a self-portrait as representative of the whole of mankind awaiting redemption; for he is struck by the stream of blood which falls directly on his head from the wounds in Christ's side. A man could hardly claim a higher theological position for himself.

Artists' memorial chapels

However there were complete memorial chapels in addition to the individual works. The Florentine architect and sculptor Bartolommeo Ammanati went blind during the last years of his life, came under the influence of Counter-Reformation austerity and devoted himself to religious exercises with the greatest zeal. He left the Jesuits a considerable fortune, but before that, when he felt his end was near, he had the Chapel of San Bartolommeo built at his own expense in the Jesuit Church of San Giovanni degli Scolapi at Florence and he found his last resting place there. He had the altar picture painted by Alessandro Allori and on it allusions to himself can be found: his patron saint, St Bartholomew, has Ammanati's features and the artist's wife is also portrayed. The sculptor Giovanni da Bologna also chose the feudal form of erecting a memorial chapel to himself. He established for himself and "all Belgians who practise the same art" a chapel in SS. Annunziata, a church of the Servite Fathers at Florence. The artist had already produced some works for this church. He built the chapel according to his own plans and the work took from 1594 to 1598. The inscription on the tombstone is dated 1599. Strangely enough the works for display in the chapel were not specially designed for it; instead, combinations of the artist's works in replica were used. There are reproductions of the six panels of the Passion which are in Genoa; the crucifix is a replica of the one which was made for the Duke of Bavaria. The allegorical figures of the active and the contemplative life in the niches, figures which are otherwise only found on princely monuments, on Michelangelo's Julius Tomb or the façade of Heidelberg Castle, are the work of Francavilla, one of his pupils. Two angels and two apostles are by Pietro Tacca. Only the two stucco angels lying on the ground are by his own hand. It is characteristic that the artist claimed as monumental and rich an ensemble for himself as the one he had executed for his noble patrons. His memorial chapel is virtually a simplified version of his main work in the Salviati Chapel in San Marco at Florence. In the decoration of his house and studio Giovanni da Bologna also threw light on the class of society to which he belonged by introducing the bust of his protector Grand Duke Ferdinand I, and his own coat of arms, on the façade. The detailed inscription on his tomb reads: "Johannes Bologna, Belgian, of noble rank and member of the court of the Medici, Knight of the Military Order of Jesus Christ, famed for his sculpture and architecture, known for his virtue, of excellent morals and piety, founded this chapel in God's honour and as a burial-place for himself and all Belgians who practise the same art, in the year of Our Lord 1599." In 1608 Giovanni da Bologna was buried in the resting place he had prepared.

Vasari's memorial chapel in S. Maria Assunta at Arezzo

Vasari cherished the most radical plans for the erection of a distinguished burial-place. He felt perfectly at home in the role of sovereign in the kingdom of the mind and art, and hero of *virtus*. This gave him the inner justification to claim for himself and his family the marks of honour which he had provided for princes and rulers when in their service. Vasari decided to erect his family's memorial chapel in Arezzo in magnificent style. We owe our knowledge of the progress of this project to the researches of Christian-Adolf Isermeyer. On 27 October 1599 Vasari addressed a petition to the *operai* of the Collegiate Church of S. Maria Assunta. Vasari was born in the diocese of the same church on 30 July 1511. He proposed to enlarge and decorate the family chapel, until then a small enclosure in the wall, at his own discretion. But in 1560 the canons offered to let him take over the chapel of the high altar as a memorial chapel. This offer was a most extraordinary honour; people were astounded: the most sacred place in God's house was to serve as the burial place of an artist! The taking over of the Cappella maior was confirmed in the contract of 28 September 1560. To treat the chapel worthily it was necessary to rearrange the interior of the whole church, so as to improve the lighting and provide the visitor with a clear overall view. The pews were removed from the nave and placed between the columns, and the floor retiled. Extensive alterations had to be made to the presbytery situated above the chapel. The small high altar in the apse painted by Pietro Lorenzetti was broken up, the barriers on the side of the adjoining house of novices were removed. The canons' stalls were transferred to the apse, which was now empty. A new altar of massive dimensions was erected in front and the relics from the old altar were transferred to it. In the process the traditional liturgical arrangement had been turned upside down: the choir of the clergy was no longer in front of the altar as in the Middle Ages, but behind it; the Cappella altaris maioris had become a choir chapel, Cappella Vasari. The bones of the artist's forefathers were laid to rest there.

Work on the large high altar took three years. The twenty-six-foot-high altar was installed on 13 April 1563 and covered with a gigantic thirty-nine-foot-high baldaquin in the following year. On 25 March 1564, Lady Day, the new high altar was consecrated by the Bishop of Arezzo, who was a friend of Vasari's. The patron saint was St George, the patron saint of the founder and builder Giorgio Vasari himself. The iconographic programme of the altar paintings exhibits certain peculiarities. The main picture facing the choir shows St George and the dragon as befitting the patron saint. But the odd thing is that Mary and St John do not stand next to the wooden crucifix as usual; the saint has been exchanged for St Cosmas, the patron saint of the Medici, Vasari's patrons. The artist confirmed in a letter that his three helpers had been Christ, Mary and Duke Cosimo, and that he had changed the saints for that reason, which people found almost blasphemous and certainly highly egocentric. But these marks of honour were not enough: in 1567 after personal negotiations in Rome, Pope Pius V, by a so-called *Motu proprio* for the perpetual care and control of the chapel, granted Vasari a richly endowed deanship whose incumbent would take first place after the archpriest. Only then were his claims, which could not have been higher, satisfied.

When Vasari died on 27 June 1574 his body was buried in the new chapel, not in the tomb of his forefathers in the centre of the chapel, but in a privileged place at the foot of and behind the high altar. In its present state the altar is considerably changed. In the first place it no longer stands in the original church; since 1865 it has been in the Badia at Arezzo which Vasari rebuilt at one time. This high altar represents a veritable compendium, for another smaller altar containing relics collected by Vasari has been inserted inside it. In other words it consists of an altar within an altar. From the point of view of historical development this altar from the period following the conclusion of the Council of Trent is the ultimate outcome of the series of altars starting with Perugino and Giulio da Sangallo and can be claimed as a predecessor of Baroque altars. The model for it was presumably the high altar of SS. Annunziata at Florence, also a double altar, which was set up in 1500 and whose accessories were perhaps designed by Leonardo da Vinci. Vasari's altar immediately served as a model. Alterations of a similar type were made in Florence to the altars of S. Maria Novella, S. Croce and the choir of S. Lorenzo, in the last named for the Medici family. Vasari himself reproduced the altar three times, in 1568 for the Camaiani family in the same church at Arezzo, then in the Badia at Florence and in the case of the high altar of the Dominican Church of S. Croce al Bosco near Alessandria, the birth- and burial-place of Pope Pius V: in other words the art form which Vasari claimed for himself was even adopted by the Pope, thus paying him this further tribute. It would be almost impossible to overestimate this triumph for the self-confident art for the artist's sake.

The tomb of Michelangelo

But no artist was so honoured and exalted after his death as Michelangelo. When this artistic and intellectual hero died in Rome on 18 February 1564, he was given the most ceremonious obsequies. At first his corpse was buried in a tomb in SS. Apostoli by the brotherhood of S. Giovanni decollato to which Michelangelo had belonged. The Pope cherished the intention of erecting a special memorial and tomb for him in St Peter's, the first church of Christendom, in the building of which Michelangelo had played such a decisive part. Yet Rome was not to keep the mortal remains of Michelangelo. Since he had not been able to have and honour Michelangelo alive, Duke Cosimo decided to have his corpse brought to Florence to show it the highest honours in death. "He was sent out secretly, packed in a bale like merchandise", to his home town.

In Florence the exequies were prepared by the Academy of which Michelangelo had shortly before been chosen joint head with Duke Cosimo. Permission was given to hold the ceremony in S. Lorenzo, the church of the Medici, "where the majority of Michelangelo's works still in Florence are preserved". The great humanist and Florentine historiographer Benedetto Varchi gave the funeral oration, which appeared in print soon afterwards. Duke Cosimo, who had also considered setting up a monument with Michelangelo's name and his bust in the Cathedral, gave orders for the erection in the Church of S. Croce "of a tomb in the place of honour since Michelangelo *p.164* had already decided in his lifetime to be buried in that church because the grave of his forefathers was there". This was done. The Duke gave Michelangelo's nephew Lionardo, who bore the remaining expenses, the white and coloured marble for the tomb. According to a drawing of Vasari's the commission for the monument was given to the sculptor Battista Lorenzi.

The significance of this tomb must be interpreted wholly in terms of Mannerist aesthetics and symbolism. It is a manifesto of the theory of the trinity of the three fine arts as defended by Vasari, Zuccari and Lomazzo in their

GIUSEPPE ARCIMBOLDO:
Allegory of Fire. Kunst-
historisches Museum,
Vienna

treatises. Sculpture, painting and architecture are characterized by three allegorical female figures sitting on the sarcophagus. But the ideological unity of these three arts is demonstrated in another, as it were practical, way in the structure of the tomb. First architecture is introduced by the tomb itself. Secondly sculpture is represented by the bust of the artist and the three allegorical figures. Thirdly *Pictura* appears as the painting above the bust and in the painting of the baldaquin which hangs down over the tomb and is pushed aside by *putti*. Finally the unity of these three arts is further symbolized by the two emblems of three intertwined crowns on either side of the bust of Michelangelo. Admittedly Michelangelo's effigy is in the centre of the whole structure, but this tomb does not only concern him. The immortal artist was considered far more as the exponent and guarantor of a universal idea, the idea of Mannerist aesthetics as such. To that extent even the greatest and most honoured personality appears as subordinate to the Idea. This was a typically Mannerist conceit and in his tomb even Michelangelo had to pay his tribute to the general literary scholarly tendency of the Mannerist style as represented by the conventional followers of the "divine genius".

Portrait of Giovanbattista della Porta from the 1623 edition of his work *Della fisonomia dell'huomo*. The first edition appeared in 1583 with the title *De humana physiognomia*

Blandus honos, virtusq́; simul delubra tenebant,
Sed binis templis vnica PORTA fuit.
Tu quoque virtutem coniunctam nactus honori,
Amborum digne PORTA vocandus erit.

The theory of the portrait

In theory the portrait as a branch of painting was rather despised during Mannerism. Because the portrait had to deal with men's individual features, the finished product did not satisfy the *Idea* freed from the dross of the earthly and individual which Mannerism was particularly intent on and proud of. So of necessity it fared badly in the hierarchy of types of picture which was built up on the criterion of the idea. It is significant that Michelangelo, the very artist who tackled the idea most intensively and exclusively, held the portrait in such low esteem that he scarcely practised in that field. Vasari says: "He fought against imitating the living unless it was of infinite beauty." There speaks aversion to everything inferior and mediocre.

In aesthetics this conception was concretely expressed by Armenini's view that it needed far more ability, effort and intelligence to paint one or more nudes so that they appeared tangibly to the spectators together with their muscles and gestures in colour and chiaroscuro than to master the couple of skills necessary to produce a portrait. The claim could even be ventured that the more an artist understands of drawing the less capable he is of painting portraits. Karel van Mander also classified portraiture as a second-rate calling. But in spite of all this theoretical opposition portraiture received a notable impetus within the bounds of Mannerism. Among the great masters we find a striking number of outstanding portrait painters. Among the Italians: Parmigianino, Pontormo, Bronzino, Salviati, Sebastiano del Piombo, Tintoretto, El Greco, Scipio Pulzone, Bartolommeo Passarotti; among the Dutch: Anthonis Mor, Pieter Pourbus, Frans Floris, Hendrik Goltzius, Cornelis Ketel, Pieter Pietersz.; among the Germans: the two Cranachs, the two tom Rings and Hans von Aachen. People wanted to have their portraits painted even more than in the Renaissance. We sometimes feel that the rulers' main aim was to have a visual record of themselves at all periods in their lives and enable the step by step development of their personalities to be followed in portraits. Thus we can follow the development of Philip II's appearance through the portraits which Titian, Anthonis Mor and Pantoja de la Cruz executed. Jehan Lhermite even drew the gout-ridden King

p. 200 sitting in his armchair. The same thing holds good of other rulers, Henri IV of France, Cosimo Medici and Ottheinrich, whose appearance has come down to us in tapestries, drawings, reliefs and busts. A curiosity significant of this attitude is that Matthäus Schwarz and his son Veit, who followed each other as book-keepers in the service of the Augsburg Fuggers, made the experiment of having themselves painted in all the clothes they had ever worn in their lives. Their wardrobes (we might call them) were portrayed in one hundred and forty costume pictures. The father even went so far as to have the series of portraits, which ended when he was sixty-three, begin when he was still in his mother's womb. In his thirtieth year he acquired an embarrassing embonpoint; so he took off his constricting clothing and had himself painted stark naked both front and back view.

The family portrait galleries of princes and systematic collections of portraits

The highly developed genealogical interest of the royal households stimulated the demand for portraits. Family portrait galleries such as those in Ambras and Baden-Baden Castles, and Castel Sant'Angelo came into being.

Bronzino painted miniatures of all the Medici since the days of Giovanni Pizzi for a private room of Cosimo's. The miniature portrait came into being and met with great approval. The engraved portrait was given an unexpected impetus. A phenomenon such as the famous portrait museum of the scholar Paolo Giovio who died at Florence in 1552 is very characteristic of the new assessment of all the various shades of personality. Giovio, Bishop of Nocera and favoured by Leo X, became celebrated through his Universal History in Latin. At an evening entertainment in the home of Cardinal Farnese Giovio gave a lecture on the painters before Cimabue which directly stimulated Vasari to write his lives of the painters; consequently Giovio is also of some importance for Mannerist biographical literature. The same Giovio founded a systematic collection of portraits of famous men. His collection mostly contained copies, but there were also some originals, among them portraits by Titian. According to a traditional scheme they were divided into scholars, poets, humanists, artists, statesmen and generals. The portraits were explained by brief biographies on cards beneath the pictures. This portrait gallery was influential for a long time afterwards. Cosimo I de Medici had much of it copied for his palace at Florence and Archduke Ferdinand of Tyrol sent his own artist to Florence to make copies of the copies. Cardinal Federigo Borromeo, the founder of the Biblioteca Ambrosiana, at Milan, also had many of the paintings in Giovio's museum reproduced. Such initiatives gave rise to the famous gallery of artists' portraits in the Uffizi. Vasari tells that there were portraits of famous men not only in the palaces of the rulers, but also in the houses of citizens, chosen according to their nationality, their family or simply the taste of the individual collector.

In order to depict the human individual Mannerism developed a specific form of portraiture which was peculiar to it and quite different from the solutions found in other epochs. The Mannerist artist who was always soaring into the lofty realms of thought even wanted to see the power and effect of the idea manifested in portraiture. He was simply incapable of making an exception to the basic rules governing his thinking. An inner conflict was inevitable owing to the sharp contrast between the idea which was divorced from true reality and the actual appearance of man inherent in his individual features, but in spite of this the Mannerists contrived a bold and brilliant solution to the difficult problem. Here again we see the ability of Mannerist man to combine the irreconcilable in an inventive and virtuoso way into a higher, complicated unity. The artist was no longer satisfied with the restful self-possessed Renaissance concept of the portrait, of the kind we know from masterly likenesses by Leonardo, Raphael, Botticelli, Ghirlandaio and Giovanni Bellini. Mannerist portraits tend to show men in an intensified, even exaggerated way. The narrow upright format which was often used suited it well. Lomazzo called on the painter to bring out the *grandezza* and *maestà* and ignore the shortcomings of the natural model. An element of over-tension and extravagance invades the human image; in biological terms we would say the sitters were overbred and highly strung. In accordance with the mental climate on which the main accent now lies, the sitters are of a cultivated elegance. They look etiquette-bound, conventionally schematic. In their chill formality they seem to keep the spectator at a distance. They are not people of flesh and blood going about their everyday affairs, rather they are cramped into stiff artificial poses and demonstrate their lofty mental attitude to life with flawless distinction. As yet the man in the Mannerist portrait does not know what it is to let himself go and enjoy life, and he no longer knows composure and relaxation in his natural environment. But neither do the portraits express the confident devotion, reliance on God and intrinsic modesty which the Italian and even the northern portraits in the Netherlands, Germany and France did at the end of the Middle Ages. Apparently the Mannerist man felt a deep-seated need for constraint; in stiff poses he represented a higher humanity which paid homage to an idea conceived by man. This was intentionally and exaggeratedly emphasized, almost anxiously sought after, as if man in his real surroundings ran the risk of forgetting and losing his human dignity. All this resulted in the unnatural, strained, markedly artificial element in the Mannerist conception of the portrait. But these portraits compel respect for the sitter; they created a conscious distance between the person portrayed and the spectator. The latter feels deeply

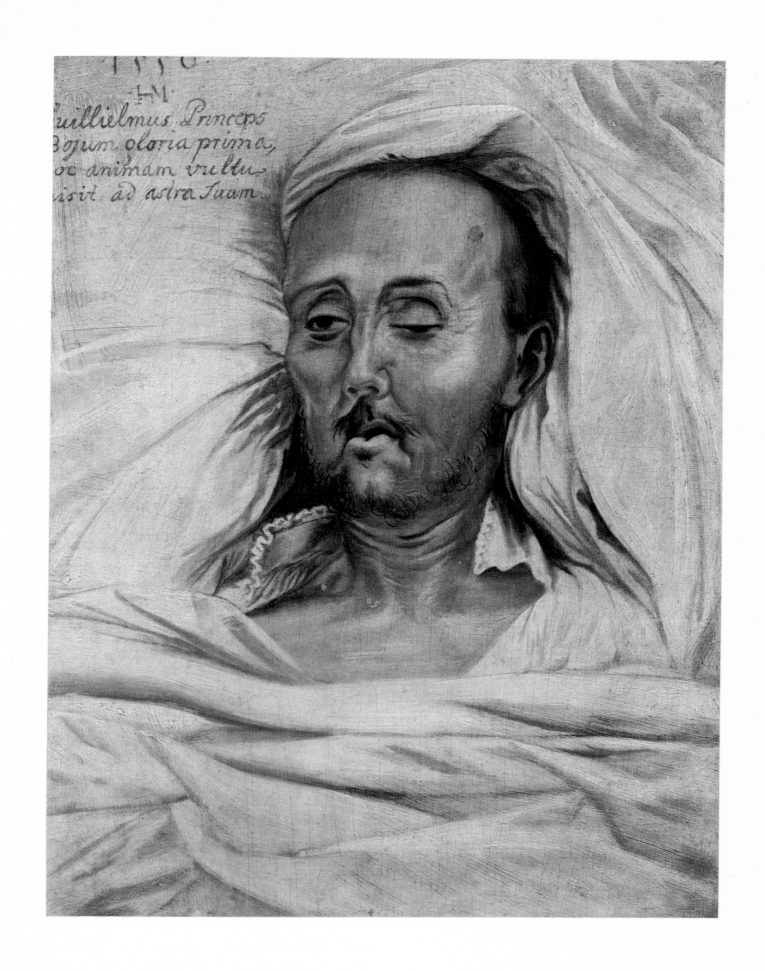

HANS MIELICH: *Duke Wilhelm IV on his deathbed*. Bavarian National Museum, Munich

affected in his normal everyday inferior existence by the nobility shown in the portraits, but he also feels a strong appeal to his spiritual side and a summons to higher things.

The Mannerist portrait does not merely aim at an exact depiction of the subject, for it represents an ideal, that of the civilized man, and even the ethical virtuous man. It is embodied in the new intellectual class. The goal of the portrait is not to render the individual, specifically personal traits of the sitter, but in every case to create a supra-individual, typical image. What we might call the élite of a new type of men developed, men who, in spite of living in a free, relaxed environment, submitted to an inner moral obligation and thereby paid tribute to an ethical ideal. As a result of such contradictions a trace of restriction and often of melancholy overshadows the men in these portraits. In a severely modified form the mediaeval conception of a class portrait survived in the Mannerist theory of portraiture, which concentrated on the spiritual and mental aspects at the expense of the external appearance. Lomazzo demanded that the person portrayed should be given the spiritual qualities befitting his profession and social position; the emperor should represent grandeur and majesty, the poet should reveal the profundity of his thoughts, women should radiate charm and amiablity. The demand for supra-individuality was carried so far that the latter even showed when the model in fact lacked the typical qualities of his class. This liking for the "ideal" picture was quite in keeping with the character of Mannerist art and its propensity for didacticism.

The social status of the portrait

The various kinds of portraits reveal an extensive graduated scale of human dignity. The great social class of intellectual personalities had its undisputed place in the middle of it, but the extremes go a good deal further, both upwards and downwards. The span reaches up to the allegorical and mythological portrait of the ruler, indeed as far as the super-human Olympian, but it also plunges down into the terrifying world of the freak and the sub-human with portraits of dwarfs and cripples. Men were caught at the height of their authority, but also in their last dying hours. The most striking contributions to human portraiture are distributed among the various countries of Europe according to their special indigenous bents: the south produced the highest achievements in glorifying great men, the north preferred to dwell on human helplessness and misery, in death-bed pictures for example. Lucas Furtnagel portrayed the features of Martin Luther on his death-bed. In 1550 Hans Mielich painted the Bavarian Duke Wilhelm IV with the most pitiless realism as his head, distorted in his death agonies, lies like *p. 193* a still-life among the pillows and sheets of his death-bed. As a conscious contrast to the pomp of the architectural and sculptural trappings of the mausoleum of Duke Ernst von Schaumburg-Lippe in the church at Stadthagen his funeral portrait, painted with unsparing naturalism, hangs as a panel picture on the wall.

The allegorical and mythological portrait of the ruler

Man reached the highest position in life in the office of ruler. In this capacity he rose into the sphere of the divine, an aspect which was duly emphasized in portraits, both paintings and statues.

Emperor Charles V

In the uppermost sphere The Emperor was pre-eminent as the worldly regent of God's dominon. Many works of this kind revolve around the figure of Emperor Charles V. The most pretentious portrait of the Hapsburg monarch with its wealth of accessories is Parmigianino's, known only through a copy in the Cook Collection at Richmond. The Emperor sits with lance and sword as the goddess of victory approaches him. Beside him a *putto* holds the whole globe to show how much territory Charles V had to keep watch over. In a free variation

p. 197 Parmigianino's nephew, Girolamo Mazzola Bedoli, followed this model in his allegorical portrait of Ranuccio Farnese at Naples. The young ruler sits on a globe the height of a chair and embraces Minerva sitting next to him. A statuette of *Fama* to trumpet the ruler's fame to the four corners of the earth is placed behind the young man as an important attribute. In the same way that the great examples of bravery from classical mythology and Christian moral philosophy were publicly displayed as sculptures (Perseus with the Medusa's head, David with the head

p. 58 of Holofernes, but also Virtue overcoming Vice, depicted by Michelangelo in his statue the *Victor* and by Giovanni da Bologna in one of his groups) the rulers themselves could assume the roles of the great conquerors and heroes.

p. 198 The sculptor Leone Leoni made a life-size allegorical group: Emperor Charles V, as the responsible Catholic representative of divine dominion on earth, conquering ignorance. In this theme the old conception of the virtuous battle or *psychomachia* is revived. Hideous ignorance lies cowering at the Emperor's feet while he stands triumphantly erect with his lance as *Miles Christianus*. The group is further distinguished by a peculiar device; the armour can be removed from the Emperor and then he stands before us like a classical nude. This transformation gives a choice between the two extremes of human appearance; on the one hand in the rigid, constricting, heavy metal armour, a reminiscence of the Middle Ages at a time when fire-arms were already in use and suits of armour had become famous showpieces, and on the other hand the man *per se* in heroic nudity and bodily vigour, which associates him with the heroes of antiquity, especially Hercules.

King Philip II

Emperor Charles V's son and successor to the Spanish throne, Philip II, had himself portrayed with allegorical exaggeration in a somewhat different situation, as the decisive link in a historical event. Titian was commissioned

p. 209 to celebrate the Battle of Lepanto in a memorial picture. In 1572 Don Juan of Austria, Philip II's half-brother, had defeated the Turks with the help of the combined Spanish-Neapolitan and Venetian fleets, and saved Europe from the assault of the East. This historical deed was to be glorified. To celebrate this event Titian used a complicated structure in the allegorical allusions, as well as in the arrangement of the accessories and the subject matter. In the coldly calculating emphasis of his apparatus he comes remarkably close to the stylistic ideal of Mannerism, something which was commoner in the large compositions of his old age, for example the big votive picture *Faith Appearing to the Doge Grimani* or the *Pietà* intended for his own tomb. In other words even Titian, whose art in general strove towards quite different goals, could not completely avoid the powerful stylistic current of Mannerist thinking and composing in terms of allegory and apparatus when the occasion demanded. Thus the Spanish King and his little son Ferdinand are removed into the heavenly sphere and the earthly event is conceived of as the emanation of supernatural powers. On a balustrade high above the sea on which we see the naval battle raging stands a table, next to it a prisoner cowers and a dead man lies on the floor. The spoils of war are grouped in painterly fashion. The King stands by the table like a high priest in front of the altar and dedicates his newborn son to the duties of a Christian ruler, while an angel plunges down from heaven and hands the palm of victory to the baby boy; the King and father looks devoutly upwards to the skies where this invasion of earthly existence by the heavenly powers began. But the King as father is conscious of the frailty of his own triumph and he wishes his own son, his successor in the defence of the Christian faith, more success and fame than he himself dared demand from history; for written on a scroll next to the palm of victory are the words: *Maiora tibi*, thou art destined for greater deeds.

As an example of the portrayal of a monarch in a mythological role we may mention the original solution to the problem by Hans Eworth (Ewoutsz.). This Flemish portrait painter came from Antwerp, but settled in London

in 1545. At first he painted in the style of Holbein the Younger and Anthonis Mor, but later he adhered more
to the Mannerist attitude.

Queen Elizabeth

His glorification of Queen Elizabeth of England shows her taking part in a judgment of Paris. Standing at the *p. 199*
top of some steps, as if she was coming out of her palace, she assumes the role of Paris. The three goddesses Juno,
Minerva and Venus shrink back from Her Highness, into the distant landscape. Behind them we see Windsor
Castle, the earthly dwelling of the mythologized Queen. But the Queen as Paris proves a most peculiar arbiter:
she has awarded herself the apple. As much as to say that the Queen is *hors concours* owing to her infallibility. This
idea was also expressed in the Latin inscription on the original frame of the painting: "Juno rules by the sceptre,
Pallas Athene by the acuteness of her brain and Venus with her rosecoloured lips. But when Elizabeth approached,
Juno was put to flight, Pallas grew pale and Venus blushed." A similar glorification of Queen Elizabeth is also
found in the literature of the time, in Giordan Bruno's *Eroici furori* (1585): The "blind" were finally made to see
by the sight of the ideal in which the trinity of perfection, namely beauty, truth and wisdom, meet (naturally this
refers to the Queen) and by baptism with that water known as the water of wisdom and the source of eternal life
in the holy scriptures. This water is completely cut off from the world in the bosom of the ocean, and there are
nymphs there. The "blind" reach the mild climate of the British Isles and the court of the beautiful captivitating
daughters of the Thames. In a song of homage these beautiful nymphs on the Thames are implored to open the
urn which the church has given "the blind" ones (the church is supposed to express matter, the urn the capacity
for transformation to higher things). In the end it is the chief nymph, Elizabeth, who opens the urn. In the con-
cluding poem it says: Neptune no longer envies Zeus his firmament; for the island on the Thames belongs to his
kingdom and is inhabited by the most beautiful nymphs. But its Queen is so sublime that Zeus will lose all enjoyment in his own sun at the sight of her. So Zeus decided to let "the sun around which the billows now roared"
to shine in his heaven among the stars, but to give the sun in the heavens to the nymphs of the Thames. A deeper
meaning lies at the basis of this form of homage: the expression of human greatness, however oddly classical
symbolism was employed.

Diana of Poitiers

Sometimes the mythological portrait could assume a very pretentious form, the person portrayed appearing as
a life-size, full-length figure. Diana of Poitiers, the mistress of the French King Henri II, was depicted by a French
painter *c*. 1550–1560 as the goddess Diana strolling through the woods with quiver, bow and arrows, accompanied *p. 213*
by a hound. The nude of the maid of honour is of an exquisite elegance, with brilliantly drawn outlines. Bronzino
painted a portrait of the master of the seas Andrea Doria as Neptune with his trident. *p. 198*

Emperor Rudolf II

Arcimboldi glorified the Emperor Rudolf II as the god Vertumnus. Folowing his other allegorical still-life head *p. 149*
arrangements, which are composed of objects suiting the subject depicted, the painter has constructed the Emperor's
head of autumn fruits. This singular metamorphosis presumably has several reasons: Rudolf II was a great lover
of gardening, like his father; moreover Vertumnus is the symbolic figure of the interchangeability of the sexes;

The ruler is raised to the level of allegory

GIROLAMO MAZZUO-
LA BEDOLI (*c* 1500–
1569): *Ranuccio Far-
nese and the allegory of
the City of Parma.*
Museo di Capodi-
monte, Naples

197

The divine right of kings leads to their equation with figures in sacred and mythological events

JUAN PANTOJA DE LA CRUZ (1551–1608): *The Spanish Queen Margaret as Mary, and her firstborn daughter as the Archangel Gabriel, in the biblical scene of the Annunciation.* Kunsthistorisches Museum, Vienna

Below:
HANS EWORTH (EWOUTSZ.): *Queen Elizabeth I confounding Juno, Minerva and Venus.* 1569. Royal Collection, Hampton Court

Rulers acquire the status of virtuous heroes or turn into mythological divinities

Far left: LEONE LEONI: *The Emperor Charles V conquering ignorance* – as a classic nude in the upper illustration, and wearing armour in the lower one. 1551–1553. Prado, Madrid

Above left: ANGELO BRONZINO (1503–1572): *The Doge Andrea Doria as Neptune.* Louvre, Paris

Below left: GIORGIO VASARI (1511–1574): *Alessandro de' Medici.* Palazzo Riccardi, Florence

199

LEONE LEONI (c 1509–1590):
The Emperor Charles V. Kunsthistorisches Museum, Vienna

BASTIANO TORRIGIANO
(d.1596): *Pope Gregory XIII*.
Staatliche Museen, Berlin

ADRIAEN DE VRIES: *The
Emperor Rudolf II*, 1607.
Kunsthistorisches Museum,
Vienna

DIETRICH SCHRO (1545–1568):
The Count Palatine Ottheinrich.
Louvre, Paris

200

ANGELO BRONZINO (1503–1572): *Ugolino Martelli*. Staatliche Museen, Berlin

LUCAS CRANACH THE YOUNGER (1515–1586): *The Electoress Anna of Saxony*. Historical Museum, Dresden

Ideal types of mankind are illustrated by portraits of intellectually or socially eminent personalities

VT NIL CONCORDI THALAMO FELICIVS OMNI IN VITA ESSE POTEST, ET SINE LITE TORO:

SIC MAGE IVCVNDVM NIHIL EST, QVAM CERNERE GNATOS CONCORDEIS NIVEO PECTORE PACE FRVI. 1561

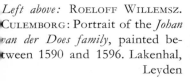

People grouped in family reunions or
social organisations

Left above: ROELOFF WILLEMSZ.
CULEMBORG: Portrait of the *Johan
van der Does family*, painted between 1590 and 1596. Lakenhal,
Leyden

Left: FRANS FLORIS: *The Van Berchem family*, 1561. Rijksmuseum,
Amsterdam

Above: CORNELIS KETEL: Sketch
for a shooting party in 1581.
Rijksmuseum, Amsterdam

Right: DIRCK BARENDSZ.: File G
of the Voetboogsdoelen. 1562.
Rijksmuseum, Amsterdam

PIETER AERTSEN (1509–1575): *Cook*. Musée des Beaux-Arts, Brussels

AERT PIETERSZ. (*c* 1550–1612): *Pieter Diercksz.*, known as Long Beard. Rijksmuseum, Amsterdam

Right: VALERIO CIOLI (1529–1599): *The Court Dwarf Pietro Barbino riding on a turtle*. Boboli Gardens, Florence

204

for it is related in Ovid's *Metamorphoses* that the god Vertumnus approached the garden nymph Pomona in various disguises, including that of an old woman. Sitters could even appear as saints; thus Jean de Dinteville, ambassador to England, appears as St George in a portrait by Primaticcio, now in the possession of G. Wildenstein in New York. Similar solutions of the portrait using the *Verfremdungseffekt* (as we might call such transformations) also took place elsewhere, for example when Lucas Cranach the Younger "replaced" the disciples in the Last Supper on his Dessau altar (1565) by a group of contemporary German reformers, Luther, Melancthon, Bugenhagen, Justus Jonas, Casbar, Cruciger and others. The Spanish Court Painter Juan Pantoja de la Cruz provides an extreme case of this kind in his painting of the *Annunciation* (1604/05) in the Kunsthistorisches Museum, Vienna. Queen Margaret of Spain has taken over the role of Mary kneeling in expectation at a *priedieu* and her first-born daughter Anna as the Archangel Gabriel announces the imminent birth of an heir to the throne, Philip IV. It is difficult to imagine a more extreme comparison, and one which verges on blasphemy, of events in the ruling house with incidents from the scriptures.

p. 199

Duke Alessandro de' Medici

p. 198 In addition there is the programmatic portrait crowded with subject matter. Vasari's portrait of Alessandro de' Medici is of this type. It is so overloaded with allusions that Vasari himself devoted a commentary to it which was as detailed as those he wrote on his profound frescoes. The gleaming of the armour is supposed to show that the affairs of the subjects are reflected in the affairs of their lord. If he had not specifically explained it no one would have suspected this interpretation of the gleaming armour. Behind the shoulder of the sitter, because it belongs to the past, we see the ruins of a house, an allusion to that year of misfortune 1530 when the Medici were exiled from Florence. Through the ruins there is a view of Florence; a blue sky covers the city as a sign of peace. The Duke sits on a round seat, which, "with no beginning and no end", alludes to the permanence of Alessandro's dominion. A red cloth on the seat betokens the blood of those who dared to fight against the house of Medici; but a small piece of purple material which covers Alessandro's knee reminds us of the murder of the innocent Giuliano de' Medici.

Portrait busts

The Mannerist conception of the portrait even resulted in the production of extraordinary portrait busts. This is strange because one would have imagined that the art form of the bust, in the way it was taken up again during the Renaissance after Donatello as a classical heritage, was not very susceptible of variation. But even it is often stifled with apparatus, whether owing to Mannerism's predilection for allegorical and other iconographical allusions, or owing to delight in decoration for its own sake. Even with busts of men an attempt was made to fit *p. 200* them into wider contexts and make then dependent on them. The bust of Emperor Charles V by Leone Leoni is divided into several storeys, as it were, and as a result is exaggeratedly tall and narrow. A slender base with two naked figures, a warrior and a woman, on either side of an eagle, is introduced beneath the Emperor's magnificent armour. These figures support the actual armour covering the chest as lightly as a Gothic console. Over the extra-long armour, which has delicately chased ornaments, a sash falls diagonally across the chest, contrasting with the Emperor's head which is slightly turned in the other direction. The structure of the head is just as delicately graduated as the bust structure as a whole. The individual forms of the face, the hair, folds and furrows are as scrupulously traced as the ornament on the armour. The Emperor's face radiates spiritual harmony and noble distinction. This bust composition glorifying the Emperor was to become a model. The bronze bust of Charles V was highly prized by his grandson Emperor Rudolf II who acquired it for his Prague residence from the estate of Cardinal Granvella. Rudolf II's Court Sculptor made a bust of him in 1603 which was obviously dependent on this work. In this way the successor to the imperial throne had the reverence he felt for his grandfather, whom he also wanted to resemble physically, given concrete expression in a work of art. In a second bust which Adriaen *p. 200* de Vries produced in 1607, the sculptor was able to seize the personal characteristics of Rudolf, grown older and stouter in the meantime, even more effectively. The head presses down harder on the short neck and consequently the broad lower part of the chin with the protruding Hapsburg lip becomes more telling. In this bust De Vries departed from the official schema and made room for the surprisingly personal animation of the sitter. Nevertheless the world of supra-individual, ideal thought is also preserved in this work of art. Allegorical recumbent figures in exaggerated poses are introduced on the armour as separate fields, as if they were taken from a series of engravings. *Fama*, a conventional motif, trumpets the Emperor's warlike fame to the four corners of the earth; yet his appearance makes it scarcely believable that he earned such fame in fact. The strength and historical mission of his period of office lay rather in the skilful deferment of smouldering conflicts and a constantly conciliatory and peace-loving policy, in which he succeeded for a long time.

In spite of the high degree of idealization which Mannerist portraiture strove to achieve, it could in contrast, as already mentioned, also seize human frailty. An alabaster bust only 6 $^5/_{16}$″ high in the Louvre, by Dietrich Schro, gives an unsparing picture of Count Palatine Ottheinrich sitting motionless in his chair because of his corpulence and holding his arms lifelessly in front of him. The man's bowed posture shows his bodily helplessness, but in spite of that he is conscious of his dignity. He wears a costume with a wide cloak, a richly embroidered collar and full puffed sleeves, fashions which further heighten the impression of massiveness. But even this "compassionate image" was decorated with all kinds of allegorical embellishments and given added significance. Lions sit on the front of the arms of the chair, on its rear side two caryatids hold a curtain apart, a pair of satyrs sit next to a medallion with the arms of the Count Palatine. The general dignity of office and the lonely destiny of man meet in conscious, deliberately exploited opposition in this likeness. The unique effect of Count Orgaz in El Greco's altar painting with the picture of his burial in 1586 depends on the same antithesis. There too the gorgeous pomp of the richly decorated vestments of St Stephen and St Augustin, Bishops of Hippo, as well as the armour of the Count himself, are in agonizing contrast to the crumpled broken figure of the dead Count, that symbol of human frailty. We see the visible encounter of the transitoriness of the temporal and the permanence of the eternal. The magnificent busts which Bastiano Torrigiano made of Popes Sixtus V, Gregory XIII and Pius IV contain the same ambiguity. The highly individual heads, conceived with penetrating psychological insight, are in each case constrained by very conventional stiff pluvials. The decorations of the pluvials become large fields on which powerful allegorical figures are displayed. The virtues under which they exercise their office were very important to the Popes. Popes Sixtus V and Gregory XIII are between justice and strength; the head of Pope Pius IV is accompanied by the powerful figures of Peter and Paul introduced as decoration on his pluvial. Whether the head itself is the groomed, erect head of a jurist, like Gregory XIII's, or a furrowed, deeply bowed peasant skull like that of Sixtus V, these are only variations and additional interpretations of the main conception dominated by the rigid embellished vestments which are scarcely susceptible of alteration. In these works too conventional costume and individual appearance are in animated conflict.

The intellectually eminent man

The most brilliant creation of Mannerist portraiture was the depiction of cultured and intellectually eminent persons. For the men who were portrayed by Pontormo, Bronzino, Salviati and the Parma-born Parmigianino there was no submission to the blows of fate, no human transitoriness as in the northern portraits of a Dirck Jacobsz. or Lutger tom Ring the Younger. In spite of their naturalism an ideal conception was paid homage to, the type of the man ennobled by intellect and demeanour. The sitters appear in precious poses and in many ways do not differ greatly from the figures in the freely invented historical paintings. Within his personal domain individual man too was intended to participate in the titanic humanity of Michelangelo. These men are strikingly slim. They nearly always walk with an over-erect carriage and are confined to stiff poses. The shape of their heads is generally a regular oval. Ugliness and deformity are removed from their facial features; their well-groomed hands which are usually conspicuous terminate in long tapering fingers. Such beauty is stiff and mask-like, and so makes an uncanny enigmatic impression. Nearly all the sitters are introduced into the format of the picture in a way which is typical of the Mannerist attitude to men. The head, as seat of the brain and crown of the body, is pushed up as close as possible to the top of the picture. This arrangement provides a visual realization of man's elevation above inferior matter and the triumph of the ethical man, so conscious of his deportment, over dull reality. The cultural background was often underlined by appropriate accessories, among them books, medals, gems and musical instruments, which were placed in the sitter's hand. In addition there were statues and statuettes which were supposed to refer to the sitter's interests and tastes. Sometimes the allusions were very specific. In the portrait by Bronzino, Ugolino Martinelli holds a volume by Pietro Bembo in his left hand and on the table stands the statue of David by Donatello. In Bronzino's portrait of Laura Battiverri, with whom the painter had exchanged verses in the style of Petrarch, a volume of Petrarch's sonnets appears. The portrait of Count San Secondo by Parmigianino in the Prado contains what is presumably a classical statue of Perseus, with a pile of books lying next to it. The statuette of an Amazon falling off a horse is introduced into the background of the portrait of a man by Salviati. The long flowing seams of clothes were often used to stress the slender elegance of the subject even more effectively. This is noticeable in Tintoretto's portraits of Venetian senators with their fur-trimmed cloaks.

p. 201

The virtuous man

Alongside the cultured man we find the man who represents the ideal of virtue. This moralizing conception of portraiture is commoner in the north than in Italy. When captions specifically point out the category of virtue to which the sitters belong, it is not a superfluous flourish. In the portrait of the Mayor of Sankt Gallen, Andreas Möhrlin, painted by Tobias Stimmer in 1566, a letter is introduced with the inscription: "To the pious, puissant, prudent and wise Mayor and Councillor of the Town of Sankt Gallen, our dear good friend." In the spandrels appear the allegories of geometry and astronomy with this Greek inscription underneath: "I was able to do everything through him who made me powerful, Christ." This ranked the sitter in higher spheres. A common practice was to point out that the person depicted in the portrait was under God's dominion. Such an inscription is found for example on the self-portrait of Lutger tom Ring the Younger painted in 1547: "Glory, praise and honour be to God alone from whom all good things must come. By his Grace I have painted myself from life. A figure of me as I appeared at the time stands above, looking to the left. All my longings are for art, I earn my living by 'Ring' painting." In the engraving which Cryspin de Passe made of Queen Elizabeth of England in 1592 is written: "Posui Deum adjutorem meum", I have taken God as my helper. Moral devices could also characterize people's conduct. In the background of a miniature of Lady Elizabeth Stanley by Nicholas Hilliard appears a sun and a pierced heart with the inscription "Facies mutabilis sed amor stabilis — semel missa semper fixa": (the face is changeable, but love is stable: once set free, for ever fixed). It is typical of this moralistic outlook that Hendrik Hondius published a collection of portraits under the title *Theatrum Honoris*. Only men who were considered worthy to be included in the concept of honour, could appear in it.

Portraits of women

Appearances played a decisive role in the Mannerist view of mankind. Coldness and etiquette go hand in hand. Dress and costume are often used lavishly and provocatively, and have a value of their own quite apart from the sitter. People frequently look as if they were inserted into their covering of clothes as an afterthought. Fashion developed exaggeratedly stiff, artificial and unnatural forms. Portraits of women are particularly distinguished by the splendour of the patterns on the material. The pleated ruffle appeared. The black of Spanish fashion was the predominant colour. We have the feeling that the sitters deliberately wanted to highlight the exaggerated fashions of the period in their portraits. Arrangements of clothes were displayed which no longer had much connection with the basic forms of the human body. The Duchess Magdalena, wife of Duke Wolfgang Wilhelm of Neuburg, *p. 217* was portrayed by the Bavarian Court Painter Pieter de Witte, known as Candid, in a half-length portrait in an especially exquisite arrangement. The aristocratic head of the Duchess is completely swallowed up in the ingenious structure of the costume. Her face is encircled and framed by a transparent fan-like collar of the finest lace. The coiffure is piled high and terminates in a point with a pearl diadem. In contrast to it the fixed look of the Duchess is lowered in a pensive tired mood. The arms emerge from the dress trimmed with a border of rich braid as if from armour. Minor accents in the form of two small black bows are skilfully introduced into the splendid colour scheme of salmon red, salmon pink and silver. It was no mere coincidence that many illustrated costume collections were published in the sixteenth century: the *Hochzeitstänzer* by Heinrich Aldegrever of 1538, Weigel's *Trachtenbuch* of 1577 with wood-cuts by Jost Amman and the series of etchings by J. J. Boissard *Habitus variarum orbis gentium* of 1581. Great importance was obviously attached to ornaments. The chains, lockets *p. 201* and brooches are not merely incidental trimmings, they are the insignia and proof of the class, wealth and dignity of the wearer. Only people of high rank or station were able to honour themselves with such precious ornaments. A theatrical exhibition of the kind found in the self-portrait of Rembrandt with his wife Saskia did not appear until the Baroque.

Portraits of children

Many artists had a special preference for portraits of children. They were able to extract a singular charm from this theme. Undoubtedly the most beautiful and best known works of this kind, a genuine enrichment of Mannerist portraiture, were painted by Bronzino and Cranach the Younger at the courts of Florence and Saxony respectively. It was not always necessary for the children to appear in the care of their parents; they were also considered worthy of being depicted in separate portraits as independent individuals. Nevertheless the modern spectator who prefers to see the child looking and behaving naturally finds it rather grotesque that the children are not portrayed spontaneously. They freeze in conventional poses and look like small-scale adults. Like the adults they too wear their rich heavy necklaces as a sign of their high rank. Boys already hold their state daggers in their hands, for example Prince Christian I, son of the Elector Augustus of Saxony, in the portrait by Cranach the Younger. In Mannerism the social status of children was more important than the qualities natural to their age. In most cases the portraits are of the children of ruling princely houses on whom the responsibilities which are their natural heritage weighed heavily from their earliest childhood. It is quite exceptional when a child emerges from his conventional stiff reserve and laughs as happily and heartily as Prince Garcia, the son of Cosimo I of Tuscany, in the portrait by Bronzino. Portraits of children are often further distinguished by special childish attributes, although they do little to release them from their stiff attitudes. Boys play with small birds and girls hold dolls in front of them. Once, in a children's portrait by Giovanni Caroto, we even find a laughing girl proudly showing the spectator a drawing of a child, presumably an unaided self-portrait.

TITIAN: *Allegory of the Battle of Lepanto*. Prado, Madrid

Combinations of men in groups and societies opened up a new branch of portraiture. Two fields call for special attention: the family portrait and the group portrait. The family portrait spread all over Europe, but with few exceptions the group portrait remained a speciality of Dutch painting. These two new kinds of commissions go hand in hand with the growing strength of the middle classes and the recognition of man as an individual who makes his own decisions. Group portraits no longer had to be included as part of altar works, merely as secondary figures, as was the rule in the Middle Ages. The saint's intermediary role as patron disappears. The sitters no longer appear as donors who rank themselves in the religious plan for the salvation of the world by Christ. Family and group portraits were linked with different mental associations and consequently developed into a separate independent branch of art. Both families and societies were recognized as self-contained organisms functioning independently and achieved a measure of self-realisation.

Family portraits

It is interesting to observe the way in which this peculiarity is first expressed in the compositional organization of family portraits. The grouping of the members of families took place according to laws which were very schematically applied. Particularly sharp genealogical divisions were made. Generally speaking there was strict differentation between the sexes: on the left of the picture the father and his sons, on the right the mother and her daughters. Even if we can recognize an echo of the arrangement which appears in donated pictures, the new principle of division has become decisive. The children are arranged according to their age, firstly the taller elder ones and then the smaller younger ones, going up or down like organ pipes. These family portraits give no fleeting insight into everyday household affairs; if anything the family symbolizes a higher meaning. They demonstrate with pride that the children overcome fleeting time, transitoriness and death. We are often astounded by the great numbers of children. For example the picture of the middle-class merchant family of Pierre Moucheron painted by Cornelis de Zeeu in 1561 shows twenty. Occasionally, depending on the circumstances, the circle of sitters is extended to those already dead. Ancestors are included in the picture by means of painted portraits hanging behind the living, as with the Van Berchem family painted by Frans Floris in 1561 or a family group which Frans Menton painted in 1577. A characteristic Latin inscription on the family portrait of Johann van der Does and his wife Elisabeth van Zuylen in the Lakenhalle at Leyden painted by Roeloff Willemsz. Culemborg gives specific information about the family: "I van der Does whom my wife *p. 202* Elisabeth of the house Zuylen has made a father twice times six. But only nine of the family survive, of which one pair was born female, the remainder being male. Half of them are like their father and half like their mother. How well it is depicted by the skilful hand of Roeloff! I who look at myself know, O God, at the sight of so many guarantees that it will come to pass that they will outlive my ashes." In other words the highest satisfaction and greatest happiness is the ability to conquer death with numerous progeny. Previously the idea had been to turn spiritual death into the blessed immortal life by piety and good works, and so enable the family too to share in the religious hope of salvation after death; now the goal was more earthly and immediate, a man was satisfied if the biological continuity of the family was assured and thereby *Vanitas* banished and overcome, for a time at least. This new idea was embodied in the conspicuous schematism of the pictorial composition which was now dominated by it, in other words, through it the composition gained a significance mainly connected with the subject matter.

Sometimes different mental associations may be stressed, the family can be placed beneath a moralizing motto referring to its communal life, for example the motto of harmony and peacefulness. Written in Latin on the frame of the portrait of the van Berchem family painted by Frans Floris in 1561 are the words: "There can be nothing happier in life than a marriage without strife". In his own way Frans Floris shows us what this desirable family state looks like. The family of thirteen is gathered round a table. In order to record middle-class material opulence a still-life of fruit is constructed in the middle of the picture on a white napkin which stands out against the dark, multi-coloured tablecloth, while a woman peels an apple. In addition music is played on the lute and table spinet. Music also brought its blessing to family circles and that was recognized as one of its tasks at the time; on the lid of a clavicembalo (a type of harpsichord) in the Rijksmuseum at Amsterdam is written: *Musica laborum dolce levamen*, music is a sweet way of alleviating toil. The older members are listening attentively to the music in rigid attitudes, only the children bring a little disorder and spontaneity into the scene; the little girl asks for a piece of the peeled apple and the puppy jumps up at the other end of the table. Portrayal of the group as they go freely to and fro about their normal business is only known on a very limited scale; the age of portraying environment in the real sense of the word has not yet dawned. In the general structure of the composition the strict law of the schematic ranking of persons prevails and is valued higher than the random, and consequently undignified, everyday activities of the family. Here too the Mannerist art form sought to conquer reality with a higher insight and help the overriding idea to break through.

Dutch group portraits

The same schematism committed to the idea is explicit in Dutch group portraits. In every case the aim is to demonstrate the idea of the individual group members' sense of belonging to the society or club. Meetings of middle-class corporations were portrayed. Mostly we find the voluntary defence companies of musketeers or arquebusiers assembled for regimental dinners or taking the field. A file, section or company may be portrayed under the command of a captain or lieutenant. Later come the portraits of governors of guilds, charitable institutions, orphanages, foundations and hospitals, and the so-called regents' and anatomical pieces; the latter show the members of the various surgeons' corporations taking part in a scientific demonstration on a body. But groups of regents and surgeons first really came into prominence at the beginning of the seventeenth century and they almost entirely avoid the genuine basic attitude of Mannerism. In the earliest anatomical picture of Doctor Sebastian Egbertsz. (1603) and the oldest known regents' group of the six Amsterdam cloth assayers (1599), both painted by Aert Pietersz., all we can see are faint traces of Mannerist characteristics in the schematic general arrangement, as well as in the deliberately twisted attitude of individuals. Group painting was especially cultivated in Amsterdam and somewhat later in Haarlem, then in the Hague, Delft, Leyden and even in smaller towns such as Gouda, Alkmaar and Hoorn. All group portraits, which hung in the assembly rooms of the various corporations, especially the shooting clubs (*doelen*), had an essentially didactic purpose to fulfil. Knowing this we can understand when the device "Vreede Eendrachtigheidt behaegt Gods Maiested" appears on the seal of file E in the shooting piece of 1563 by Dirck Jacobsz. These words could stand as a superscription for all Dutch group portraits because they state the moral duty of these meetings most clearly. The schematic arrangement of the figures is the time-honoured method of depicting piety and harmony in the compositions. This solidarity is captured by giving equal emphasis to each member in a formal planimetric design. The almost mathematically calculated arrangement can be either staggered like a chess-board or consist of simple juxtaposition. The individual member is always conscious of being a part of the group mentality of the whole. Each individual is given due recognition (the cost of these group portraits was shared among the members) in that his face is generally turned towards the spectator regardless of what is happening. Only a few deviations from this basic procedure can be observed in individual paintings. From this point of view it is significant that genre treatments, in so far as they are used at all, always remain in embryo. They are never allowed to snatch the reins of the composition and seriously endanger the rule of schematization. This would be an unforgivable offence against the harmony of the idea. The men in the group portraits by Dirck Jacobsz., Cornelis Teunissen and Dirck Barendsz. hold the most varied objects in their hands: whole guns, gun barrels, arrows, skulls, gloves, writing materials *p. 203* and slips of paper on which *In vino veritas* may be written, and at banquets the appropriate goblets, bowls, tankards, glasses, pastry and herrings. All these things have an almost classical attributive meaning, just as the saints in the past had had their distinguishing marks, and still fitted in with the others when they appeared in company. But these supplementary artefacts were never used by their owners to distract attention from the sacrosanct arrangement decreed by the overriding idea of solidarity.

Towards the end of the sixteenth century the schematization of the arrangement relaxed in favour of a more genre-like and natural conception. Arrangements dominated by the idea began to break up. More space was placed at the disposal of the figures and they could behave more spontaneously. Now there was enough space for flags too to be depicted and cross the pictorial field, as they do in the shooting pieces by Cornelis Cornelisz. van Haarlem and Aert Pietersz. painted in 1583 and 1603 respectively. This motif was still retained in the early shooting pieces by Frans Hals. Yet this relaxation was partially counteracted because the adoption of the intrinsically Italian ideal figure created a new artificiality. Sitters are caught in unnaturally distorted acrobatic postures; they subscribe to an affected language of gesture. A significant result of the "aristocratization" of the figure which goes hand in hand with it is that troops are no longer the only subject; reunions of officers were also portrayed, for example the banquet after parrot shooting painted in 1599 by Cornelis Cornelisz. van Haarlem. Cornelis Ketel painted the most striking examples of complicated attitudes in his two full figure pictures of military companies setting forth dated 1581 and 1588. We might think that the arrangements of the two scenes had been taken from the cycle of historical pictures which Tintoretto painted for the Gonzagas and transferred to the quite different problem facing Dutch group portrait painting to judge by the exaggerated solemnity and gesturing of Ketel's treatment of the business of taking the field.

Portraits of people of the lower classes

It is a sociological fact that through the custom of the Dutch group picture the distinction of being portrayed was conferred on people from social classes who would scarcely have been used as subjects if this branch of painting had not existed. We find genuinely popular lower-class human types, especially from the early epoch until shortly after the middle of the century. In their vivid immediacy they are typical representatives of their class. Broad strata of the population met in the defence companies of arquebusiers and musketeers; the retailer and the big merchant stood next to each other on the same footing. The portrait which had previously been the almost exclusive privilege of the higher intellectual, ecclesiastical and noble classes began to embrace larger circles of the population. Naturally enough this sociological extension did not take place without voices being raised against it. They came from Italy which was still thinking on more exclusive and aristocratic lines at the time. In 1545 Pietro Aretino complained that it was a disgrace that now even tailors and butchers were painted from life. Only famous people ought to be portrayed. Lomazzo expressed himself in similar terms in 1584. In spite of such protests, from then on minor figures in the social sense were portrayed at their work in individual portraits. We can include falconers among them. In 1533 Holbein the Younger painted Henry VIII's falconer, Robert Cheseman, holding the bird on his hand and stroking it cautiously. There is also a portrait of a falconer by Frans Floris. Giovanni Battista Moroni painted a tailor at work. The expressive portrait of a standard bearer by Hendrik Goltzius has been preserved. Karel van Mander confirms that Goltzius painted portraits of people from the lower classes, although for his own pleasure. He mentions the portrait of a peasant woman from the

School of FONTAINEBLEAU: *Diane de Poitiers as the Goddess Diana*. Louvre, Paris

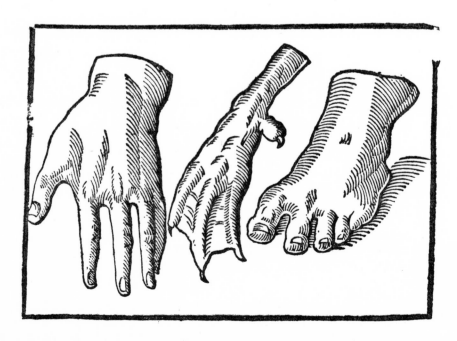

Ass's head and human head; flexing
muscles and plucked hen; hand, claw,
foot. From a 1623 edition of *Della
fisonomia dell'huomo* by Giovanbattista
della Porta

214

north and actually names the picture of a certain Jan Govertsen who lived at Haarlem and was a mussel gatherer. He has a mother of pearl mussel in his hand and several sea snails lie next to him. In 1573 a woman called Kenou Simons Hasselaer was captured in a portrait because she "had piously fought the Spanish tyrants in days gone by". This popular heroine was portrayed by a Dutch master. The woman displays her ordinary rough honest face furrowed by life's cares, her simple hood and the weapons which she used in her fight for freedom. The desire to portray men and women of the people meant that even cooks could appear in solemn paintings. Pieter Aertsen and his nephew Joachim Bueckelaer were specialists in this genre. The cooks were shown at their work as half- or full-length figures in the midst of pots, jugs, stools and large joints of meat in baskets, or preparing or roasting chickens in the fireplace. Surprisingly enough these figures are portrayed with considerable artistic pretention; they adopt the same swaggering poses as Tintoretto's generals, they make the same negligent gestures with their arms and show the backs of their hands in the same Michelangelesque manner. Altogether they appear to have the same self-possession and pride as people of the upper classes. In these pictures the artist even applied the grandiose formula of introducing architectural details, such as handsomely curved consoles next to the figure. And we do not find it disturbing when a commonplace cabbage is tucked under the cook's arm like a helmet under the arm of a knight. The painting of the materials of bodices, aprons and skirts shows virtuouso technique. In this way a kitchen background is made to yield a strangely official ceremonial atmosphere. In Mannerism the stylistic form with its basic emphasis on distinction and exclusiveness was so strong that it even spread to subjects who were quite unentitled to such elevating characteristics and attributes.

p. 204 Mannerism also took pleasure in freaks of nature. In 1583 Aert Pietersz. painted Pieter Diercksz. whose only claim to fame was that he had let his beard grow to an excessive length. It was so long that Diercksz. could hold the tip in his hand with the loop touching the ground. It was part of the normal duties of a Court Painter to portray court jesters and dwarfs. Bronzino had to reproduce Morgante, Duke Cosimo's dwarf, "life size and naked", seen from the front on one side of the picture and from the rear on the other. Sculptors, too, often carved Morgante with his colleague the Court Dwarf Barbino. Pietro Barbino became famous through the statue of him riding on a turtle in all his shapeless obesity with which Valerio Cioli da Settignano, a Florentine sculptor who mainly produced garden figures, immortalized him in 1560. Recently Gustav Künstler has established that the burlesque figure of Barbino has a literary model. In *Orlando Furioso* by Lodovico Ariosto the fat chief of the wicked fairy Alcina's band is described as riding on a turtle. In the 63rd stanza of the 6th canto of *Orlando Furioso* there is a reference to the drunken Silenus, the companion of Dionysus. The following is a prose version of it: "Now the chief of the band appears with bloated belly and fat cheeks. He sits on the neck of the biggest turtle which only takes one slow step. One man has to catch hold of him here, another there, for he is drunk and his head is lolling. One man has to wipe his forehead, another his chin; another flaps cloths to keep him cool."

The figure of the jester also played an important role in the poems and theatrical productions of the Dutch Rederijkern (or lovers of letters), the middle-class associations for the encouragement of popular national literature. The jester commented on the play on the stage and explained to the audience what they could learn from it. The jesters were not mere buffoons, they were called *wyze nar* or *wyze man* (wise fool or wise man). Sometimes they made a Rederijker Chamber famous, as was the case with the Haarlem jester Piero. That is why his portrait was painted by Cornelis Cornelisz. van Haarlem. (There is a copy of it in the Lakenhal at Leyden.) Anthonis Mor painted Cardinal Granvella's Court Jester standing next to an enormous dog. There was method in such a juxtaposition; people were interested in comparisons with animals. In his book *De humana*

p. 214 *physiognomia* published in 1583 the Italian natural philosopher Giovanni Battista della Porta established the correspondence between men's facial features and those of certain animals and assessed them from the point of view of character. At all events the Mannerist picture of mankind also included pitiable creatures such as dwarfs and cripples in its scale of values. In other words the range of people worthy of representation was greatly extended owing to this morbid interest in the sensational and curious: it went from the glorification of emperors and popes to the bizarre depictions of monsters.

The distinction between "gloria" and "memoria"

In Late Mannerism we come across the subtle distinction between the purposes for which portraits were painted. There were two possible aims: either the artist wanted to confer fame, *gloria*, on the sitter or he simply intended to keep his memory, *memoria*, alive. In the portrait of himself and his wife painted in 1601 Joachim Wtewael admitted what his aim was in the inscription: "Non gloria, sed memoria." There speaks middle-class modesty, although it does not quite come through in the style. The swaggering precious gestures of the sitters, which are resonant with more than a little *gloria* and Mannerist thinking, contradict it. But in conclusion we can make the general statement that the end of exalted Mannerist portraiture came at a time when the unnaturally exaggerated postures of sitters relaxed and the portrayal of everyday normal features became common, in other words when the natural came into prominence as a stylistic ideal. For then fame or *gloria* was no longer the dominant principle; the likeness alone, the pure memory of *memoria* prevailed without a higher idealistic meaning. This became the rule in the next period, the Baroque.

PIETER DE WITTE, known as CANDID: *The Duchess Magdalena*. Alte Pinakothek, Munich

Human destiny and the power of nature in Mannerist art

During the centuries of the Middle Ages man took it for granted that he was a part of the Christian order of salvation. He accepted its shelter without much inner conflict because it satisfied his spiritual and moral needs, whatever might happen on earth. Indeed it did not pay much attention to specifically earthly, everyday practical needs. It was more concerned with life after death than the state of man during his earthly existence. Admittedly there were certain moral principles which he had to observe during his life on earth, but they were not unduly emphasized. All that was radically changed during the sixteenth century.

Man began to see and recognize himself in his specific human predicament. Admittedly it had been one of the goals of the Renaissance for man to make himself the centre of his thought and activities, but at first he did so with a certain vigour, refreshing unconcern and naivety. This enlightened mood largely disappeared in the sixteenth century; it gave way to a more introspective fearful attitude to the world. Man sought a new support in the environment in which he now felt insecure. We can clearly sense how difficult it was for man to orientate himself in the new situation. On the one hand he experienced the reality of life and nature with hitherto unknown immediacy and tension, his specific problem being to master the world in its rational actual state and make himself at home in it. But on the other hand he had not yet succeeded in submitting to the laws of rationally perceived nature with a degree of wise equanimity and allowing them to take their course, as happened later in the Baroque period and the eighteenth and nineteenth centuries. To be able to face this dilemma, man felt forced to look round for higher rules and seek guidance in ethical ideas. Then he applied these theoretical directives to practical world conditions in order to master them. There is something ambivalent about such a way of life; it contains an unresolved element of uncertainty and inner strife, even of contradiction. But precisely such divergent features characterize Mannerist man, who, starting from a rational basis, fights for the idea which is the highest thing on earth to him.

Human life and the power of fate

Over wide areas painting also undertook the new task of acting as a prop to man in his vacillating and consequently difficult relationship with the world. For this reason pictures were often of a moralizing and didactic nature. A large part of the repertoire of Mannerist didactic thinking does not occur in the higher spheres of panel pictures or even frescoes, but is expressed at length in the astonishingly large production of engravings and woodcuts. With their copious sequences and explanatory captions they form part of the overall stylistic picture of Mannerism, indeed its mental attitude often comes more directly to life in this graphic production than in the high panegyric art of panel pictures and frescoes. Dutch Mannerist graphic art achieved extraordinary things in the field of moral enlightenment. Its masters are Martin van Heemskerck and Hendrik Goltzius.

Virtues and vices

Engravings have an extremely wide range of themes. The mediaeval allegories of the virtues and vices are retained, but they are used even more incisively and lavishly. They appear wherever possible in Dutch series of engravings, but also in the great Italian fresco cycles, on palace façades, in Gobelin tapestries and paintings. At times the accent changes in engravings depending on whether more importance is attached to the allegory or more to bringing out the practical consequences of virtue and vice. Thus Hendrik Goltzius stressed allegory in his sequence of virtues and vices, whereas Bruegel the Elder concentrated more on reality in his plates. In his series of drawings made in 1590 which have the vices as their theme, Jacopo Ligozzi produced very realistically conceived allegorical figures. The accent on the importance of the different virtues could also be shifted according to the patron's opinion of them. When the Count Palatine Ottheinrich ordered his tapestry of *Prudentia* in Brussels in 1531 he put more emphasis on sagacity than on faith or *fides*, which he eliminated from the programme.

Happiness and ruin

Sixteenth-century men were seized with a new longing to find happiness on earth and this also shows in their

p. 232 pictures. For example in 1582 Hendrik Goltzius engraved a series of four plates which deal with "the way to happiness" and have the following contents: Plate 1: Firstly, powerful figures are shown as an acknowledgement of productive human activity. We see work, *labor*, and diligence, *diligentia*, with which it must be carried out if it is to bear the appropriate fruits. Plate 2: Next, something about the nature of work ist stated. Even in practice, *usus*, the higher idea must also be kept in mind. Earthly activity is praised as a gift of the heavenly powers, of *ars*. Plate 3: In continuation, an account of the consequences of good conduct is given. A man will reap honour, *honos*, achieve prosperity and be materially secure. Plate 4: But more than that, a man can indulge in relaxation, spiritual repose. This is embodied by the female figure of rest, *quies*, who broods reflectively.

In the same way Late Mannerism in the north enjoyed making ingenious extensions of the so-called *tabula Cebetis*. The ancient philosopher Cebes wrote a dialogue about an imaginary mural in which the temptations of this world and also purification by the virtues were portrayed. Many painters and illustrators adopted this table of virtues, Holbein the Younger, Lambert Lombard, Hendrik Goltzius and the Dutchman Joris van Schooten.

p. 169 More modest in its deployment of subject matter is the *Victory of Wisdom* by Bartholomeus Spranger. The graceful ideal figure of Wisdom is introduced in the midst of a host of real-life contemporaries. Wisdom appears as a quality which must belong to every man if he does not want to perish in the world of deceitful appearances.

Such themes may also refer to conduct; man confronted with a moral decision. But powers are also depicted to which he is involuntarily exposed, such as love and death, or the goddess of destiny, *Fortuna*. Frequently biblical scenes are chosen. They serve as moral directives rather than portrayals of the actual events and are supposed to have a higher significance for mankind. The great theme of the control of sensual pleasure was treated over and over again, often coupled with the theme of marriage. Of this type are scenes such as Susanna at the bath and the two elders, Joseph and Potiphar's wife, Lot and his daughters, or Christ and the woman taken in adultery, as well as Tarquinius and Lucretia from Roman history. For it was a favourite practice to discuss the dangers which beset man on his way through life in very general terms. The frequently painted story of the prodigal

p. 229 son offered a suitable pretext for this. A picture like *Loose Company* by Jan van Hemessen warns against the temptations of false love. It shows women tempting a man to drink and gamble: the effects of drunkenness are shown in the toothless old hag lolling over the table and holding the lid of her tankard open. But the man shrinks

219

back from the enticements of the whore who is trying to ingratiate herself with him and raises a warning hand to us. Almost without our realising it, this man taken from life, as the main figure in the scene, assumes a prophetic role. The striking isolation of his face by the large framing shape of the scarf which hangs down from his headgear accentuates this impression. In his relation to the conflicting choice between good and evil the moralising man does not fit smoothly into the composition, thus underlining the dichotomy even more. The Mannerist pictorial form vacillating between reality and idea possessed definite qualities which made it suitable for the treatment of moralising themes.

A theme such as *Christ with Mary and Martha* was a direct challenge to make the division between profane reality and lofty idea visible in the composition as well. The solution found by Pieter Aertsen shows this most impressively. In the foreground of his picture we look at quite close range into the reality, the objective world, which surrounds us. Our gaze falls first on two tabletops which are covered with all kinds of objects — baskets, flower vases and plates. The actual biblical scene of Mary crouching at the feet of Christ as he teaches only appears in the background. The sacred scene theoretically takes precedence by virtue of its spiritual value, but this is scarcely credible in practice because the material world almost swamps the significant part of the picture with the exuberance of the still-life. The artist can no longer resist showing his skill in portraying his environment and accurate knowledge of objects; but for all that he does not want to conceal the higher insight which flows from Christ's words. However minor it may appear, this central group cannot be overlooked. The opposition of reality to it deliberately provokes tension. The Mannerist artist always left this conflict unresolved. Yet there are paintings which at first sight seem to be completely contained in the sphere of dull reality. In Bruegel's *Fools' Paradise* the *p. 230* men themselves become still-lifes, clumsy inanimate objects. Nevertheless we feel that the figures of the knight, the peasant and the citizen lying lazily on the ground are ennobled by the delicate drawing; for all their "dehumanization" we can still sense a higher existence.

The beauty of the female body

Pictures which refer to the mutual relations of the sexes and love-life take a prominent place. For the first time since the end of the Middle Ages the Mannerist style was able to give pictorial expression to a highly developed refined sensuality. It was helped in this by its sensitive feeling for line and also by its special gift for achieving the most subtle gradations of colour, which was the special province of this style. But this particular kind of picture was mainly encouraged in the courtly atmosphere of the most varied European royal residences where this refined artistic style met with particular approval. Female beauty with its supple suggestive elegance and exaggerated grace literally became one of the main goals of artistic admiration. Many figures from classical mythology were called on to reveal the specifically Mannerist idea of beauty; besides pictures of Venus we have others of Leda, Danaë or charming nymphs. Such themes are found in famous masterpieces by Italian, French, Dutch and German artists; for example Pontormo, Bronzino, Tintoretto, Jacopo Zucchi, Giovanni da Bologna, Adriaen de Vries, Martin van Heemskerck, Hendrik Goltzius, Bartholomeus Spranger, Hans Baldung Grien and Lucas Cranach. The School of Fontainebleau had a predilection for portraying women sitting in bath tubs; in them the female figures are seen in a remarkably stiff and doll-like way in comparison with the backgrounds which luxuriate in naturalistic still-lifes of flowers and fruit. Michelangelo took up the theme of Leda in a drawing. Inspired by it, Ammanati used it in a relief. The young Rubens also followed this tradition. We find variations of the same subject by Tintoretto. In 1603 Hendrik Goltzius painted a Danaë embellished with many precious accessories, and Parmigianino painted his Cupid carving a bow, a boy almost out of his childhood who no longer seems

Niccolò dell'Abbate: *Portrait of a man with a parrot.* Kunsthistorisches Museum, Vienna

quite suited for the role of the putto-like childish Cupid. Bronzino enlarged the motif of Venus and Cupid by adding the figures of Time and Folly in his painting *Venus, Cupid, Time and Folly*. The main figures in this composition *p. 173* are pressed together in remarkable distortions. The arm of Saturn, who, seething with rage and glaring balefully, is on the point of tearing away the curtain behind which the figures of Venus and Cupid are caressing each other, is introduced almost as a contrasting motif. The demonical and the beautiful clash with unusual directness. The bitingly cold, bright colouring makes its own contribution to this in every way elegantly portrayed scene. There is a combination of five interrelated compositions by Bartholomeus Spranger which deal with unhappy loving couples from classical mythology following Ovid's *Metamorphoses*. Both Tintoretto and Martin van Heemskerck chose the moment when Venus and Mars were surprised by Vulcan. *p. 177*

Social life

But Mannerism also developed a very special feeling for sociability pure and simple, in addition to the most intimate sexual unions. It preferred to represent carousing, music and dancing as taking place in higher spheres depicted with a certain fantasy. The best examples of this are the countless banquets of the gods and feasts painted by Giulio Romano, Primaticcio, Niccolò dell'Abbate and the Dutch Mannerists Bartholomeus Spranger, Joos van Winghe, Karel van Mander, Cornelis Cornelisz. van Haarlem, Gerrit Pietersz., Abraham Bloemart and Joachim *p. 113* Wtewael. The marriage of Cupid and Psyche or that of Peleus and Thetis was frequently chosen as a theme for both frescoes and panel pictures. But sometimes artists were content merely to preserve the supernatural Olympian atmosphere in general terms and to portray festive companies of dallying couples who are iconographically indeterminate. Specific accessories were often introduced to heighten the festive atmosphere. In pictures of *al fresco* meals cloths were stretched from tree to tree or streaks of cloud with *putti* introduced between the trees. The guests were depicted in the most swaggering and affected attitudes, and were dressed in the most unusual costumes. Oddly enough those biblical scenes which come under the heading of social pictures also experience its enchantment. Thus a painting such as *Herod's Banquet* from the circle of the Fleming Joos van Winghe has a fluctuating *p. 181* broken up composition. The event in the picture itself is most originally dissolved into small individual scenes by frameworks (for coupled columns, balustrade and staircase have that effect) and as a result of this typically Mannerist division into compartments we scarcely have the impression of a spatially coherent, freely developing banquet scene. With the help of many sources of light an amusing play of details spotlighted in different places is achieved in this nocturnal revel. A few of the guests standing together are gesticulating. The small group of half-length figures appears abruptly in the foreground. The only really full-length group is that of Salome carrying the salver with the head of John the Baptist and conversing with her attendant who is also very fashionably dressed. A magnificent candelabrum, a triumph of the Mannerist goldsmith's art, hangs over the festive board in the background.

The transitoriness of everything

Representations of death were just as popular as scenes of love and society. Man recognized the relative limitation of the time on earth allotted as his life span. Consequently he had to come to terms with the transitoriness of everything, with birth and death, but most of all with dying as such. Transitoriness, the dreaded *Vanitas*, had not yet become a familiar fact with which he had to reckon as a matter of course. Knowledge of the frailty of the human body experienced by all became a disturbing phenomenon which had to be looked fearlessly in the eye once more.

It had become a pressing and unavoidable concern for men to take this new stage in the knowledge of human existence into account and reorientate themselves in relation to the world accordingly. The best philosophers of the day, Michel de Montaigne (1533–1592) and Francis Bacon (1561–1626), speculated about it. Montaigne attempted to rationalize his attitude to dying: "God shows mercy to the man from whom he removes life piece by piece. That is the sole good in old age. Then the last death is less painful and violent. It is only killing half or a quarter of a man. One of my teeth fell out quite easily and painlessly. It was the natural end of its period of service. This part of my being, like many others, was already dead; others again, which in my heyday played the leading role, are half dead. Thus I diminish and disappear. How stupid it would be of me if I felt this fall to be a fall from the height of my powers! My consolation in thinking of death is that it is completely in the order of nature. What I would obtain or desire from fate beyond that would be a favour which did not belong to me by right. In my opinion human happiness does not rest on a happy death, as Antisthenes would have it, but on a happy life; I am especially bound to thank my fate because every single thing has come at the right time in my life...and likewise my wisdom has developed differently according to the various stages of its growth."

But man not only recognized death as a division, as a break between temporality and eternity, he was also conscious of the lapse of time by stages. This insight stimulated him to depict the ages of man. They first appeared in German illustrations in the second quarter of the sixteenth century. In a woodcut by Hans Schäuffelin the ages of man are still linked with the hope of salvation held out by the church. In the later humanist woodcut of the stages in the life of man by Jörg Breu the Younger and in the two series of woodcuts each consisting of five plates, the *Ages*

p. 156 *of Man* and the *Ages of Woman*, by Tobias Stimmer the artist concentrates on the idea of the progressive unfolding of life. For Tobias Stimmer the gradual approach of death is a natural process, which is further illustrated by the introduction of trees in various stages of growth in the background: i.e. men had the same stages of growth as trees. Dutch engravings followed: the *Theatrum vitae humanae* by Wiericx, published by Peter Balten at Antwerp in 1577, and the *Septem planetae 7 hominis aetatibus respondentes* of 1581 by Martin de Vos, in which the ages of man were related to the planets: childhood, *infantia*, for example, is associated with the moon, *luna*. In 1544 Hans

p. 231 Baldung Grien painted his picture, with full-length figures, of the seven stages in the life of woman. The painting in the Prado (*c.* 1540) introduces the same ideas in abbreviated form. In it the painter also tried to bring out the passage of time in the combination of the figures. The two women and death are closely entwined, but the child lying on the ground is also drawn into the group by echoing the shape of the broken lance of Death, which he is touching with his hand, and by his leg which he is stretching out towards the young woman. An ambivalent stylistic purpose makes itself felt in this composition and in its conscious artificiality the exquisite play of lines is on a level with similar treatments by the Florentine Mannerists, such as Pontormo and Bronzino. Yet Baldung Grien's point of departure was the old German tradition of shapes, which in such late works and within its national setting was perfectly suited to the contemporary intellectual art. The painting as a whole, with a narrow upright format, has assumed something of the fragility of death. The thin female figures with their tapering limbs hold their ground obstinately; death and they are linked, yet each of them is pulling away from the other so that action is obstructed. Bad-tempered and haggard, each of the figures is looking in a different direction. The general colouring matches the hopeless situation; it has a morbidly grey, uncannily unreal corpse-like pallor.

The three Fates

The classical Greek conception of the three Fates who spin the thread of life is intimately linked with death. So we can understand why this theme occurs over and over again in specific contexts during the sixteenth century.

Sometimes this motif is called on to open the great cycles of princely life. The three Fates appear in this capacity in the ceiling picture on the first landing of Trausnitz Castle by Friedrich Sustris, at the beginning of the *Lives of the Good and Bad Knights* in the ceiling painting at Baden-Baden Castle by Tobias Stimmer and even in the first picture by Rubens in the Medici Gallery. Francesco Salviati portrayed the three Fates most impressively in a panel picture in the Palazzo Pitti at Florence. Salviati chose powerful types of women, marked with age, so that they would suit his responsible task and give the pictorial idea sufficent weight. He took Michelangelo's Sybils as a model. With heavy hands they slowly and deliberately accomplish their fateful activity of spinning and cutting the thread of life; the two sisters in the front seek mutual counsel with serious looks. Above this pair there is a ghostly strip of light which diffuses an uncertain play of light and shade. The third figure, almost disappearing in the darkness of the background, looks straight ahead with half-open mouth, her face distorted with pain. What are they thinking about? The anxiety of men, who are afraid of their destiny, is reflected in the figures of the three Fates. They, as the arbiters of life and death, should actually be free of the effect of the sentence they pronounce on men. Yet the penetrating, frightening effect of this picture depends precisely on this psychological interpretation of the theme with its emotional cross-references.

The goddess Fortuna

Once man with a personal destiny had become a subject for discussion, the concept of the goddess *Fortuna* also increased in importance. As the world power which hovers over earthly activity she may signify either luck or misfortune and is very comparable to the fickleness of human destiny. In literature *Fortuna* appears as the power which rules everything. When the French poet Pierre Ronsard wrote a comedy for carnival at Fontainebleau, he produced a *Theatrum mundi* in which the men appear as actors and *Fortuna* as producer, who also prepares the costumes. In Rabelais' *Pantagruel* there is a discussion as to whether virtue is more important for men than *Fortuna* whose workings cannot be influenced deliberately. *Fortuna* also plays an important role in Montaigne's philosophy of life, which aims at the natural adjustment of the way of the world, and Francis Bacon wrote two essays, one on fortune, the other on misfortune, in which he enquires to what extent a man can direct his own destiny.

It is typical that in the course of the sixteenth century the representation of virtue was increasingly displaced in favour of the vaguer figure of *Fortuna*. Vasari gave *Fortuna* pride of place in the fresco scheme for his studio at *p. 163* Arezzo. She is the dominant power who rules over the painter's conduct. In the big allegory of *Felicità* by Bronzino in the Uffizi *Fortuna* with her wheel appears at the feet of Happiness as a sign that happiness too depends on the benevolence of *Fortuna*. In addition to the somewhat crude and general personifications of *Fortuna* or Time, subtler distinctions could appear, e.g. the idea of the right moment, the favourable opportunity, the *occasione*. A painting by Girolamo da Carpi depicts it. In it the *occasione* is very fittingly combined with Patience, *Patientia*. Biding one's time, not hurrying unduly, were also necessary for the success of an undertaking. In a painting by Cornelis Cornelisz. van Haarlem of 1590 *Fortuna* stands on a pedestal in the midst of mankind and strews treasures on the earth: wealth, money, silver and gold. Men reach avidly for them. Adam Elsheimer used it for his well-known composition *The Search for Happiness*. It is characteristic of the Dutch painter Hendrik Goltzius that he placed the finely drawn figure of *Fortuna* above a naturalistic seascape and so identified the goddess of fortune directly with *p. 233* natural events and the weather. To the left rages a wild storm which destroys the ships and to the right the calm sea extends in beautiful sunshine. The obvious stylistic tension which arose from such a combination of figure and landscape in no way disturbed the Mannerists.

TINTORETTO: *The rescue of the body of St Mark*. Accademia di Belle Arti, Venice

Nature and the cosmic world feeling. The concept of nature

The Mannerist concept of nature is very complicated. The strictly scientific system of interpreting nature which developed in the centuries to come did not yet exist; the most varied conceptions circulated. Undeniably the idea was valued higher than nature representationally. This attitude is clearly expressed in the explanation of the concept of the *Idea* in Cesare Ripa's *Iconology*, in which nature plays a subordinate role. It is dependent on the Idea and he demonstrates how nature is held at Idea's breast so that she can "give it milk like a cow". There were numerous ways in which what we understand today by nature or landscape as a concrete view of our actual surroundings could be interpreted. The span goes from the allegorical general concept of nature to the specific individual scene which varies with the seasons. The points of view adopted in an attempt to comprehend nature and in a broader sense the cosmos are partly allegorical, partly mythological and partly rational. For nature taken as a whole a classical allegory was to hand: the many-breasted goddess of Ephesus. Vasari used her when he had the naturalistic side of activity in mind as opposed to the Idea. Consequently we find this goddess included in the design for the studio rooms in his palaces at Florence and Arezzo. In the programme of garden figures for the Villa d'Este at Tivoli the statue of nature is pushed to one side on the last and lowest terrace of the garden lay-out; all the other gods and figures rank before her in importance.

Owing to his idealistic personifying method of representation the Mannerist artist is even able to make a very tangible portrayal of a cosmic event such as the origin of the Milky Way in the heavens. Probably the man who ordered it, a Doctor Tommaso Rangoni da Ravenna, supplied the details for this theme and Tintoretto produced *p. 145* his magnificent picture after them. The picture relates the Greek myth that when his wife Hera was asleep Zeus put Hercules at her breast so as to make him the adopted son of a goddess against the sleeper's will. The young Hercules drank so greedily that milk spurted in all directions; the drops which shot upwards formed the stars of the Milky Way and lilies sprouted from those which fell to earth. Thanks to Tintoretto's high art the figures in this event seem to be suspended supernaturally; we ourselves feel drawn out into space and are seduced into accepting this Mannerist composition as a cosmic event.

The four elements

The physical inventory of the phenomena of our world was comprised in the four elements, earth, air, fire and water. The four elements were such a familiar idea that they could occur in the most peculiar contexts. When Lomazzo compared artists with pictures of animals he called Leonardo a lion, Michelangelo a dragon, and Titian an ox. The dragon was composed of the four elements because it crept out of the earth's primaeval slime, imitates the waves of the sea with its jagged figure, flames and smoulders inside and rises into the air with its wings. Lomazzo sees a similar mixture of the elements in Michelangelo. Giuseppe Arcimboldi painted the four elements as allegorical figures. The figure of fire is solely composed of objects which are connected with that element: flints, candles, *p. 189* tongs, tapers, lamps, the barrels of guns and cannons. Jacques de Gheyn painted the four elements as half-length figures in genre pictures as cook, hunter, fowler and fisherman. We see an original combination of historical scenes in a landscape with allegories of the four elements in a painting on which the landscape painter Denis van Alsloot and the figure painter Hendrick de Clerck collaborated. The landscape, which depicts Paradise with its *p. 233* plants and animals, includes figurative scenes in the middleground; the appearance of God the Father in the clouds, the creation of Eve, the Fall and the expulsion from Paradise. In the foreground personifications of the four elements are also introduced to interpret nature allegorically, over and above the idyllic landscape scenery.

The four allegorical figures are distributed ingeniously and symmetrically in pairs in the frontal plane of the picture. The female figures of water and earth lie on the ground surrounded by mussels, fish, fruit and flowers in lavish splendour and above them float male nudes representing air and fire. The figures of Adam and Eve dallying, which thematically belong to the biblical scenes unfolding on earth, fit surprisingly well into the design because of their rhythmic movements. This drawing clearly shows how Mannerism was able to combine apparently incompatible themes into a whole, creating a self-contained ingenious pictorial idea.

The four continents, the four seasons and the four ages of the world

Geographically our earth was divided into the four continents of Asia, Europe, Africa and America. Martin de Vos drew a series of full-length figures of them. The changing appearance of the earth's surface during the course of the year was made clear by representations of the four seasons or the twelve months. Arcimboldi also produced allegorical figures of the seasons in two cycles which have been preserved; once again they are composed of appropriate objects. The French painter Antoine Caron introduced the triumphal chariot of the season into the *p. 235* landscape which fitted it. The triumphal chariot of *Winter* moves through a town scene including the Temple of Janus. It is drawn by storks and preceded by a festive procession of decorative figures including Mercury. The whole scene is covered in snow. Again painters used personifications which were supposed to emphasize the special qualities of the earth: fertility, for example, which was embodied by the goddess Ceres. In 1576 the French painter Noblet painted a Michelangelesque full-length figure as an allegory of Ceres, which is now in the Louvre. On the original frame was written: *Officium commune Ceres et terra tuentur* (Ceres and earth discharge their common office). The floral display with which the earth bedecks itself is characterized by the allegory of *Flora*. The four ages of the earth, gold, silver, bronze and iron, were familiar to the Mannerists from Ovid's *Metamorphoses*. Jacopo Zucchi *p. 231* painted three allegories of the golden, silver and bronze ages. The golden age was supposed to show that ideal blessed world when no laws were necessary and "Men lived without care in agreeable repose"; when the earth "was still untouched by the rake, not yet wounded by the plough" and "eternal spring" reigned. Such a theme might have been made for a Mannerist wanting to place his nude figures in an ideal landscape. Christian counterparts to this ideal state of human existence are the depictions of paradise, of which there are examples by Lucas Cranach the Elder, Jan Brueghel the Elder and Roelandt Savery.

The Mannerists had no conception of what we call landscape in the narrow sense, i.e. as a part of nature. Michelangelo despised landscape as much as he did portraiture. None of his works is devoted substantially to the problem of reproducing scenic contexts. His landscapes as the necessary stage for the figurative composition are mostly bare and bleak. Here Vasari's description of the landscape in Michelangelo's frescoes in the Cappella Paolina is instructive: "Michelangelo's endeavour was…solely directed towards the highest perfection of art; thus we find here neither landscapes nor trees, and not even a certain variety and artistic charm, which he did not value; perhaps he did not want to demean his lofty mind with such things."

The theory of landscape painting

The idealist Mannerist aesthetic would not yet allow landscape validity as a separate branch of painting. Thus Lomazzo, on the subject of composing landscapes, tells us how the artist divides them into the three picture planes and how the accessories should look, but never writes of landscape as a special realm cut off from history. These theoretical views correspond to the actual state of contemporary landscape painting. It was not so much a question of counterfeiting nature in landscapes, *ritrarre*, as of heightening and transfiguring, *imitare*, the natural model according to the preconceived idea in the idealistic sense. Armenini and Lomazzo are agreed on one thing: man should compensate for the errors of nature by the power of art. The conception of the universal landscape, as *p. 234* created by Leonardo, was retained. The multifarious aspects of the earth's surface in his pictures went half-way to meet Mannerism's endeavour to comprehend subjects in their entirety. There is even a contemporary theory which establishes the circulation of water in the universal landscape as a unified conception: rivers come from the mountains and flow into the sea; they evaporate in the sea and return to the mountains so that in their course they confirm the words of the Bible: "They return to the place whence they came." In his book *Osservazioni della pittura* which appeared in Venice in 1585, Christophoro Sorte sets forth this natural-philosophical theory of the universal landscape. But the surface of the earth itself becomes the stage for superhuman divine activity. Mythological tales and biblical events are introduced into the landscape. Thus Niccolò dell'Abbate depicted the rape of Proserpina *p. 235* by Pluto in a magnificently designed landscape. The wild formation of the scenery matches the dramatic mythological event; clouds gather, shafts of light suddenly illuminate several strips of land, many small castle and crags break up the smooth expanse of the plain. The features of the landscape are agitated, like the excited gestures of Proserpina's attendants. Below a mound of earth in the foreground reclines a female figure, probably a goddess of nature, who concentrates the action on the figurative aspect once more. As yet Mannerist landscape art did not know how to introduce human figures smoothly and harmoniously into landscapes. Even in the smallest of them we feel that the human figure is valued more highly than the landscape; the figures have more strength in their shapes than the landscape formations. Even in Pieter Bruegel the Elder's pictures of the months in Vienna, men are to some extent foreign bodies in their environment, for all their inclusion in the rhythm of nature. Very often the strong local colours of their clothes are in contrast to the colours of the earth and the vegetation; the forms of the figures are as flat as playing cards compared with the greater sensitivity to space shown in their surroundings. The "natural" portrayal of landscape and figure without harsh contrasts and different scales of values which arrived with the Baroque was unknown in the Mannerist landscape.

The Mannerists even subjected trees to their special conception of form. Trunks of trees and branches were deliberately twisted and turned in artificial elegant shapes. The landscape drawings of Jacques de Gheyn or the engravings of Hieronymus Cock provide impressive examples of this. In them something similar to the ideal of the *figura serpentinata* emerges, if we are entitled to compare figures with scenic accessories. Karel van Mander devotes long passages to foliage and says in conclusion: "…there intelligent art appears to be merely a dreaming being; for leaves, hail, air and matter are nothing but spirit and the spirit teaches them to produce." Thus artificial images also appear in Mannerism's depiction of landscape. Formalization divorced from nature was the aim, rather as in figurative art. Yet in this case it does not reduce the expressiveness of the subject matter, but rather the opposite. Mannerist landscape painting is distinguished by far-fetched mountain formations. Here too, as in all other forms, the artist's inventive gifts had to be shown off. In El Greco's landscape, where Moses appears with the tables of the law, towering mountains form the wild scenery. He paid little attention to the fact that the jagged mountains could not have stood up at all in reality, but would have inevitably collapsed.

It is a well known fact that the practical applications of observations of delicate shades of atmosphere increased. Pieter Bruegel the Elder was able to capture specific atmospheric nuances, dreary wetness in *Gloomy Day* and the icy cold of a winter snowscape which he portrayed in his picture of a hunter in the snow. Antoine Caron also captured the feeling of cold in his *Allegory of Winter*. In Caron's painting we feel that the light covering of snow will not last very long and that the magic of nature is made all the more astonishing by it. With typical Mannerist incongruity the figures in this picture pay absolutely no attention to the low temperature and appear as usual in

Man caught in the moral dilemma between good and bad

JAN VAN HEMESSEN (c 1500–1566): *Loose Company*. Staatliche Kunsthalle, Karlsruhe

PIETER AERTSEN (1509–1575): *Christ with Mary and Martha*. Boymans-Van Beuningen Museum, Rotterdam

Far left: PIETER BRUEGEL THE ELDER: *Fools' Paradise*, 1568. Alte Pinakothek, Munich

Far left, below: ALBRECHT ALTDORFER: *Lot and his Daughter*, 1538. Kunsthistorisches Museum, Vienna

Left: HANS BALDUNG GRIEN: *Death and the Ages of Woman. c* 1540. Prado, Madrid

Below: JACOPO ZUCCHI (*c* 1541–1590): *The Golden Age*. Uffizi, Florence

Labor *Diligentia*

.I. .1582.

Henricus Goltzius inuen et sculpsit, proprÿsum Harlemi

Cum Labor, & socia iungunt Industria palmas, | Daermen geen Arbeit spaert noch gheen Diligentie
Ars quoq Palladiam meditatur pectore curam. | Sietmen dat Conste baert diuersche Jnuentie.

Ars *Vsus*

HG. fe

Quisquis amore bonas exercet sedulus arteis, | Diemet staden bemind Consten t'Exerceren
Congeret obryzum multa cum laude metallum. | Hon beladen beuint met veel Ryckdom in Eeren

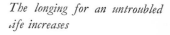

The longing for an untroubled life increases

HENDRIK GOLTZIUS: *The way to happiness:* engravings, dated 1582. Work and Diligence, Art and Practice, Honour and Wealth, Repose

Honor *Opulentia*

3. Hcoltzius fecit.

Mutua Diuitic et laus si inodo fœdera nectunt, | Als Ryckdom ende Eer haer in liefden vergare
Optatam parient homini sine lite Quidem. | Ons leuen naer t'begheer zy vyen van beswa

Quies

HG. fecit. 4

Mens quoq Terrigenum curis distenditur ægra, | Dat menschelyck verstant altyt sorchuuldich
Certior æternam quò posset adire quietem. | Nae rust aen elcken cant, daer naer geduldich waert

232

Nature is systematically comprehended and allegorically represented as a whole

HENDRIK GOLTZIUS (1558–1617): *Fortuna, soaring above a seascape divided into night and day.* Staatliche Gemäldegalerie, Stuttgart

HENDRICK DE CLERCK (figures) and DENIS ALSLOOT (landscape): *Paradise* – with the creation of Eve, the consummation and the consequences of the Fall, and the allegories of the four elements. Alte Pinakothek, Munich

233

MARTIN VAN HEEMSKERCK (1498–1574): *The Colossus of Rhodes*. From the series of engravings of the Seven Wonders of the World
Below: TOBIAS VERHAECHT: *Mountainous landscape* (as a universal landscape), 1612. Alte Pinakothek, Munich

TINTORETTO: *Santa Maria Aegyptiaca*, detail of the landscape. *c* 1583. Scuola di San Rocco, Venice

234

Architecture, together with imaginary landscapes, universal landscapes which represent
the self-contained unity of nature, mythological ideal landscapes and the atmospheric magic
of landscape–all go to make up the Mannerist
concept of landscape

NICCOLÒ DELL'ABBATE (c 1509–1571):
The Rape of Proserpina. Louvre, Paris

Below: ANTOINE CARON (c 1520–1599):
Allegory of Winter. Private collection,
Paris

The group crowning this composition of figures is not only an allegory of sculpture, but embodies art in general. Arranged below it are the three fine arts: Sculpture, Painting and Architecture; to which are annexed Incisoria, the art of engraving, and Anatomia, the knowledge of the structure of the human body

JAN VAN DER STRAAT, known as Giovanni Stradanus: *The artist's workshop with his pupils*. Dated 1578, engraved by Cornelis Cort

236

ideal nudity or scanty drapery. Now artists also ventured to include the actual process of snowing, the curtain of flakes, in the picture. Both Bruegel and Lucas van Valckenborch experimented with this special atmospheric condition which so altered the normal look of things.

Lighting effects

Lighting effects were very much to the fore. The urge for the sensational and mysterious could be fully exploited in them. The short work by Christophoro Sorte already mentioned deals almost exclusively with landscape painting, but it is mainly concerned with colours and the atmospheric effects of light, for example sunrise, reflected light, nocturnal lighting and double illumination by the moon and torchlight. The reproduction of the sea at various times of day and in different seasons, changing weather effects, fires, ice-bound scenes and snowfalls were also discussed. The theoretician claimed that his observations could be used for such themes as the Burning of Troy, the Rape of Orythia in the Snowstorm, Phaëthon and the Transfiguration and there are several examples of these subjects painted by his contemporaries. There is a painting of Troy burning by night by Kerstiaen de Keuninck in Courtrai Museum; Desiderio Monsù also used this theme, while Albrecht Altdorfer painted the

pp. 185, 230 burning of Sodom in his picture *Lot and his Daughters*. At times far too much importance was attached to lighting effects. Lighting by torches or lightning ruthlessly disrupted the organized unity of the rest of the composition. El Greco painted Toledo in a storm in a picture now in the Metropolitan Museum of New York. The sky is haunted by streaks of cloud, now glaringly lit up, now dark, ghostly silhouettes. Lights suddenly flash forth on the ground as well as on walls and towers, and the grass and the trees join in the ecstatic frenzied whirl of forms.

Tintoretto also frequently dramatized his paintings by strong effects of light, such as the summer lightning seen in Upper Italy and the bright-red glaring of the sky after a raging storm. Similar violent treatments were even introduced in designs which did not necessarily require such exceptional meteorological conditions. Compositions were supposed to be striking, broken up and full of effects. In this dispersal and mutilation there is a certain parallel with the frequently expansive gestures of the figures which are also intended to exclude any self-contained coherent general impression. Tintoretto developed the fantastic side of lighting effects with the utmost virtuosity. His technique raised the few landscapes he painted to a dreamlike atmosphere. The pictures of *Santa Maria Aegyptiaca* and *Santa Maria Magdelena* in the Scuola di San Rocco at Venice were painted *c.* 1583–1584. In an astonishing way they reveal the landscape of a different world; as if they were molten, even the thick trunks of the trees melt into broad flashing streaks of light. The leaves become a shower of flakes in the pointilliste manner. The physical

p. 234 condition of the river bank on which Santa Maria Aegyptiaca is sitting is transfigured into a fantastic vision. The flashing lights lead a ghostly dance in the otherwise gloomy dark greenish-blue atmosphere making it all the more uncanny as a result. These two landscapes by Tintoretto have a mysterious splendour. There is a Christian apocalyptic feeling about their fitfully illuminated gloom which is the highest goal of the meditations of the two women. The atmospheric intensity of Tintoretto's landscape recurs in the forest landscapes of Gillis van Coninxloo, Frederik van Valckenborch and Kerstiaen de Keuninck, all landscape painters who represent a quite definite stage in Late Mannerist northern, especially Flemish, landscape art. Dramatic unreal atmospheric effects are mixed in these inherently naturalistic forest interiors; there are Will-o'-the-wisps in the branches, nature gives her own firework display and achieves a fairylike ingenious ghostly enchantment. A subject such as the magic garden of Armida from Tasso's *Gerusalemme liberata* in a picture by Kerstiaen de Keuninck serves perfectly as the culmination of the style. Mannerist landscape paintings were mainly distinguished by the fact that they always had a dash of the fantastic, artificial and unusual. However we must also remember that it was precisely during the sixteenth

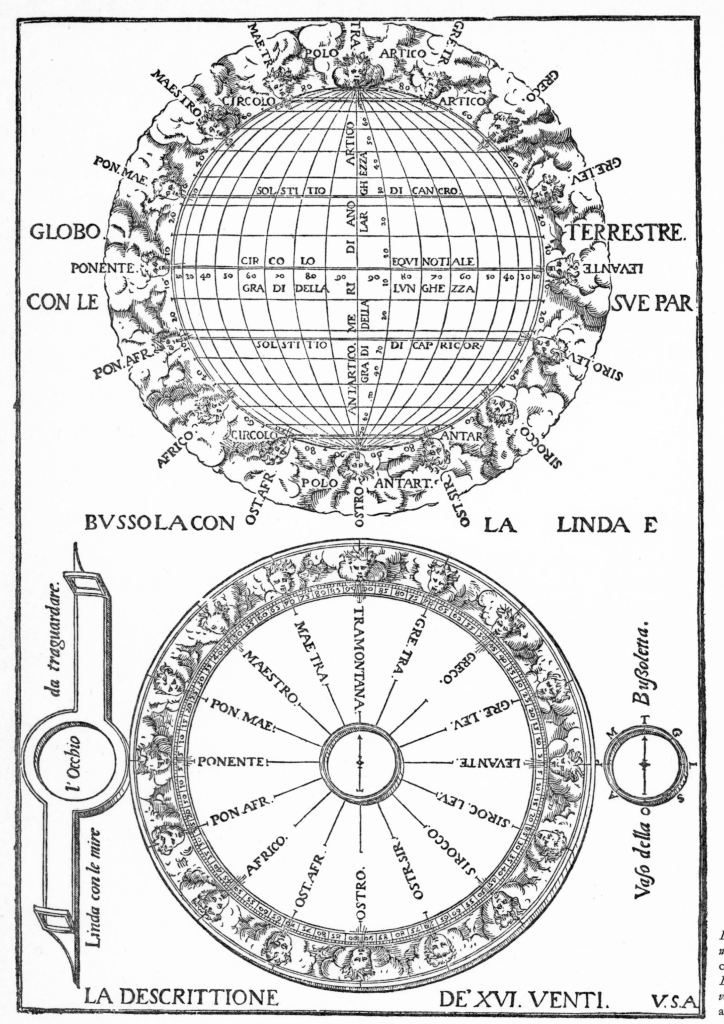

GLOBO. TERRESTRE.

CON LE SVE PAR

BVSSOLACON LA LINDA E

LA DESCRITTIONE DE' XVI. VENTI. V.S.A

Description of the sixteen winds. Woodcut by Vincenzo Scamozzi from *L'idea dell'architettura universale.* The first edition appeared in Venice in 1615

238

century that solid purely imitative topographical landscape painting was much more widely appreciated. Hans Bol and Georg Hoefnagel are representatives of this tendency. But it is typical of the general contemporary attitude to the problem of what the landscape should look like that especially attractive epithets were even held in readiness for perfectly normal landscapes. Thus in the drawings of Georg Hoefnagel typical captions are appended such as *amoenissimus...prospectus* or *elegantissimus prospectus*, as if a landscape could be elegant in itself. Just as the figures of Mannerism were interpreted with regard to these qualities, this kind of landscape art showed the general features of the style, at least in the wording of the captions. The Mannerists remained idealists and visionaries to the end, having more regard for the inner vision than the outward appearance.

El Greco's vision of Toledo

p. 240 When El Greco was commissioned in his last creative years *c.* 1608 to paint a view of Toledo, the town which he himself had elected to work and live in, a higher vision appeared to him. He did everything to prevent the actual view of Toledo from dominating the picture. He put the figure of the river god of the Tagus in the left foreground. He also removed the monastery, which lay outside the town and for which he presumably painted the view of the town, from reality by transferring it from *terra firma* to a bright airy cloud. Above it he painted the vision of Mary borne high over the town by angels, as the Mother of Heaven and patroness. Not content with that, the painter further distorted the view of Toledo and the unequivocal reality of the scenery by the addition of the half-length figure of a boy holding out the plan of Toledo to the spectator. A town plan can be rolled up and unrolled, and projected like this one can hold the whole dimensions of the real landscape in one's outstretched arms in imagination. This picture achieves the feat of making man master of the actual landscape by confining it to the town plan and in it El Greco celebrates the triumph of the Idea over matter.

But even the view of the actual town is removed into a dream landscape for the painter. Its colours submerge it in a strange atmosphere: grey, olive green and yellow tones are mixed; what we have are not the familiar browns and greens: the earth is transfigured by a ghostly colouring, mainly yellow and gold, which has the effect of dissolving matter. But the most surprising thing is that in this case the "de-materialized" atmosphere can hardly be attributed to a transformation by the artist; for remarkably enough the landscape of the Castilian plateau really does look unreal and vision-steeped. El Greco in fact stuck surprisingly close to his natural model. But the most significant thing about such reflections is that the Mannerist El Greco had chosen a region for his creative work and dwelling place which already possessed an "unreal" appearance by nature. This master who pushed his radical Mannerism as far as possible into the new century of Baroque naturalism held fast to the end to the "Idea" and the belief in something higher than reality. He was one of those true Mannerists whose love of the idea was far stronger than the pull of everyday drab reality. Not that reality was unknown to them, but the crucial factor was that they did not believe in reality as the only possibility and did not consider it as governing their activity.

EL GRECO: *View and plan of Toledo*. Museo del Greco, Toledo